GW01406544

The North Sea Bridge

Ferry Connections between Scandinavia and Britain 1820-2014

Ferry Publications

Published by:
Ferry Publications, PO Box 33, Ramsey, Isle of Man IM99 4LP
Tel: +44 (0) 1624 898445 Fax: +44 (0) 1624 898449
E-mail: ferrypubs@manx.net Website: www.ferrypubs.co.uk

The last Norway-UK ferry in regular service, the ***Queen of Scandinavia***, arriving in Bergen in summer 2007. *(Marko Stampehl)*

Acknowledgments

This book, perhaps more so than any other book that I've written as the sole author so far, has only been possible with the generous assistance of numerous individuals and associations more knowledgeble in the subject than I am.

First of all thanks to my colleagues at Ulkomatala at the time the article series that served as the point of departure for this book was published: Lassi Liikanen, Jussi Littunen, Sergei Pennonen and Olli Tuominen, as well as the magazine's regular fact-checkers and proofreaders Jukka Koskimies and Juhani Mehto.

While the entire text you are about to read is my own, it would not have been possible without the help of several individuals and organisations, who did research on my behalf, loaned or even gave me relevant publications (and in one case, an unpublished book manuscript) I would not have otherwise had access to. Thus, special thanks are in order to Agnar Jónas Jónsson of the Reykjavík Maritime Museum, Anders Bergenek, Alan Dumelow, Bård Kolltveit, Harald Oanes, The Ship Historical Society of Finland, Bernt Arild Torstrup, and Rami Wirrankoski.

For a completely different reason but just as importantly, special thanks go to The Association of Finnish Non-fiction Writers for the generous writing grant that allowed me to finish this book.

More regular-sized thanks go to Jocelyn Anderson-Wood of the Hull Maritime Museum, Dag Bakka Jr, Ian Boyle, John Bryant, Krzysztof Brzoza, Miles Cowsill, Martin Cox, Matt Davies, Elísabet Pétursdóttir, Tor Eriksen, Per Gisle Galåen of the Norwegian Maritime Museum, Henriette Gavnholdt Jakobsen of the Maritime Museum of Denmark, Ambrose Greenway, Per Jensen, Richard Kirkman, Klubb Maritim, Joonas Kortelainen, Marko Laine, Simona Mitmann, Bruce Peter, Sverre Andreas Rud, Rickard Sahlsten, Marko Stampehl and David Trevor-Jones for helping out in various ways along the way.

Finally, as always, I would like to thank my wife Maria Id for her continued love and support, our son Tarmo for at least occasionally letting me work in peace, and our now-deceased cat Ville, alongside his successors Sisu and Urho, for mostly staying off the keyboard and only occasionally deleting chunks of text while I wasn't looking.

Dedicated to my mother

The author's work was supported by The Association of Finnish Non-Fiction Writers

Contents

Preface	6
Chapter 1: Scandinavia to Britain: An Overview	10
Chapter 2: Finland to Britain: The White Ships and The Red Ships	21
Chapter 3: Sweden to Britain: Large and Luxurious	43
Chapter 4: Norway to Britain: Competition and Innovation	77
Chapter 5: Iceland and Faroe Islands to Britain: Lifeline By-Product	112
Chapter 6: Denmark to Britain: DFDS Domination	123
Chapter 7: Dreams of Restoration	154
Bibliography	159

Produced and designed by Ferry Publications trading as Lily Publications Ltd
PO Box 33, Ramsey, Isle of Man, British Isles, IM99 4LP
Tel: +44 (0) 1624 898446
www.ferrypubs.co.uk e mail: info@lilypublications.co.uk
Printed and bound by Gomer Press Ltd., Wales, UK +44 (0) 1559 362371

Published November 2019

ISBN: 978-1-911268-25-3

The ***Tor Britannia***, seen here passing the Hoek van Holland-Harwich ferry ***Prinses Beatrix***, and her sister ***Tor Scandinavia*** were arguably the ultimate Scandinavia-UK ferries in terms of design. While failures for their original owner Tor Line, after takeover by DFDS they went on to provide successful service on the routes from Sweden, Denmark and Norway to the UK, being one of the select few ferries to sail to all three countries. *(FotoFlite)*

Sealink
DFDS TOR LINE

Preface

In 2014, DFDS Seaways terminated the last seaborne passenger link between the Nordic countries and the United Kingdom, when the Esbjerg-Harwich route operated by the *Sirena Seaways* was closed down. A nearly 200-year old link thus ceased. In an editorial meeting of the Finnish maritime magazine Ulkomatala, we decided to publish not only an article about the closure of the Esbjerg-Harwich route, but also a series of articles about the history of the Scandinavia-UK passenger links. As I had majored in history, this job naturally fell to me.

I quickly discovered that the subject matter was not only fascinating but also more complex than I had presumed. If anything, the trans-North Sea routes to the UK resembled the fabled North Atlantic link in miniature form: each country had its own "national carrier" – sometimes several – trying to outdo the others in terms of luxury, speed, or both. Often, the vessels discussed were true national flagships in terms of size, speed and comfort. But, again like the transatlantic liners, while luxury was often emphasised, for much of the history of the link it was migrants who counted; for many, the journey across the North Sea was just an overture to a much longer transatlantic crossing to North America. Whereas the transatlantic liner trade fizzled to almost nothing following the introduction of the jet airplane, the North Sea services were transformed by the arrival of the roll on-roll off car-passenger ferry in the 1960s and (with the exception of the Finland-UK link) persisted until the 21st century as genuine liner services, whereas the transatlantic trade was turned into an americanised, Las Vegas -esque re-interpretation of the original for the amusement of the wealthy. Yet, while books about the transatlantic liner service are too many to count – let alone read – those about its 'little cousin' across the North Sea are few and far between.

Following the good reception of the Ulkomatala articles, I soon had the idea that the series – which, despite my attempts to be brief, bloated from a planned four to seven parts and ran for a total of 74 pages – could be translated and expanded into a book. Work on this begun in earnest in 2017, amidst other projects and now, finally, it is completed in book form. I hope it will be an enjoyable and, more importantly, informative read.

Structure

As you have probably noticed from a glance at the Contents page, the "beef"of this book are Chapters 2 through 6, which detail the histories of passenger shipping links between each individual Nordic country and the UK. These are arranged in chronological order by the closure of the service; thus, we start with Finland (which lost the UK link by 1986 at latest) and end with Denmark. For practical reasons, the services to the Faroe Islands – an autonomous country under Denmark – are grouped together with those of Iceland, as not only did the Faroe-UK services have more in common with those from Iceland than those from Denmark, very often the same route served both island groups.

Some lines discussed in this book served several countries: those from Finland called at Danish and sometimes Swedish ports along the way, services from Sweden at times included intermediate calls in Norway, and those from Norway occasionally called in Danish ports. As a rule of the thumb, these are discussed in detail in the chapters relevant to the final destination country; thus, for instance, the Finland-Denmark-UK services are described in the chapter for Finland.

In general, I have chosen to include only dedicated Nordics-UK services. Lines that linked Nordic countries to Britain as a part of a longer route to other destinations have been either ignored or are only briefly discussed; including, for example, all passenger services from UK to ports on the Baltic Sea that sailed via Copenhagen would have simply made this book too long to publish. A notable exception to this rule are the Leningrad-London services of the Soviet Union's Baltiyskoye Morskoye Parokhodstvo, or the Baltic Shipping Company, which sailed via numerous Nordic ports. After World War II, these were the sole passenger shipping connection from Finland to the UK and I felt their inclusion warranted.

The first and last chapters are more general ones. Chapter 1 looks at the development of the passenger services between the Nordic countries and the UK as a whole, charting out the broad trends that effected the development of the routes, and in the process will hopefully help the reader better contextualise the subsequent, more detailed chapters. Chapter 7, on the other hand, looks briefly at the various attempts that have been made to restore the passenger link between Scandinavia and Britain, and analyses the likelihood of these plans becoming reality.

Definitions

The definition of what actually is a passenger ship is difficult. Very few ships in liner service actually carried only passengers and no cargo, and separating the development of passenger services from the cargo carried alongside is impossible. While I have concentrated mostly on the development of services from the passenger point of view, this should not obscure the fact that cargo was often equally, if nor more, important. As for what ships and services to include, I have gone with the definition that vessels with a capacity for more than 12 passengers are are considered passenger vessels, even when their primary focus was the carriage of cargo. For older vessels and services, the precise passenger capacities are difficult to discover and, as such, my decisions

Svenska Lloyd's ***Suecia*** and ***Britannia*** were the mainstays of Sweden-UK services from 1929 until 1966. The ***Britannia*** is photographed here towards the end of her career in 1959. *(FotoFlite)*

on what is included in this book should not be considered definitive by any means.

Although they are often used as synonyms, the terms "Scandinavia" and the "Nordic countries" are not always used to refer to the same thing. In common usage, both lack a firmly established definition. I have chosen to go with what most people from the Nordic countries agree is the correct way: Scandinavia refers to the three geographically Scandinavian countries – Denmark, Norway and Sweden – while the Nordic countries (or simply Nordics) refer to the five culturally Scandinavian countries that also form the membership of the Nordic Council: Denmark, Finland, Iceland, Norway and Sweden. My chosen definition should, however, not be taken as universal. Often, Scandinavia is used to refer to the five countries I am referring to as the Nordics, while in the recent years, the definition of the Nordic countries has been extended to include Estonia and at times even Latvia and Lithuania.

I have used the terms United Kingdom (or 'the UK'), Great Britain and Britain in this book as shorthand for the United Kingdom of Great Britain and Northern Ireland; the former term should not be confused with the United Kingdom**s** of Sweden and Norway that existed in 1814-1905. All terms always refer to the area of the sovereign state (rather than just the individual island known as Great Britain), thus including – crucially from the point of view of this book – the Shetland Islands, which long enjoyed passenger shipping links to Denmark in the south, as well as the Faroe Islands and Iceland in the north.

Notes on Russian cyrillic names

Due to the inclusion of ships belonging to the Baltiyskoye Morskoye Parokhodstvo (probably more familiar to readers under the English-language name Baltic Shipping Company) in

Ship development immediately after World War II was either nonexistent or superficial; the ***Blenheim*** (2) of 1951 was a conventional cargo-passenger vessel with a streamlined exterior. *(Joonas Kortelainen collection)*

Wilson Line were the dominant operator on the Scandinavia-UK trades until World War I. The ***Spero*** (3), seen here, was their last attempt of running a passenger service, operated between Sweden and the UK 1966-1972. *(Maritime Museum: Hull Museums)*

The ***Dana Sirena*** (2) was originally envisioned as a Mediterranean ropax, but she was refitted into a more passenger-oriented form for DFDS' Esbjerg-Harwich route. Later renamed ***Sirena Seaways***, she was destined to be the last passenger ship on Scandinavia-UK routes. *(John Bryant)*

The ***Jupiter*** (4), previously the ***Dana Gloria*** (1) and ***Color Viking***, is an example of the second-hand tonnage that became increasingly common on the Scandinavia-UK routes from the 1980s onwards. *(Marko Stampehl)*

The link from the UK to the Faroe Islands and Iceland was converted to car-passenger ferries exceptionally late. The former Baltic ferry ***Norröna*** (1) served on the route for three decades. *(FotoFlite)*

this book, I have had to familiarise myself with the transliteration of Russian Cyrillic text into English. Unfortunately, there is no unified standard on of Russian-to-English transliteration, and even academic texts take a slapdash approach by not citing which system is used, often using several different approaches within the same text, and almost never including the original cyrillic forms that would be vital if one wanted to look at the original Russian-language sources.

For the purposes of this book, I have chosen to use the United States Board on Geographic Names/Permanent Committee on Geographical Names (BGN/PCGN) system, which is relatively intuitive for English-speakers. This may result in certain names of ships, people or companies being in slightly different form than has been used in other publications.

For the sake of completeness, whenever a ship, company or individual from Russia or the Soviet Union is first mentioned in this book, the original Russian Cyrillic form of the name is included alongside the transliterated one. This has the advantage of allowing readers from non-english-speaking countries to transliterate the original name to their own language according to the relevant rules – for example, the ship (and person) named Вячеслав Молотов in the original Russian becomes *Vyacheslav Molotov* in (BGN/PCGN) English, *Vjatšeslav Molotov* in (my native language) Finnish and *Wjatscheslaw Molotow* in German – and allowing readers to look for information on the relevant ships from Russian-language sources.

The ***Tor Britannia*** and ***Tor Scandinavia*** (pictured) were unusually sleek to achieve a high service speed, linking Sweden to the UK in less than 24 hours. However, being designed before the first oil crisis, their high fuel consumption kept them from being as successful as had been hoped. *(FotoFlite)*

Chapter one

Scandinavia to Britain: An Overview

Before moving to more detailed looks on services to and from each Nordic country in the subsequent chapters, this chapter looks at the general development of the Scandinavia-UK services. In addition to the overarching international economic development that effected all routes, which are explored here, developments on most or all routes connecting Britain to Scandinavia were similar when it came to things such as tonnage renewal. This chapter will help placing the more detailed information provided in the following chapters into the general framework of the development of Scandinavia-UK routes.

British beginnings

With the exception of Iceland and the Faroe Islands, the first companies to operate regular passenger services from the UK to the Nordic countries were based in the British port of Hull: the Wilson Line, who linked their home port to Denmark, Norway and Sweden from the mid-1800s, and Bailey & Leetham, who linked to Finland (and Denmark) starting from 1869. In Iceland and the Faroe islands the story was different, as these islands connection to the UK was more in the nature of a by-product of the need to the link them to Denmark, and as such they were operated by DFDS (formed in 1866). The early years of the regular passenger links during the 19th century were dominated by cargo vessels transporting a limited number of passengers in basic accommodation. It should be borne in mind while reading the following pages that on the routes discussed here – as indeed on almost all seaborn passenger services to have existed to date – the passengers carried were just one part (albeit the most visible one) of the operation, with much of the income coming from mail contracts (often the most lucrative part of the operation) and the carriage of cargo. Furthermore, the carriage of cargo and passengers were to a degree interlinked: outside the main tourists season(s), the main passenger group in the higher-class accommodation were businessmen travelling to make trade deals – for example, purchasing people of British book and newspaper printers travelling to Sweden or Finland to sign contracts to buy paper, or their conterparts in the food industry going to Norway to buy cod in bulk – with the cargo thus secured often travelling on the same ships.

While the traditional explanation (at least in English-language literature) to the initial British dominance has been the fact Britain was more industrially advanced, this is only half the truth. A major factor was also the fact that Britain was rarely the most important trade partner for the Nordic countries. At the same time, Britain was considered to be a cultural backwater, with Germany held to be the leading light of Europe when it came to culture and science. Therefore, when the first passenger connections further afield than the nearest neighbour were established by Nordic shipping companies, these were generally links to Germany, which was considered to be of utmost importance for both trade and culture. Linking to Britain was a secondary consideration.

In Denmark, Finland, Norway and Sweden, local companies did eventually rise to challenge the British hegemony in passenger and cargo transport during the second half of the 19th century: Det almindelige danske Dampskibsselskab in Denmark in 1856, Ångfartygs AB Göteborg-London in Sweden in 1865, Østlandske Lloyd and P.G. Halvorsen in Norway in 1880, and Finska Ångfartygs Aktiebolaget (or FÅA for short) in Finland in 1891. With the exception of the last-named, all these companies either went bankrupt or were absorbed into larger players relatively quickly, but they laid the groundwork for the subsequent Nordic companies, which would eventually go on eclipse the British.

From here on, services developed among different lines in different countries: for Denmark, Finland, Iceland and the Faroe Islands, services became either a monopoly or joint service by former competitors. On the routes from Sweden and Norway, however, competition between Wilson Line and the local companies was the norm, resulting in ever-larger ships being completed in an attempt to out-do the competition in size, speed and quality. Thus, ships on the Sweden-UK and Norway-UK routes were, during the late 19th and early 20th century, large and luxurious, especially on the former routes: Wilson Line's Sweden-UK ships tended to be the largest on the North Sea, while their competitor Ångfartygs AB Thule's vessels were often the largest under the Swedish flag.

A major contributing factor to the overall growth of passenger numbers on the Nordics-UK services, particularly when it came to Iceland, Norway and (to a lesser extent) Sweden, was the cultural trend of romanticism, with its glorification of the past – particularly the medieval era – and "unspoiled", rugged nature. All the things favoured by romanticism were found in the Nordic countries mentioned, with the added bonus of the Vikings, which resonated heavily with the romanticist ideas – even more so in the after the publication of Norse sagas translated into English by William Morris and Eiríkr Magnússon between 1869 and 1875 – and thus Iceland, Norway and Sweden became major tourist destinations for the wealthy. There is some irony in the fact that romanticsm was born as a counterreaction to industrialisation, and yet tourists were carried to the "unspoiled" North with steamship made possible by that same industrial revolution.

Even with the importance of tourism, it should not be forgotten that a large (and lucrative) part of the passenger

The Hull-based Wilson Line dominated the early decades of Scandinavia-UK passenger services. The 1874-vintage ***Angelo***, used on the Christiania (present-day Oslo)-Hull route is a representative of the combined cargo-passenger liners of the era. *(Maritime Museum: Hull Museums)*

operation was the carriage of migrants bound for North America, who travelled in simple accommodation far removed from the luxury of first class.

Consolidation into Nordic hands

In the years leading up to World War I, a gradual process of consolidation had taken place, with the services ending up in the hands of fewer and fewer companies. The decimation of Wilson Line's (renamed Ellerman's Wilson Line following a change of ownership in 1916) passenger fleets during the war (only one passenger ship survived, and even that was not deemed worthy of repair) and their inability to rebuild afterwards meant that, after the end of World War I, there were five major players in the passenger trades between Scandinavia and the UK: FÅA from Finland, Svenska Lloyd from Sweden, Det Bergenske Dampskibsselskab (BDS) and Fred. Olsen from Norway, and Det Forenede Dampskibsselskab (DFDS) from Denmark (who also served Iceland and the Faroe Islands). These companies were supplemented in the second half of the 1920s by the Soviet Union's Baltiyskoye Morskoye Parokhodstvo (Балтийское морское пароходство, BMP for short, or Baltic Shipping Company in English), which initiated services linking Leningrad with London via various Nordic ports.

The short post-war economic boom saw a small number of new ships completed, often similar or even identical to their pre-war fleetmates. They were designed to carry relatively larger numbers of migrants; however, as the United States radically curtailed immigration in the early 1920s, the previously lucrative trade dried up. This change was reflected in the new tonnage delivered during the economic upturn of the second half of the decade, with different operators choosing somewhat different approaches. FÅA, DFDS and the

The 1896-built ***Ficaria*** of DFDS was the first ship built specifically for the needs of the Denmark-UK link. *(Bruce Peter collection)*

This postcard of the ***Oslo*** of 1906 demonstrates the colourful livery favoured by Wilson Line, which earned their ships the nickname "Wilson's parrots." *(Ian Boyle collection)*

DFDS' ***Jylland*** of 1926, the second of four ships in the class, is a representative of the cargo-oriented vessels favoured by BMP, DFDS and FÅA during the 1920 and 30s. *(Museet for Søfart (CC-BY-NC-SA))*

Loading and unloading in the era before roll on-roll off ferries was time-consuming. Here, stevedores carry barrels of butter onboard DFDS' brand-new ***Parkeston*** of 1925 at Esbjerg. *(Museet for Søfart (CC-BY-NC-SA))*

Svenska Lloyd's ***Suecia*** of 1929 is a representative of the more passenger-focused tonnage favoured by BDS, Fred. Olsen and Svenska Lloyd, allowing for higher service frequency from shorter loading and unloading times. *(Anders Bergenek collection)*

newcomer BMP all opted for relatively simple tonnage primarily designed to carry cargo: FÅA's *Oberon* of 1925, DFDS' four-strong *Parkeston*-class of 1925-32 and *Dronning Alexandrine* of 1927, and BMP's six-strong *Jan Rudzutak* (Ян Рудзутак) -class of 1927-30. In Sweden and Norway, meanwhile, shipping companies opted for vessels primarily designed to carry passengers (though with limited capacity for cargo alongside), and were thus relatively fast: Svenska Lloyd's *Suecia* and *Britannia* of 1929, and BDS' *Venus* (2) of 1931. In order to attract the relatively affluent passengers – who became the main demographic of the services in the post-migrant era – the three last-mentioned in particular were opulently outfitted by leading interior designers of the day. The trend of hiring well-known design talents continued until the 1970s.

Initially, the new tonnage ordered during the latter years of the 1920s seemed something of a mis-investment, as the ships were delivered just before or during The Great Depression, the worldwide economic downturn that had begun in the United States in 1929, which resulted in an overall slowdown of international trade. However, the ramifications of the depression should not be exaggerated, as Britain and the Nordic Countries suffered relatively little compared to, for instance, the United States, France or Germany. For the shipping companies operating between the Nordic countries and Britain, there was an interval of smaller profits or even losses, which meant that, in some cases, investments were put on hold – but by the middle of the 1930s, passenger and cargo numbers were on the rise again and invesment recommenced.

As the decade progressed, new tonnage was contracted for all services linking the Nordic countries to the UK (with the exception of services to Iceland); this next generation of

Nordics-UK ships tended to be more passenger-oriented and better appointed than theor predecessors. As fate would have it, several of these were only completed during, or after, World War II. The generation was started by FÅA's *Aallotar* of 1937, followed by BDS' *Vega* (2) and Fred. Olsen's *Black Prince* (1), both in 1938, and the latter's sister *Black Watch* (2) in 1939. Completed when war had already broken out were BMP's *Iosif Stalin* (Иосиф Сталин, which sank as a troopship, never carrying regular passengers) and *Vyacheslav Molotov* (Вячеслав Молотов) of 1940, alongside FÅA's *Astrea* of 1941 (which never entered passenger service for her original owners, but did enter Norway-UK trades for DBS after the war). Two ships that we contracted before the war but completed after it were Svenska Lloyd's *Saga* (2) and DFDS' *Kronprins Frederik*, both entering service in 1946.

Post-war rebuilding and changing passenger demographics

Unlike the years following the first World War, those after World War II saw nearly uninterrupted economic growth, resulting in a demand for more passenger vessels for the Nordics-UK trades. The immediate post-war generation again followed the precedent of the ships designed before the war: DFDS' *Kronprinsesse Ingrid*, Icelandic newcomer Eimskip's *Gullfoss*, EWL's *Borodino*, Svenska Lloyd's *Patricia* (3), Fred. Olsen's *Blenheim* (2) and *Braemar* (1), and BDS's *Leda* (2), all delivered between 1949 and 1953, were traditional liners, with changes to the previous era only visible in their exterior design, if at all. Absent from this list are ships of FÅA, who did not re-initiate passenger services to the UK after the war. BMP continued sailing from Finland to the UK, initially using old FÅA tonnage received as war reparations. The Soviet company only took delivery of new tonnage for the Leningrad-London service in 1958-1963, when three new *Mikhail Kalinin* (Михаил Калинин) class ships arrived: the *Mikhail Kalinin*, *Estoniya* (Эстония) and *Nadezhda Krupskaya* (Надежда Крупска). Arguably, this trio (part of a 19-ship series built in East Germany) was outdated from the start, as the car ferry revolution was looming just around the corner.

During the post-war era, the heavy seasonality of passenger services between the Nordic countries and the British Isles effected vessel deployment more than before: most, though not all, perators ran reduced services during the off-season, sending the superfluous vessels either cruising or on liner services in warmer waters.

For the post-war era, several overarching and overlapping factors effected the development of the Nordic countries-UK ferry services:

First, Britain became a more attractive travel destination than perhaps ever before (or after); while its political and military power waned, culturally Britain became increasingly dominant in (Northern) Europe, with "Swinging London" becoming **the** destination for Nordic youth to travel to. In Denmark and Norway, Britain had gained notable goodwill for its participation in the defeat of Nazi Germany and also in ending the German occupation of these countries, further increasing its attraction as a travel destination (things were different in Sweden, which had been neutral, and in Finland, which had allied with Germany and been at war with Britain). At the same time, the economic fluctuations and changes in the value of currencies meant that the Nordic countries were relatively cheap for British tourists to visit during the 1960s, resulting in good travel flows in both directions.

Second, air travel rose to challenge sea travel as a viable alternative for the first time in the 1950s. However, before the ascent of low-cost airlines, air travel was an option only for the more affluent travellers, which required shipping companies to alter their product and concentrate on the passengers looking for an economic way of travelling – for example, the youth mentioned above. BDS' *Leda* (2) was a prime example of this thinking, as was Svenska Lloyd's refit of their aged *Suecia* and *Britannia* in 1956 from first-class dominated ships to catering primarily for tourist class.

Icelandic Eimskip's sole passenger newbuild for the UK trades, the ***Gullfoss*** of 1950, is an example of the immediate post-war generation, with virtually no development from the pre-war predecessors. *(Museet for Søfart (CC-BY-NC-SA))*

BMP's ***Mikhail Kalinin*** and her sisters arrived in 1958-1963, but failed to anticipate the car ferry revolution that was just about to start. *(FotoFlite)*

Third, with car ownership skyrocketing across the region, the ships' capacities to carry cars (and trucks, as these became more and more important for moving cargo) became an increasingly important factor. For people wishing to go on holiday with their own car, air travel was not an option (except to the precious few who could afford the car-carrying airplanes

First-generation Scandinavia-UK ferries, Fred. Olsen's 1966-built ***Black Prince*** (right) and DFDS' 1967-vintage ***Winston Churchill***, passing outside Harwich, likely on the occasion of the latter's maiden voyage. *(FotoFlite)*

experimented with at the time) and thus motorists became an important, perhaps even the most important, passenger group.

Thus, in order to continue services, the existing passenger operators had to change their mode of operation from traditional passenger liners (with limited cargo capacity) to car-passenger ferries with roll on-roll off (roro) cargo decks, and from passenger facilities aimed at the elites to what the lower social classes considered aspirational. Most operators on the Scandinavia-UK trades were able to do just that, as we shall see below.

Dawn of the car ferry

In the relatively short timespan between 1964 and 1970, the passenger routes from Scandinavia to Britain were converted almost entirely to car-passenger ferry services. Although the primary subject here is passenger services, the change particularly effected the cargo side: until now, time-consuming practices of loading and unloading cargos had meant that vessels carrying passengers and cargo had two alternatives: either build large cargo holds (such as had been done by BMP, DFDS and FÅA) and accept long harbour times, detrimental to service frequency, or build ships comparative small cargo capacity (such as had been done by Svenska Lloyd and BDS), giving shorter harbour times and better service frequencies – but also diminished income from freight. The roll-on, roll-off cargo arrangement solved this problem: with cargo now loaded and unloaded on their own wheels, relatively large amounts of freight could be discharged within hours, when the conventional arrangement would have required days for the same volume to be shifted.

Despite the obvious advantages of roro freight handling, different operators chose different approaches. The North Sea

Svenska Lloyd's ***Saga*** (3) and her running mates were attractive for passengers, but their impractical cargo-handling systems doomed them as commercial failures. *(Postcard, Joonas Kortelainen collection)*

The newcomer Tor Line's Sweden-UK ferries ***Tor Anglia*** and ***Tor Hollandia*** were more conventional car-passenger ferries and highly successful. *(Postcard, Kalle Id collection)*

The large, fast and well-appointed ***Tor Britannia*** (pictured) and ***Tor Scandinavia*** of 1975-1976 secured Tor Line victory in the struggle for Sweden-UK passenger service but their high running expenses forced Tor Line to seek a merger with DFDS just a few years later. *(Krzysztof Brzoza collection)*

car ferry pioneer, DFDS' *England* (2) of 1964, could only carry private cars, and even her 1967 consort *Winston Churchill* only had space for a small number of commercial vehicles, primarily relying on increasingly outdated solutions for the carriage of cargo. BDS, Fred. Olsen and the newcomer Tor Line all opted for state-of-the-art designs with full-height cargo decks for trucks, while the England-Sweden Line (ESL) consortium (formed by Svenska Lloyd, EWL and newcomer Rederi AB Svea) chose an innovative but ultimately failed design where the cargo decks were designed for the carriage of containers rather than commercial vehicles. The ships owned jointly by BDS and Fred. Olsen were particularly innovative: during the summers they operated as passenger-car ferries on the North Sea, but converted to combined cruise ship/reefers (refrigerated cargo ships) during the winters. This dual deployment continued until the 1980s – in a break from the general trend, as the other operators abandoned off-season cruising by the early 1970s.

At this time, operators of the different services chose – or were forced to – adapt different approaches towards their competitors: the Denmark-UK service was by now a monopoly of DFDS, on Norway-UK routes the two operators – BDS and Fred. Olsen – co-operated and eventually formed a joint venture in 1975, but on Sweden-UK routes the era was marked by fierce competition, first between Tor Line and the ESL consortium and, after Svenska Lloyd left the latter, between Tor Line, Svenska Lloyd and ESL. In this struggle, Tor Line eventually triumphed.

The wide ramps of the ***Tor Britannia*** and ***Tor Scandinavia*** (the latter is seen here in the later guise as the ***Princess of Scandinavia***) meant cargo could be quickly discharged, a stark contrast with the laborous loading and unloading of the pre-roro era. *(Søren Lund Hviid)*

Apogee

Arguably, the apogee of North Sea passenger ships was the 1970s, despite the fact just four new ships we delivered for the

BMP's attractive ***Baltika*** was the last "traditional passenger steamer" on the routes linking the Nordic countries with the UK, a remnant of an earlier era after all the other services had been transformed to modern car-passenger ferry links. This fine aerial view shows the ship at the very end of her career in 1986. *(FotoFlite)*

The ***Dana Anglia*** was the last passenger vessel specifically designed for the Scandinavia-UK routes. While she was very efficient, her design process was clearly made on the basis of the most economic solutions, which both her exterior and interiors less attractive than those of the previous vessels. *(FotoFlite)*

services during the decade. DFDS and Tor Line had contracted new vessels before the oil crisis, and these appeared in 1974 (*Dana Regina*), 1975 (*Tor Britannia*) and 1976 (*Tor Scandinavia*). In keeping with the growing affluence of the primarily middle-class passenger demographic, all were better-appointed and larger than the previous generation. (It should be kept in mind, when using terms such as middle-class, that the Nordic countries have notably more flexible class divisions than Britain, and what a British reader associates with the term is not nescessarily the same as a Nordic reader would).

This new generation of larger ferries with higher-quality accommodation arrived both at an opportune and at an inopportune moment. On one hand, the skyrocketing price of fuel had a negative impact particularly on the fast but fuel-hungry new Tor Line ships. On the other hand, the recession resulting from the oil crisis (which in the UK was felt particularly keenly) created demand for mini-cruises on the North Sea, as travellers were now looking for relatively cheaper vacation options close to home. Naturally, tax free shopping onboard was an added allure. The more luxurious new ships of the 1970s, as well as those of Fred. Olsen and BDS from the 1960s, were well suited for the new, more leisure-oriented onboard product. These dual trends were also reflected in the final vessel built during the decade (and indeed, the last newbuilt ship designed for Scandinavia-UK services), DFDS' *Dana Anglia* in 1978.

On the routes from Finland, Iceland and the Faroe Islands, the conversion to car ferry service took place later, and due to the nature of these routes, the mini-cruise product was not as important. The Finland-UK trade gained its first car-passenger ferry in 1973 – but the ship, Finnlines' *Finnfellow*, was primarily a cargo carrier with space for only 48 passengers. The *Finnfellow* moved to other services already in 1975, replaced by a pure cargo vessel. She remains the sole car-passenger ferry to connect Finland to the UK, as the Soviets never upgraded their Leningrad-London route to this ship type, instead opting to continue operations with the elderly *Baltika* (Балтика, ex-*Vyacheslav Molotov*) until the closure of the service (the newer *Mikhail Kalinin* class ships having been converted to full-time cruising in the mid-70s). The Faroe Islands only gained a car-passenger ferry link to the UK in 1975, with the second-hand ferry *Smyril*, and the Iceland-UK routes were only upgraded to car ferries in 1983, with the twin arrivals of the successful *Norröna* (1) of the newcomer Smyril Line, and the unsuccessful *Edda* of Farskip, which sailed for just one season.

Stagnation

DFDS entered an expansion drive in the early 1980s, attempting to gain a monopoly of the long-haul North Sea passenger services. This was briefly successful, as the company gained control of the Sweden-UK and Norway-UK routes (as well as those linking West Germany to the UK, which lie outside the scope of this book) in addition to the Denmark-UK routes they already controlled. However, DFDS' old stronghold of the Iceland and Faroe Islands to UK services stayed out of their hands, and the company were forced to

On the routes to Norway, operators changed many times over the years, with ships passing from one to the other. Seen here is the ***Jupiter*** (3) of 1966, in the livery of her fourth and final operator Norway Line. *(Hilton T. Davis)*

give up the Norway-UK services in the mid-80s following financial difficulties caused by their overexpansion.

DFDS' expansion came at a particularly inopportune time as it was was followed by diminishing passenger numbers. The early-1980s recession was particularly keenly felt in Britain and Sweden, and also resulted in the Nordic countries becoming comparatively expensive for British travellers. At the same time, the riots and other instability caused by the recession in Britain (arguably made worse by actions of the British govenment) made Britain a less attractive destination for Nordic travellers, while flying to warmer holiday destinations in southern Europe became more affordable and was seen as more aspirational than travelling to (what was at least perceived to be) a grim Britain. What undoubtedly also had an effect was the fact the trans-North Sea routes were never particularly well suited for the minicruise product, with long crossings and short harbour times, combined with the often tempestuous weather. While these factors effected passenger services, local production of various goods in Britain decreased and imports increased. Thus, the cargo services between the Nordic countries and Britain benifited and more cargo-only tonnage continued to be built, with the passenger services becoming more and more a secondary consideration.

This stagnation meant no new ships were built for the Nordics-Britain services. With the exception of a small number of vessels acquired second-hand, the routes continued to be operated by the tonnage build in the 1960s and 70s. Most of the 60s-vintage ships were eventually replaced by second-hand acquisitions in the 1990s, while the 70s-vintage vessels continued in service into the 2000s. It is telling that while larger and more opulent tonnage was constructed for almost all passenger shipping routes linking to the Nordic countries during the economic upturn of the latter part of the 1980s and the early 90s, none appeared for the Scandinavia-UK routes. Instead, the number passenger-carrying routes and the ships employed on them declined from the mid-80s until the mid-90s, by which time each Nordic country had just one route linking to the UK, operated by just one ship (with the exception of Finland, which had already lost its passenger link to Britain): for Denmark Esbjerg-Harwich, for Sweden Gothenburg-Harwich (after 1999 Gothenburg-Kristiansand-Newcastle), for Norway Bergen-Stavanger-Newcastle, and for Iceland and the Faroe Islands Seydisfördur-Tórshavn-Lerwick-Hanstholm. This latter route, which continued to be operated by Smyril Line, saw the last purpose-built ship arrive for Scandinavia-Britain routes in 2003: the *Norröna* (2) – although it should be kept in mind that the UK connection was only a byproduct of the need to connect Iceland and the Faroes to Denmark, and arguably

The ship of many names: the ***Dana Gloria*** (1) sailed on Denmark/Sweden-UK routes in 1981-83, then reappearing on the Norway-UK routes in 1994-2005, first as the ***Color Viking*** and then from 1998 as the ***Jupiter*** (4), as seen here. *(Marko Stampehl)*

Smyril Line's ***Norröna*** of 2003 was primarily commissioned for the Denmark-Faroes-Iceland link, but also connected the Faroe Islands to the UK, making her the last newbuilt ship on the routes between the Nordic countries and the UK. *(Marko Stampehl)*

Modern cargo handling: trucks are positioned to drive out within minutes of berthing on the cargo deck of the ***Dana Sirena*** (2). Contrast with the picture of her predecessor Parkeston being loaded on page 12. *(John Bryant)*

The ***Sirena Seaways***, ex-***Dana Sirena*** (2) approaching Esbjerg during the final weeks of the last Scandinavia-UK passenger link in summer 2014. *(Bruce Peter)*

the last ship designed from the outset to connect a Nordic country to the UK was the *Dana Anglia* of 1978.

It should have been clear that the demand for a product oriented towards mini cruises had diminished to such a point that radically different thinking was needed but, strangely, a chance in the mode of operation only took place on the Denmark-UK route. DFDS chose to replace their long-serving Esbjerg-Harwich ferry *Dana Anglia* by a newbuilt ropax (acquired in mid-construction) *Dana Gloria* (2) in 2002, which was in turn replaced by the near-sister *Dana Sirena*, which had been rebuilt with larger passenger accommodation, the next year. However, despite the importance of freight services between Scandinavia and Britain – particularly on the Sweden-UK routes – this remained the sole connection converted to ropax operations.

The end

Between 2006 and 2014, the remaining passenger services between the Nordic Countries and Britain were all closed. The contributing factors to all these were two-fold: rising fuel costs made the operation of long-haul passenger-oriented routes uneconomic, especially with older, more fuel-hungry tonnage; at the same time, passenger numbers dwindled as the rise of low-cost airlines made air travel an option to almost all travellers, regardless of their income, and Britain failing to join the Schengen agreement made travel to Britain less appealing than countries within the Schengen area after all the Nordic countries joined Schengen in 2001.

The first to go was the Gothenburg-Kristiansand-Newcastle route, still operated by the 1976-vintage *Princess of Scandinavia* (ex-*Tor Scandinavia*), which was nearing the end of her economic lifespan in northern European service. While studies of converting the route to a ropax service looked "promising", especially considering the high numbers of cargo being conveyed (on DFDS' own ships) between Sweden and Britain, this option was never pursued and the route was closed down in 2006.

Coinciding with the closure of the Sweden-UK service, DFDS purchased the Bergen-Stavanger-Newcastle route and its sole ship, the 1986-built *Fjord Norway*, from Fjord Line (which had taken over the service in 1997, the route having changed owners several times during the previous two decades) which was renamed *Princess of Norway*. While DFDS had high hopes for the route, especially its potential as a mini cruise product, these proved false and the service was closed already in 2008. Despite the short time under DFDS operation, the ship used on the route had been changed and the last ship to offer regular passenger service between Norway and the UK was the *Queen of Scandinavia* of 1981.

Also discontinued in 2008 was Smyril Line's link from the Faroe Islands to Britain. Calls at Lerwick, in the Shetland Islands, had ceased in 2006, but these had been replaced by a service to the port of Scrabster in the Scottish mainland. Although the route experienced promising growth, Smyril Line's financial difficulties forced the company to reorganise their sailing schedules, concentrating solely on the core route linking the Faroe Islands to Denmark in the south and Iceland in the North.

Thus, after 2008, just one Scandinavia-UK service remained, the Esbjerg-Harwich route operated by the ropax *Dana Sirena*. Even with ropax tonnage, the route struggled to make a profit. With new International Maritime Organisation - imposed regulations on sulphur emissions from ships, and resulting projected higher fuel costs, due to come for Northern Europe in 2015, DFDS calculated the route would start making a loss, and it was closed down at the end of the 2014 summer season.

Thus, after nearly 200 years, the passenger link between the Nordic countries and Britain ceased. These sea routes are now the sole domain of freighters, which carry the cargoes which previously co-existed with passengers. Yet, the stories of the different passenger services were more complex than this overview lets on, and next we will look at services to Britain from each of the Nordic countries in more detail.

Chapter Two

Finland to Britain: The White Ships and the Red Ships

The Finland-UK liner ***Capella*** of 1888, seen here unloading in Helsinki, was FÅA's first vessel with limited passenger accommodation and rudimentary ice reinforcements. *(Alexander Eugen Maconi, Helsingin kaupunginmuseo (CC BY 4.0))*

The services between Finland and the United Kingdom differ notably from those from the other Nordic Countries. From Finland, ships not only had to traverse the North Sea, but also an equally long stretch of the Baltic Sea to reach Britain – and in order to maintain an around-the-year service, ships had to be reinforced for ice navigation. Thus it is not perhaps a surprise that not only was Finland the last Nordic country to gain a dedicated UK passenger connection, it was also the first to lose it. Further unusual features were the dominance of Soviet shipping companies in the Finland-UK services after World War II, and the (related) fact the routes were never properly converted to operation with car-passenger ferries.

From British to Finnish keels

During the mid-19th century, passenger services between Finland – then an autonomous grand duchy ruled by the tsar of Russia – and the UK were not a priority to the few Finnish steamship operators, who concentrated their efforts to linking Finnish ports to Russia, Sweden and Germany. The first Finnish steamer to have carried passengers and cargo from the UK to Finland was the *Constantin* of Sydfinska Ångfartygs Aktiebolaget (literally the Southern Finnish Steamship Company; Swedish was the language of the Finnish upper classes at the time and, therefore, the names of most Finnish shipping companies were in Swedish rather than Finnish) in July 1866. This was, however, simply a way for the owners to

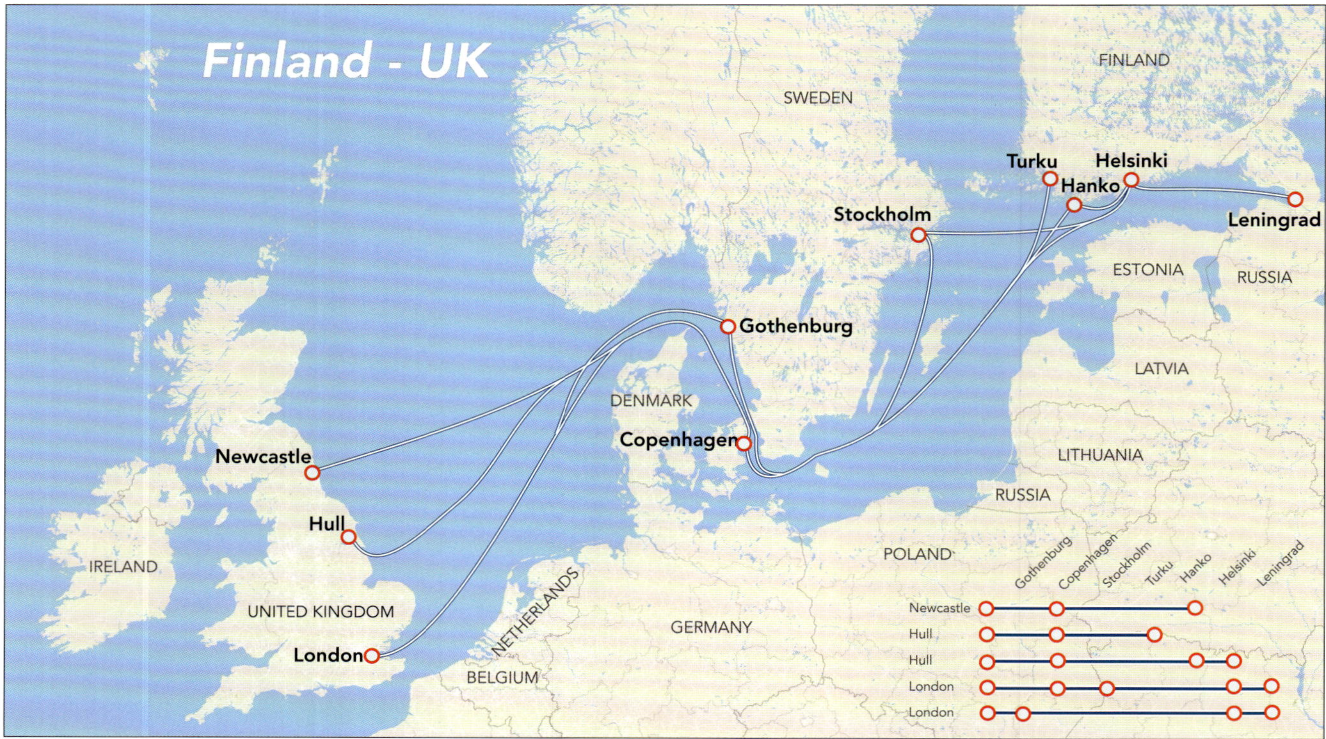

get some additional money from her delivery voyage before placing her on a regular service within the confines of the Baltic Sea.

Yet, the UK was an important trade partner for Finland, being the second-largest recipient of Finnish exports (after Russia, who dominated at circa 50%) and the third-largest source of imports (after Russia and Germany).

During the late age of sail Finland had been a small but notable seafaring nation, being amongst the top-ranking countries in the world in terms of ships per capita – though it should be remembered Finland's population was small, estimated at just 1.5 million in the middle of the 19th century. One source consulted for this book even claimed that, at most extensive, Finland's merchant fleet would have accounted for no less than 80 percent of the merchant fleet of the entire Russian Empire(!), though this seems dubious. The factors that made Finland a success story in age of sail seafaring were hard to transfer to steam navigation, however: sailing vessels had been locally built from local materials (with little need for hard currency), they were largely used for cross trading (rather than serving the needs of Finnish exports), and they were often old on for further trading quickly, sometimes at the end of their first voyage. Thus, the end of the age of sail meant a decline for Finnish seafaring, and the initiation of regular services to areas outwidth the Baltic were left to foreign companies.

The first known regular services that carried passengers between Finland and the UK were initiated in 1869 by the UK company Bailey & Leetham, who offered passenger accommodation on their vessels. How many passengers were truly carried is unknown; Finnish literature indicates they did carry at least limited numbers passengers, and the company did advertise their "first-class steamers" in Finnish newspapers, but there is no mention of passenger services in Arthur Credland and Richard Greenwood's fleet history of the company. Of course, at the time it was common for even relatively larger numbers of passengers to be carried onboard cargo vessels.

Bailey & Leetham was a major Hull-based company, established in 1854 by William Bailey and William Leetham to operate cargo steamers from Hull to Saint Petersburg via Riga and Reval (present-day Tallinn), beginning operations in 1856. By the time they started serving Finland, the company had a large route network linking Hull, Newcastle and London to ports in the Baltic, North Sea, Portugal, Mediterranean and Africa. Services from Hull to Helsinki were weekly and London to Helsinki every ten days, operated outside the winter season. An intermediate call at Reval was included from 1972. The first Bailey & Leetham ship to serve Finland was the 1854-built *Leal* of 565 gross register tons, but he company's ships were rotated between services and there was no regular vessels assigned to the routes to Finland – at least 19 different vessels are recorded to have been used on the services to Finland during the two decades Bailey & Leetham operated passenger services between Finland and the UK.

In 1873, a competitor for Bailey & Leetham was established in Finland: the Wasa-Nordsjö Ångbåts Aktiebolaget (lit. Vaasa-North Sea Steamboat Company), based in the Finnish port of Nikolaistad (present-day Vaasa), founded for the sole purpose of establishing a Finnish-flagged shipping connection linking Nikolaistad to Hull via other Finnish ports and Copenhagen. Wasa-Nordsjö started operations in 1874 with the purpose-built steamer *Fennia*. This was the first time a Finnish company operated a liner service to ports outside the Baltic Sea. The

Above: The ***Una*** of 1873 was one of Bailey & Leetham's more regular visitors to Finland. This painting by J.W. Usher illustrates why the company funnel colours earned them the nickname "Tombstone Line." *(Maritime Museum: Hull Museums)*

Left: The 1890-built ***Constantia*** is an example of the cargo steamers both Wasa-Nordsjö and FÅA used on the Finland-UK link around the turn of the century. *(Rosenlewin museo/Suomen laivahistoriallinen yhdistys)*

Middle left: FÅA's first proper passenger vessel, the ***Urania*** (1) of 1891, photographed in Helsinki in the original, rather funereal livery. *(Helsingin kaupunginmuseo (CC BY 4.0))*

Bottom left: Erkki Riimala's drawing showing the 1891 ***Astræa*** in the white-hulled livery applied around the turn of the century, which earned FÅA's passenger fleet the popular nickname "The White Ships." *(Suomen laivahistoriallinen yhdistys)*

Below: The migration to North America often turned to a festive affair, as people were away from the close-knit communities and their enforced moral standards for the first time in their life. This 1893 photo by the ***Urania***'s (1) captain J.A. Rosqvist shows the migrant passengers dancing on deck. *(J.A. Rosqvist, Museovirasto)*

Fennia and almost all subsequent Wasa-Nordsjö ships were cargo carriers with little to no provisions for the carriage of passengers.

As already indicated, the traffic to and from Finland was restricted to an extended summer season, as during the winters months the Baltic Sea froze over, rendering all Finnish ports inaccessible to the ships of the era.

In April 1883, a new shipping company was established in Finland's capital Helsinki: Finska Ångfartygs Aktiebolaget, or FÅA for short (traditionally, the name is translated into English as Finland Steamship Company, although the literal translation would be Finnish Steamship Company). The purpose of the new company was "to establish a direct steamship link between English ports and those on [Finnish coast of] the Gulf of Finland", with the goal of carrying Finnish goods on Finnish keels. FÅA immediately contracted a pair general cargo steamers, the *Sirius* (2) and *Orion* (also giving birth to FÅA's stellar nomenclature). Initially, these were placed on a Turku-Copenhagen-Hull service in 1884 in a joint service with Wasa-Nordsjö (ironically not serving any ports on the Gulf of Finland). The prime cargos were butter, which was at the time one of Finland's most important exports to the UK, and paper products. Wood and tar were also exported from Finland to the UK, but they were of relatively low value for their weight and thus usually shipped with cheaper but slower sailing ships (and later with slower dedicated cargo ships).

The importance of Britain for Finnish foreign trade begun to grow soon after FÅA had begun operations. The biggest factor in this was Russia raising custom duties for imports from Finland in 1885, which led to a gradual decline of Russia's importance as a trading partner, and the UK growing to eventually rival Russia as the biggest receiver of Finnish exports, receiving almost one-third of the total. However, the trade was somewhat unbalanced, as in terms of imports Britain was not nearly as important – in this field, it was Russia and Germany that dominated, with Britain's share in overall Finnish exports at only around ten percent of the total, and Britain's share of imports to Finland actually diminished, rather than grew, as the century progressed. Perhaps because of the relatively small number of British goods carried, the competition from Finnish operators led to Bailey & Leetham cutting down their service frequency: in 1887, the company advertised fortnightly from Hull to Helsinki, with some sailings routed via Turku. Subsequently, services ceased entirely. Bailey & Leetham itself was taken over by the Wilson Line (of which more in subsequent chapters) in 1903.

FÅA begins passenger services

FÅA made their first overture to the carriage of passengers in 1888, when the new *Capella* of 1,102 grt was delivered from the Schiffswerft von Henry Koch in Lübeck, Germany. She had dedicated passenger accommodation of 18 berths in first class, as well as rudimentary hull reinforcements to allow extension of the sailing season in early winter and late spring. She was, however, just the first step.

In 1891 FÅA took delivery of their first proper passenger liners for Finland-UK routes: the *Urania* (1) and *Astræa,* both from Wigham Richardson & Co in Newcastle. In terms of gross tonnage (somewhat in excess of 1,100), they were only slightly larger that FÅA's older cargo carriers, but could carry 252 in three classes (22 in first, 34 in second and 186 in third) alongside cargo. In practice it was not unusual for double the specified number to be carried, with the excess number being allocated to "deck class". The ships were funded by a "loan" from the Finnish Senate, which FÅA did not need to repay if they maintained an around-the-year service for transport of butter and passengers between Finland and the UK for a decade (which they did). To ensure this, the hulls, propellers and rudders of the *Urania* (1) and *Astræa* were heavily reinforced, allowing them a limited degree of autonomous operation in ice-infested waters, and making them strong enough to withstand the ice pressure when assisted by an icebreaker in more challenging conditions. The first Finnish icebreaker, the *Murtaja* (literally "breaker") had been delivered in 1890, which made around-the-year services possible for ships with ice-reinforced hulls. As the *Murtaja* was based in Hanko, the port at Finland's southernmost tip, the *Urania* (1) and *Astræa* sailed from there during the winters, offering a weekly service. Outside the ice season, they continued onwards to Helsinki and Turku on alternating weeks.

The majority of passengers sailing from Hanko to Hull were migrants bound for North America. As Finnish autonomy came under attack during the later decades of the 19th century – particularly during the reign of Tsar Nikolay II (Николай II, more commonly known in English as Nicholas II, and in Finnish as Nikolai II, who ruled 1894-1917) – many Finns opted to emigrate. Drawing from the nationalist ideas that came to dominate European discourse at the time, a regime of Russification was imposed on minorities across the multicultural empire (only about half of the inhabitants of the Russian Empire were ethinically Russian), which resulted in FÅA attracting migrants from all over the Empire; the company had sales offices for migrants as far away as Odessa. The importance of non-Finnish passengers in the migrant trade was such that FÅA printed information for potential migrants in Finnish, Russian and Hebrew – Hanko was a major departure port for Russian Jews bound for North America.

As far as the migrants were concerned, the Hanko-Hull line was a feeder service for the transatlantic liners bound for the United States and Canada. FÅA acted as the Finnish and Russian agents for many transatlantic liner operators, for instance Allan Line, Anchor Line, Cunard Line, Dominion Line and White Star Line.

Years of competition

As both passenger and cargo numbers were growing fast on the Finland-UK route, additional vessels were delivered during the last years of the 19th century. Wasa-Nordsjö, perhaps encouraged by FÅA's success, took delivery of their first and only passenger vessel for open-sea services, specifically designed to carry migrants from Finland to the UK: the *Vega* (2), built in 1898 by Wasa-Nordsjö's favoured shipyard Murdoch & Murray in Glasgow. At 610 grt, the ship was relatively small; she is recorded as having carried both first-class passengers and migrants, but the precise capacity was not discovered when making this book. When, later on, she joined the DFDS fleet (of which more in Chapter 5), she was listed as carrying 353 passengers. Despite being owned by a company dedicated to the port of Nikolaistad, the *Vega* (2) seems to have primarily sailed between Hanko and Hull (in addition to which she made ailings on coastal services linking Finnish ports to Saint Petersburg).

More substantial newbuildings arrived in 1899, when FÅA took delivery of a second pair of cargo-passenger liners, the circa 2,000 grt *Arcturus* (2) and *Polaris* (1), from the Gourlay Bros. & Co. yard in Dundee. Growth compared to the previous generation ships was mostly in terms of cargo volume (and also included a "cooled" cargo hold for butter transport), as the passenger capacity was only slightly higher at 265 (80 first, 18 second and 167 third class), but the new ships did not replace the older pair; therefore FÅA's passenger capacity doubled. The *Arcturus* (2) and *Polaris* (1) sailed on the Helsinki-Hanko-Copenhagen-Hull route (Helsinki still only outside the winter season), while the *Urania* (1) and *Astræa* sailed from Turku to Hull via Copenhagen around the year, thanks to Turku having been opened for winter navigation that same year (with the arrival of the locally-owned icebreaker *Avance*). At the same time, intermediate calls at Reval (Tallinn) were added to some sailings, particularly during the winter season, when most ships regularly sailing between Reval and the Finnish ports had to suspend services. The routes to both Turku and Reval failed to make a profit and were quickly closed down in favour of expanded services from Hanko and Helsinki.

FÅA's success in the state-subvented service attracted others to try their luck. In 1899, a group of shipowners in Turku had made a proposal to the Finnish Senate for around-the-year services from their home city to the United Kingdom, asking for financial support. While the Senate's view of the proposal was tentatively positive, no agreement could be reached (FÅA's decision to introduce the Turku service mentioned above may have been a response to this plan).

Things changed in 1902, when the state-subvented butter transports from Hanko to the UK came up for tender for the ten-year period from 1903 onwards. After recruiting further investments, the people behind the 1899 proposal formed Ångfartygs Ab Nord ("Steamship Company North") and submitted a bid to run a three-ship service from Hanko to Newcastle via Copenhagen, also calling at Turku "when possible". Nord won the concession, their victory being explained in different sources with either Nord asking for a lower level of state support than FÅA, or by political concerns: several of FÅA's owners were known supporters of (passive) resistance to Russia's attempts of restricting Finnish autonomy, whereas Nord's owners political leaning were held to be more pro-Russian.

The new operator contracted three identical ships – the *Nord I*, *Nord II* and *Nord III* – at the Sir Raylton, Dixon & Co yard in Middlesbrough. These were 1,400 tonners with a capacity for 189 passengers (24 first class, 28 second and 137 third). Unfortunately, the ships had been ordered too late to actually make the planned traffic start in the beginning of 1903. The *Nord I* was delivered in an incomplete state in November 1902, after which it sailed to Helsinki for hasty completion at the Hietalahti shipyard. In its absence, chartered cargo tonnage maintained the service.

Problems did not end there. When the *Nord I* was finally about to embark on her maiden voyage in early January 1903, she was withheld certification for carrying passengers due to an insufficient number of watertight bulkheads and thus had to sail without passengers. The *Nord IIm* delivered later in the same month, also lacked the required number of watertight compartments, but her arrival allowed for the *Nord I* to be rebuilt so that carriage of passengers could begin. Only the *Nord III*, delivered in June, fulfilled requirements from the start.

A briefly grey-hulled ***Astræa*** stuck in ice outside Hanko, with the 1891-built icebreaker Murtaja arriving to assist on the right. *(Hangon museo/Suomen laivahistoriallinen yhdistys)*

The only know surviving photo of Wasa-Nordsjö's ***Vega*** (2), closest to the camera, with two FÅA coastal steamers ahead of her. *(Matti Pietikäinen collection, Suomen laivahistoriallinen yhdistys)*

In contrast with the ships of FÅA, which carried fairly sombre liveries of a black funnel and initially black but later white hulls, Ångfartygs Ab Nord chose more lively and nationalistic funnel colours to accompany their black hulls: yellow with a black top, and a wide red band between the two. At the time, the red and gold colours of the Finnish coat of arms were widely considered to be the national colours of Finland (particularly amongst the Swedish-speaking elite, who were behind all Finnish shipping companies of note at the time); it was only after the events of the Finnish Civil War of 1918 (described below) that while and blue colours came to dominate and were eventually chosen for the Finnish national flag.

Despite the loss of the state contract to Nord, FÅA did not reduce their services on the Finland-UK run – the UK route was their most profitable, and they were unwilling to give up without a fight. Under these circumstances, the FÅA leadership must have been pleased to see the Nord ships struggle while their own quartet of steamers ran like clockwork, providing two departures from both Hanko and Hull every week. In this period of intense competition, the first loser was Wasa-Nordsjö with their sole passenger vessel *Vega* (2). Unable to find passengers or cargoes on the Hanko-Hull route, Wasa-Nordsjö sold the ship in spring 1904 to DFDS, who used the ship on their Denmark-UK-Faroes-Iceland routes (of which more in Chapter 5). A part reason for the failure of the *Vega*'s (2) failure – and one that very much affected Nord, too – was the fact that FÅA continued to be the Finnish and Russian agents for the majority of transatlantic passenger steamers sailing from UK ports, which meant that even without the state subvention, they continued to siphon most of the lucrative migrant trade.

Ångfartygs Ab Nord did not survive much longer: although they received additional state support, the owners had no choice but to accept when FÅA offered to buy the entire company in Autumn 1904. FÅA's leadership held the trio of Nord ships to be "entirely unsuitable" in terms of design and construction, and instead of being employed in FÅA's growing route network they were laid up and put for sale, still officially registered under Nord ownership. Perhaps the assessment was accurate, as it took several months to find a buyer for the almost new ships – and even then FÅA was forced to accept loss-making prices to be rid of them.

Titania – "largest and most beautiful"

The political instability in Russia raised passengers numbers on FÅA's UK services during the new century; many chose to migrate to North America, often choosing FÅA ships to begin their voyage. To meet with the growing demand, in 1908 FÅA introduced the largest Finnish vessel hitherto, the 3,500 grt *Titania*, which could carry 739 passengers (86 first, 68 second and 585 third class). The *Titania* was also to retain the title of largest Finnish passenger vessel for an exceptionally long time (though the ship herself was short-lived, as we shall see): only in 1961 was a larger passenger vessel built for Finnish owners, and the *Titania*'s number of cabin berths was only surpassed in 1975. FÅA's "stellar" naming tradition was perpetuated, as Titania is one of the moons of Uranus. Contemporaries considered the *Titania* sleek and beautiful; her first captain, Johan Rosqvist, was quoted saying "it is unlikely that a more beautiful ship will ever be seen". Rosqvist later claimed FÅA had ambitions to use the *Titania* to start a transatlantic service of their own, but if true, this idea was never acted on – possibly because they would have competed directly with the DFDS-owned Skandinavien-Amerikalinien (Scandinavian America Line). By this time DFDS and FÅA enjoyed very cordial relationships: DFDS had recently abandoned their Copenhagen-Helsinki service in favour of FÅA, and both acted as each others' agents in their homelands.

Tragedy met the Hull service in January 1913, when the *Urania* (1) sank in the Kattegat after colliding with the Norwegian cargo carrier *Fancy* in thick fog. All passengers and

The ***Arcturus*** (2) at wintery Hanko, with the 1898-built icebreaker ***Sampo*** berthed astern. Hanko was specifically built as Finland's rail-connected winter harbour in 1873, but traffic only begun in earnest with the arrival of the first icebreaker in 1891. *(Suomen laivahistoriallinen yhdistys)*

Above: An ice-encrusted ***Arcturus*** (2) loading at Helsinki in the 1920s. An open sea in sub-zero temperatures would create such potentially dangerous ice cover on the ship. *(K.O. Broström, Helsingin kaupunginmuseo (CC BY 4.0))*

Left: The ***Arcturus*** (2) at Hanko on Midsummer 1902, with traditional birch tree saplings decorating the railings. Note the original FÅA jack, which combined elements of the Union Jack and the jack of the Imperial Russian Navy. *(Erkki Riimala collection, Suomen laivahistoriallinen yhdistys)*

Bottom left: The ***Nord I*** in grey undercoat, likely photographed during the rushed completion works at the Hietalahti shipyard in Helsinki around new year 1903. *(Suomen laivahistoriallinen yhdistys)*

Bottom right: The ***Nord III*** in Turku, showing the final black-hulled livery. *(Alex Federley, Sjöhistoriska institutet vid Åbo Akademi)*

The brand-new ***Titania***, flagged overall, displaying her sleek lines in what is likely her builder's publicity photo. *(Suomen laivahistoriallinen yhdistys)*

The ***Titania***'s first class dining room was opulently decorated in the classical style favoured at the time of her completion. *(Joonas Kortelainen collection)*

A late-winter view of the ***Urania*** (2). Unfortunately, the photo gives no clue of the location, though the ice suggests this must be a Finnish port. *(Suomen laivahistoriallinen yhdistys)*

crew were safely evacuated. As a replacement, FÅA acquired from France the Societé Generale des Transports Maritimes à Vapeur -owned, 1897-built passenger steamer *Russie* of 1,900 grt and 600 passengers (102 first, 48 second and 450 third class); she inherited the name *Urania*. Prior to entering service on the Helsinki-Hanko-Copenhagen-Hull line, the *Urania* (2) was drydocked and rebuilt at Earle's in Hull, where her hull, propellers and rudders were reinforced for ice navigation.

World War I and the Finnish Civil War

Both the *Titania* and *Urania* (2) were short-lived. When World War I broke out, Finland, as a part of the Russian Empire, was drawn into the conflict as a part of the Entente. While Finland was spared fighting (until the Finnish Civil War, discussed below), Finnish ships were requisitioned by the Entente Powers. The *Titania* was requisitioned by the British Admiralty and became the auxiliary cruiser HMS *Tithonus*. She was sunk by a German U-boat in winter 1918. Meanwhile, the *Urania* (2) had been chartered to the Imperial Russian Navy and struck a mine in 1915. When the *Polaris* (1) had been also requisitioned by the Russian Navy and remained in Soviet Russia after the October Revolution (which made it impossible for Finnish owners to retrieve their ships for the time being), only the *Astræa* and *Arcturus* (2) remained of the UK route ships at the end of the war.

Finland unilaterally declared itself independent from Russia on 6 December 1917. Technically, the declaration was within the Finnish Parliament's rights as, by terms of the Finnish constitution, Finland was tied to Russia by the person of the Tsar, and Nikolay II's abdication in February 1917 had sewered this link. Russia's new Bolshevik rulers accepted Finnish independence in the end of 1917; for the Finns, the Bolsheviks' rise to power had been blessing in disguise, as they were the only major political force in Russia in favour of Finnish independence. Of course, Lenin and his comrades expected that Finnish workers – like those of every other capitalist country – would soon rise in revolution, just as those in Russia had done. A Finnish civil war did break out in spring 1918, between social democrat -dominated "Red" forces and conservative "Whites," but the Whites triumphed, in part thanks to a military intervention from Germany. (As a result of the alliance between the Whites and Germany, British forces clashed with White Finnish troops in Russian Karelia).

FÅA's *Arcturus* (2) played a small but important role in the conflict: during World War I, many dissatisfied Finns had left the country and joined the German army with hopes that Germany would help Finland become independent (committing treason in the process). After the civil war broke out, Germany discharged the Finnish fighters, the vast majority of whom opted to join the White side and were taken to Vaasa, formerly Nikolaistad (the temporary capital of the White side), onboard the *Arcturus* (2). As Finns had been exempt from military service since 1905 (and before that only 10% of the population had been selected for military service), the German-trained soldiers in part helped the white side gain the upper hand.

The era of rebuilding

The Helsinki-Hanko-Copenhagen-Hull service reopened in 1919, operated by the war survivors *Astræa* and *Arcturus* (2), alongside the small cargo-only steamer *Baltic*. During the winter seasons they were supplemented by the *Ariadne* (1) of 1914, which had been built with the Helsinki-Tallinn-Stettin service in mind, and indeed sailed to Germany outside the winter season (Reval was renamed Tallinn after Estonia became independent in 1918, although the use of the old form continued alongside the new one for many decades). The link to Germany was different from the UK route: whereas the latter attracted mainly migrants, the former primarily saw business from wealthy travellers and Finland's cultural elite. Reflecting the differences, the 2,900 grt *Ariadne* catered to just first and second class passengers, and first class was disproportionately larger: no less than 178 of the 236 passenger berths were in first class. This, naturally, made her something of a misfit on the Hull service, where third-class passengers were the largest group.

Even after the fall of the German Empire, the upper social strata in Finland saw Germany as the advanced country to emulate in terms of culture and technology (although, fortunately, not in politics), and Germany enjoyed notable goodwill for their help to the White side in the Finnish Civil War. In contrast, Britain was seen as an "egotistical country" to which good relations needed to be maintained out of nescessity; Britain had opposed the White side in the Finnish Civil War, and the Royal Navy had recruited circa 1,000 former "Red" fighters – including Oskari Tokoi, a central Social Democrat politician – during and after the Civil War to fight in the North Russia intervention. Britain was only willing to recognise Finnish independence on the condition that these

A 1930s view of the ***Ariadne*** arriving in Helsinki. She remained in the FÅA fleet until her scrapping in 1969, serving on all of the company's major routes. Notice the new design of the FÅA jack, similar to that of P&O, but with FÅA's star emblem in the center. *(Kurt Illimisky, Suomen laivahistoriallinen yhdistys)*

The French-built ***Oberon*** of 1925 was externally still fairly similar to the pre-war generation, but her art deco style interiors, refrigerated cargo holds and exceptionally strong ice reinforcements set her apart from her predecessors. *(Rami Wirrankoski collection)*

The first class lounge onboard the ***Oberon***, displaying the simple, geometric forms of decor favoured by the forward-looking elites of the inter-war era. *(Roos, Suomen laivahistoriallinen yhdistys)*

"The attention shown to the third class passengers onboard the ***Oberon*** is gratifying", wrote the Finnish newspaper Hufvudstadsbladet when the ship was delivered. Seen here is the third class dining room. *(Roos, Suomen laivahistoriallinen yhdistys)*

fighters would be either pardoned or allowed exile in Canada – despite the fact they were considered traitors by White Finland. Fenno-British relations were thus understandably strained.

Passenger patterns on the Hanko-Hull service changed after World War I. Following the rise of Soviet rule in Russia, the previously lucrative migrant market from Russia dried up: not only did the Soviets curtail foreign travel, but the various ethnic minorities of the former Empire were granted either independence or autonomy, which naturally made people less eager to migrate (of course, the freedoms granted to various non-Russian nationalities were temporary, as Stalin would later go on to impose worse Russification policies than those of Imperial Russia had ever been). A second blow followed in 1921, when the United States radically curtailed the number of migrants accepted into the country. To improve passenger loadings on the Finland-UK service, and to make use of their extensive connections to transatlantic operators, FÅA begun to market holidays in Finland to British and American travellers. The company also continued to market return trips from North America to Finland to migrants who had not found life in the new continent to their liking – an important passenger group largely neglected in the story of the transatlantic migrant service. But the new passenger groups could not replace the migrants in terms of sheer numbers. At the same time, Britain became the central trade partner for Finland (despite the political mistrust outlined above): during the inter-war era, Britain was the largest recipient of Finnish exports by some margin, receiving approximately 40 percent of the total. Imports from Britain also grew, but to "only" circa 20 percent of the total, with Germany now the biggest source of imports.

Curtailing the migrant trade was reflected in the design of

FÅA's next new ship for the Hull service, the *Oberon* from Ateliers et Chantiers de Saint-Nazaire Penhoët (later famous under the name Chantiers de l'Atlantique), delivered in 1925 (as with the *Titania*, the *Oberon* was named after a moon of Uranus). At 3,000 grt, she was the largest Finnish-flagged passenger ship of the time (although, of course, smaller than the *Titania* had been), but carried only 372 passengers,126 in first class and 246 in third; second class was eliminated completely (third class was later "rebranded" as second). She was fitted with refrigerated cargo holds, a first for FÅA, to ease the export of butter. The *Oberon* was most notable, however, for her interior design, which was by French architects in what is known today as art deco style, making her one of the first passenger vessels to be decorated in this manner. Indeed, the *Oberon* predated the French transatlantic liner *Île de France* – credited for revolutionising shipboard interiors with her art deco stylings – by two years. The *Oberon* replaced the *Astræa* on the Finland-UK route, though the older ship did return to the route occasionally before her sale in 1929.

Red sun rising

In the years following the October Revolution, Soviet Russia and later the Soviet Union (formed in 1922, when the previously independent bolshevik-ruled Russia, Belarus, Ukraine and Transcaucasia became a federation) had been largely absent from the international passenger trades. Things changed with Stalin's rise to power and the adoption of the policy of "socialism in one country" (as opposed attempting to encourage an international proletarian revolution) in 1926. Thus, when the Sovetskiy Torgovaya Flot (Советский Торговая Флот, or Sovtorgflot for short, also known as the Soviet Trade Fleet in English) took delivery of a large number of new cargo-passenger liners in 1927-30, they were placed on services to Northern Europe and the Mediterranean. Of these, six ships built by the Severney shipyard in Leningrad were allocated to the Baltiyskoye Morskoye Parokhodstvo (Балтийское морское пароходство, BMP for short, or Baltic Shipping Company in English) for Leningrad-London service via various Nordic ports: the *Jan Rudzutak* (Ян Рудзутак), *Aleksey Rykov* (Алексей Рыков), *Smolnyy* (Смольный), *Feliks Dzerzhinskiy* (Феликс Дзержинский), *Kooperatsiya* (Кооперация) and *Sibir* (Сибирь). All were of circa 3,800 grt and could carry 292 passengers in three classes (28 in first, 24 in second and the rest in third). They were also fitted with refrigerated cargo holds. In contrast to the ships used by FÅA, the Soviets specified cheaper-to-operate diesel propulsion. The first three were built with counter sterns and the rest with cruiser sterns.

The meanings of the ships' names are perhaps of interest: Jan Rudzutak (or Jānis Rudzutaks in his native Latvian) was the then-People's Commissar for Railways; Aleksey Rykov was the Chairman of the Council of People's Commissars (in other words the prime minister of the USSR); the Smolny Institute in then-Petrograd had been the Bolshevik headquarters during and after the October Revolution; Feliks Dzerzhinskiy (Feliks Dzierżyński in his native Polish) had been the Soviet Minister of the Interior and head of the OGPU, the predecessor to the KGB, before he passed away in 1926; while Kooperatsiya and Sibir are Russian for "cooperation" and "Siberia", respectively.

Unsurprisingly, considering the events under Stalin's leadership of the Soviet Union, the ships named after prominent bolsheviks received new names in the 1930s: both Aleksey Rykov and Jan Rudzutak had found their positions in the party diminished after Stalin's rise to power (in the case of the latter, despite him being a supporter of Stalin – simply being an ethnic Latvian made him suspicious in Stalin's eyes), until both were arrested on faked charges of treason in 1937 and executed the next year. Following the arrests, the *Aleksey Rykov* became the *Andrey Zhdanov* (Андрей Жданов), after the Chairman of the Supreme Soviets and Stalin's second in command, while the *Jan Rudzutak* became the *Mariya Ulyanova* (1; Мария Ульянова) after both Lenin's mother and his sister. At the same time, the *Feliks Dzerzhinskiy* was renamed *Ural* (Урал) for reasons unknown (possibly to make the other renamings look less like an excercise in revisionism).

At least initially, the Soviet sextet did not call at Finnish ports en-route, although it is possible the Finnish port was included in the itinerary on an ad hoc basis. As we shall see, the BMP would subsequently become the sole shipping company operating passenger vessels between Finland and the UK, and therefore the early era of these services is included here.

Losses and newbuildings for FÅA

The worst disaster in the history of FÅA took place in 1930: the *Oberon*, bound from Copenhagen to Hull, and the *Arcturus* (2), sailing in the opposite direction, collided in thick fog on the Kattegat. The *Arcturus* (2) remained afloat, but the five-year-old *Oberon* sank, taking with her 42 passengers and crew – including Captain Eric Hjelt, his wife, and their young daughter.

This left just the *Arcturus* (2) to offer regular Hanko-Hull passenger sailings. Supplementing her were the 1927-built *Wellamo* (1) of 1,900 grt (71 first and 106 second class passengers) and the 1929-built *Ilmatar* of 2,400 grt (90 first and 60 second class passengers), which alternated between the UK service and those from Finland to Germany and Sweden (both ships were named after characters in Finnish mythology, a break from FÅA's previous naming tradition). FÅA were in no hurry to acquire a permanent replacement for the *Oberon*, as passenger loadings on the Finland-UK route werelow, in part as an effect of The Great Depression (or pula-aika, roughly translating as "time of shortage(s)", as it was known in Finland) – but it should be noted that both Britain and Finland escaped the effects of the depression relatively lightly, and diminishing passenger numbers in the Finland-UK routes were a longer trend.

Finally, a new vessel for the Finland-UK routes was acquired in 1933 in the form of the *Preussen* purchased from Rud. Christ. Gribel, FÅA's partners on the Finland-Germany routes. The 1912-built steamer – available at a low price due to the ongoing depression – was renamed *Polaris* (2). She could carry just 78 passengers, 60 first class and the remainder in second, but this was deemed acceptable as

Above: The ***Sibir*** was the last of BMP's sextet of Leningrad-London cargo passenger liners. In contrast with FÅA, BMP specified diesel propulsion, with the engines built locally in Leningrad. *(M. Cassar, Rami Wirrankoski collection)*

Left: A postcard view of the ***Aleksey Rykov***. Notice the counter stern of the first ships of the class, compared to the cruiser stern on the ***Sibir*** above. *(Postcard, Rami Wirrankoski collection)*

Middle left: An undated and unlocated view of the ***Feliks Dzerzhinskiy***, though the construction scaffolding around her bow and the incomplete boats aft suggest this is either taken at the Severney shipyard in Leningrad when the ship was under construction, or at a later date when the ship was in need of repairs. *(Rami Wirrankoski collection)*

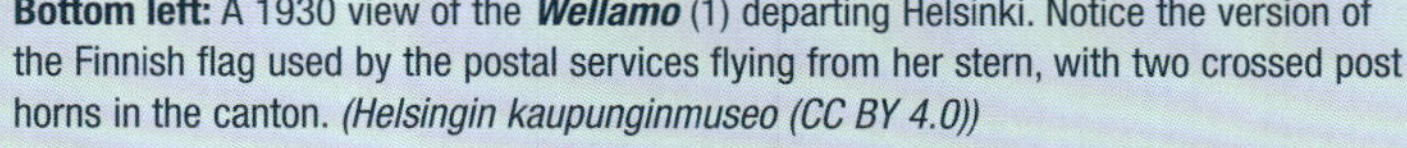

Bottom left: A 1930 view of the ***Wellamo*** (1) departing Helsinki. Notice the version of the Finnish flag used by the postal services flying from her stern, with two crossed post horns in the canton. *(Helsingin kaupunginmuseo (CC BY 4.0))*

Below: The small cargo-oriented ***Polaris*** (2) was acquired to replace the sunken ***Oberon***, but proved too small almost immediately. *(Helsingin kaupunginmuseo (CC BY 4.0))*

This side view of the 1937 ***Aallotar*** nicely illustrates the gradual development of exterior design, with a taller, moderately streamlined superstructure and higher bow compared to the previous generation. *(Kurt Illimisky, Suomen laivahistoriallinen yhdistys)*

focus on the UK service was switching more and more to cargo.

The drop in passenger numbers proved only temporary, however. In 1934, the Finnish state moved the terminal for exporting butter from Hanko to Turku. This prompted FÅA to open a Turku-Hull cargo service, operated around the year, but also a summers-only Turku-Copenhagen-Hull passenger route, operated by the *Wellamo* (1). The effects of the international depression were easing towards the mid-1930s, with passenger numbers starting to rise again in 1935. Finland's trade with the UK had also been encouraged by the tying of the value of the Finnish Markka to the British Pound in 1933. In the new situation, the *Polaris* (2) proved something of a misinvestment, proving too small for the growing passenger numbers. In the new situation, FÅA contracted a new vessel

The ***Aallotar*** somewhere in Danish waters, possibly taken during her sea trials. *(Museet for Søfart)*

A line-up of current and former UK ships in Helsinki: from left to right ***Ilmatar***, ***Aallotar*** and ***Ariadne***. Notice the altered livery on the ***Aallotar***, with the bridge now painted a brown woodish shade and less of the same shade along the main deck compared to the images above. *(Roos, Suomen laivahistoriallinen yhdistys)*

The lights are going out: wartime neutrality markings being painted on the ***Polaris*** (2) in 1939. *(Hede Foto, Suomen laivahistoriallinen yhdistys)*

for the Finland-UK services from Helsingør Skibsværft og Maskinbyggeri in Helsingør (Elsinore), Denmark, for delivery in 1937. While waiting for the new ship, the *Ilmatar* was moved back to the UK routes in place of the *Polaris* (2), sailing alongside the *Arcturus* (2) on the Helsinki-Hanko-Copenhagen-Hull service, offering weekly departures.

The new vessel for the Helsinki-Hull route, named *Aallotar* (again after a Finnish mythology character), was delivered in 1937 from Helsingør. At 2,900 gross register tons, the ship was of similar size to her predecessors, but carried fewer passengers: 97 in first class and 84 in second. In contrast to most other Nordic operators, Finnish shipping companies continued to specify ships with steam propulsion, and the *Aallotar* was no exception. The reason for this was the fact that steamers were better suited for ice navigation, whereas – with technology available at the time – a successful diesel-engined ice-going vessel would have needed expensive electric transmission. On arrival of the *Aallotar*, the *Wellamo* (1) appears to have moved to the Finland-Sweden routes, while the *Arcturus* and *Ilmatar* remained on the UK routes alongside the *Aallotar*.

Wartime newbuildings

World War II broke out in Europe on 1 September 1939, when Germany declared war on Poland and, in turn, Britain and France declared war on Germany. Not wishing to see a repeat of the events of World War I, when many Finnish ships had been left in foreign ports and requisitioned for military use by foreign navies, FÅA immediately recalled all their ships. Although not known at the time, FÅA's Finland-UK passenger link would never be restored. The Soviet Union also declared war on Poland on 17 September, which resulted in the cessation of Soviet passenger services (Britain and France did not declare war on the Soviet Union).

In October, the Soviets invited Finns to Moscow to discuss territorial exchanges: the Soviets wanted to move the border on the Karelian Isthmus further from Leningrad, and to rent Hanko as a military base. In exchange, the Soviets offered Repola and Porajärvi, Finnish-inhabited municipalities in Eastern Karelia on the Finnish border (Finland had occupied these in 1918-1921), with an area more than twice of that demanded by the Soviets. After the negotiations failed, the Soviet Union staged a faked Finnish artillery attack on the village of Mainila, the so-called Shelling of Mainila, in late November, providing an excuse for an attack. Unsurprisingly, Finland lost the 105-day-long Winter War, and was forced to cede 11% of its territory (much more than the Soviets had demanded before the war), including the country's second-biggest city Vyborg (or Viipuri in Finnish), and rent Hanko as a military base. A second war – The Continuation War – was fought in 1941-1944 between Finland and the Soviet Union, with Finland now attacking the Soviet Union as a de facto ally of Germany to regain the territories lost in 1940 (a legal fiction of Finland fighting a separate war was maintained in an attempt of preserving relations to the western Allies. This was not entirely successful: Britain declared war on Finland and the Royal Air Force assisted the Soviet assaults on Finnish forces). This war, too, ended in Finnish defeat and further territorial concessions. The final conflict of the era for Finland was the Lapland War of 1944-45, where Finns attacked their former German allies at the insistence of the Soviet Union.

Like many other liner operators, neither FÅA nor BMP saw the clouds of war gathering over Europe and contracted new ships for their passenger services in the late 1930s, delivered only after hostilities had begun.

The BMP contracted a pair of liners for the Leningrad-London service from the Nederlandsche Dok & Scheepsbouw in Amsterdam (some sources claim they were originally designed for Far Eastern waters). The 7,500 grt and 450 passenger ships were the largest Soviet passenger vessels hitherto, and were suitably named by the then-leaders of the Soviet Union: *Iosif Stalin* (осиф Стали , General Secretary of the Central Committee of the Communist Party) and *Vyacheslav Molotov* (Вячеслав Молото , Chairman of the Council of People's Commissars). In contrast to the older vessels, these were equipped with steam turbines and electric transmission.

The pair were only delivered in spring 1940, when Europe was already at war. Both were used as troop transports on the Baltic Sea and were seriously damaged in 1941: the *Iosif Stalin* (which had been renamed *-521*, or *VT-521* in latin script) when evacuating Hanko in the beginning of the Continuation

War and the *Vyacheslav Molotov* (renamed *VT-509*) when evacuating Tallinn before the imminent German occupation. The *Iosif Stalin/VT-521* sunk on the coast of Estonia (her wreck is still visible in shallow waters), but the *Vyacheslav Molotov* fared better, as we shall see below.

FÅA also contracted a new passenger ship, this time for the Turku-Copenhagen-Hull route, in the late 1930s. This was built at the Crichton-Vulcan yard in Turku – the first time FÅA had contracted a passenger liner from a Finnish yard, and the first time they specified diesel propulsion on a passenger vessel. Reflecting the increased cargo focus on the UK service, the *Astrea* (note the different spelling from the previous *Astræa*) was specified to carry just 34 passengers in first class and 16 in third, despite being the largest ship for the routes since the *Titania* in terms of gross tonnage at 3,300 grt.

By the time the *Astrea* was delivered in May 1941, Finland was enjoying the so-called interim peace between the Winter War and the Continuation War, but there was no hope using the ship in a commercial service and she was laid up. In early 1944, she was sold to Stockholms Rederi AB Svea, FÅA's long-standing partners on the Finland-Sweden routes. The sale allowed FÅA to repay a previous loan taken in Swedish Krona, which was becoming a financial burder due to the sinking value of the Finnish Markka. However, political matters may have also been at play, as the sale meant the *Astrea* would not be handed over to the Soviet Union as a war reparation. Possibly the idea had even been that FÅA could buy her back after war reparations had been paid; FÅA's managing director Henrik Ramsay was the Foreign Minister in Finland's wartime cabinet and therefore well aware of the peace negotiations with the Soviet Union (Ramsay was later sentenced to prison as one of the parties responsible for the Continuation War, despite the fact he became a cabinet minister *after* hostilities broke out. While in prison, he wrote the definitive book on early Finnish winter navigation – one of the sources used when writing this chapter). If the intention had been to keep the *Astrea* available for FÅA, this did not happen: in 1945, Svea sold her to Det Bergenske Dampskibsselskab in Norway, who rebuilt the ship with a larger passenger capacity and used her in Norway-UK services. Her later career is explored in more detail in Chapter 4.

If there were fears of losing ships as war reparations, they were well-founded: by the terms of the interim peace treaty that ended the Continuation War in Autumn 1944 (final peace was signed in Paris in 1948), 89 prime vessels of the Finnish merchant fleet had to be handed over to the Soviets. Initially, FÅA were specified to turn over the 1914-built *Ariadne* (1), the 1912-built *Polaris* (2) and the 1929-built *Ilmatar*, all familiar from the UK services, alongside a number of cargo vessels. However, when the *Ariadne* grounded in Finnish waters while on delivery voyage to Leningrad, the Soviets demanded the newer *Aallotar* in her stead. Rumour has it that the *Ariadne's* (1) crew grounded the ship on purpose to stop her falling into Soviet hands – if so, the plan backfired as the *Aallotar* was a superior ship. Furthermore, the Soviets demanded a number of new vessels built as war reparation during a five-year period (later extended to seven years). Had the *Astrea* been returned to FÅA after the initial war reparations had been delivered, it is likely the Soviets would have taken offense and demanded the retroactive handing over of the essentially new ship.

Under the red flag

After hostilities ceased, FÅA's leadership did not see the re-establishment of a passenger link to the UK as a sensible use of their limited resources. The route was re-opened with cargo-only liners, and 1939 remained the last time FÅA operated passenger vessels to UK ports. Post-war, FÅA did run a passenger service outside the Baltic Sea on the Helsinki-Kiel-Antwerp route from 1949, but this was closed in 1957 as FÅA concluded that "there is no future for the once popular passenger lines from Finland to the North Sea ports." FÅA continued as a successful operator of passenger ferries within confines of the Baltic (and cargo vessels worldwide) until 1990, when a complex process of mergers and demergers saw the cargo operations pass to Finnlines and the passenger operations to EffJohn. Today, the remains of the company are

Class reunion: the ***Wellamo*** (1, left) and ***Sestrorestk,*** ex-***Polaris*** (2), now a Soviet ship, at Helsinki in the early 1950s. The building between the two ships with the Dutch-style steep roof is the FÅA headquarters. *(Eino Heinonen, Helsingin kaupunginmuseo (CC BY 4.0))*

Top: The former ***Vyacheslav Molotov***, now renamed the ***Baltika,*** photographed in 1982 but still externally unchanged from her original appearance. *(FotoFlite)*

Above left: The ***Astrea,*** the Finland-UK ship that never was, laid up in Turku during World War II. *(Suomen laivahistoriallinen yhdistys)*

Above right: The former pride of FÅA, ***Aallotar,*** as the Soviet Leningrad-London ship ***Beloostrov***, still with the immediate post-war black-and-red Soviet funnel colours, which were later altered to white-and-red. (*Rami Wirrankoski collection)*

Below: A 1983 view of the ***Baltika*** in Helsinki, where she was a regular visitor for three decades. *(Krzysztof Brzoza)*

owned by Estonia's Tallink Grupp.

FÅA's decision to withdraw from passenger services to the United Kingdom did not mean the end of the Finland-UK passenger link. BMP restarted their passenger route between Leningrad and London after the end of hostilities, now regularly sailing via Helsinki. The precise routes varied through the years and not all route variants are recorded here for the sake of brevity. It appears that the most common post-war route was Leningrad-Helsinki-Stockholm-Copenhagen-London, but at times additional intermediate calls were made at least in Rostock, Tallinn, Gdansk and Gothenburg. The opening of the port of Helsinki for winter navigation in 1956 allowed for around-the-year services (previously, the port has been kept open on an ad hoc basis as the ice situation allowed).

The immediate post-war tonnage on the route was very familiar, as the *Beloostrov* (Белоостров) and *Sestroretsk* (Сестрорецк) were the former *Aallotar* and *Polaris* (2), respectively, now renamed after villages on the Karelian isthmus. Of BMP's 1920s-built sextet, only the *Kooperatsiya* and *Smolnyy* had survived the war, but as far as can be ascertained they did not rejoin the Leningrad-London service. Passenger numbers from Finland during the initial post-war years were limited by, on one hand, the precarious Finnish

Passengers reading on the veranda of the ***Baltika***. *(Henry Casciaro collection)*

The stair vestibule of the ***Baltika***. *(Henry Casciaro collection)*

The ***Baltika*** at Millwall Docks in 1957, being was fitted with new British-made propellers. *(Nordisk Pressefoto/Museet for Søfart (CC-BY-NC-SA))*

financial position, made worse by the heavy war reparations to the Soviet Union, but on the other hand also by the general negative perception of Britain's actions (and inactions) during World War II: many Finns saw the British (and French) failure to act on their promise of large-scale military assistance during the Winter War as a betrayal, a view that seemed to be confirmed when Britain sided with the Soviet Union in the Continuation War. Gradually, these offenses were forgotten, but even so, Finland's primary post-war affiliation (apart from the close relations to the Soviet Union, born out of political realism) was with the other Nordic countries and West Germany. At the same time, the importance of Britain for Finnish foreign trade diminished: from an initial post-war share of circa 25 percent, Britain's importance as a trade partner gradually declined, slipping to just four percent of all Finnish exports in 2018, while on imports Britain initially provided circa 15% in the late 1940s, but by 2018 the figure had dropped to less than three percent.

Neither the *Beloostrov* nor the *Sestroretsk* remained on the Leningrad-London route for long. The latter was transferred to the fleet of the Murmanskoye Morskoye Parokhodstvo (Мурманское морское пароходство, Murmansk Shipping Company) in 1954. Interestingly, the already 42-year-old ship was given an extensive refit, including replacing her steam engines with diesels. She continued to service the Murmanskoye Morskoye Parokhodstvo until 1970. The *Beloostrov* left in 1956, transferred to the fleet of the Chernomorskoye Morskoye Parokhodstvo (Черноморское морское пароходство, Black Sea Shipping Company, known commonly in English with the abbreviation Blasco). In return, BMP received from Dalnevostochnoe Morskoye Parokhodstvo (Дальневосточное морское пароходство, the Far-Eastern Shipping Company, also known as Fesco in English) the 1940-built *Vyacheslav Molotov* discussed above, which would become the mainstay of the Leningrad-London service until its closure. After a brief service on the route, the ship was refitted in East Germany in 1957. During the same year, the *Vyacheslav Molotov* was renamed *Baltika* (Балтика); while the new name was well-suited for the route (and the former name likely carried negative associations amongst the non-Soviet passengers), the reason for the name change was (again) the Soviet Union's internal politics: Molotov fell from favour in 1957 when he attempted to oust Nikita Khrushchëv (Никита Хрущёв) from the position of First Secretary of the Communist Party.

New ships from East Germany

Between 1958 and 1964 the VEB Mathias-Thesen-Werft in East Germany built a series of no less than 19 passenger liners for the various Soviet shipping companies. The very first ship in the class, the *Mikhail Kalinin* (Михаил Калинин) of 1958, was assigned to the BMP, as were the subsequent *Estoniya* (Эстония) of 1960 and the *Nadezhda Krupskaya* (Надежда Крупская) of 1963. Furthermore, in 1963 the BMP received from the Severnoye Morskoye Parokhodstvo (Северное морское пароходство, or the Northern Shipping Company, based in Archangelsk) the 1959-built sister *Mariya Ulyanova* (2; Мария Ульянова). The precise dimensions and capabilities of the vessels varied, but their dimensions were roughly 122 by 16 metres, with a gross register tonnage of circa 5,200 and a passenger capacity of approximately 335.

Of the BMP quartet, the *Mikhail Kalinin, Estoniya* and *Nadezhda Krupskaya* are known to have sailed to the UK, serving alongside the *Baltika*. However, they also carried out other duties, such as supplying the Soviet research base in Antarctica. In 1960, the precise route was Leningrad-Helsinki-Stockholm-Gdynia-Copenhagen-London-Le Havre. With the exception of the self-explanatory *Estoniya*, the new BMP ships were named after Soviet historical figures: Mikhail Kalinin was the first head of state of both Soviet Russia and the Soviet Union, Nadezhda Krupskaya (Lenin's wife) was an important Bolshevik politician, and (as noted above) Mariya Ulyanova was the name of both Lenin's mother and his sister.

The *Mikhail Kalinin* class arrived at an inopportune time. Competition from airlines was growing, as was their competitive advantage in speed due to spreading use of jet airplanes (Finnair, the Finnish state-owned national carrier, had become the first small airline to start using jet airliners in 1960). A larger section of the travelling public chose to do so

During the 1950s and 1960s, the Soviets relied heavily on East German yards for both building and refitting their passenger vessels. The East German-built ***Mikhail Kalinin*** class ships (the ***Nadezhda Krupskaya*** pictured) modernised the tonnage of the Leningrad-London route from the late 1950s onwards. *(FotoFlite)*

The ***Ivan Franko*** was the lead ship of a new, larger class of East German-built ships. Despite being destined for the Black Sea, she briefly sailed on the Leningrad-London route in 1965. *(FotoFlite)*

by air, and the sea route became more and more a budget service for those who could not afford to fly.

Despite the arrival of the newer *Mikhail Kalinin* class ships, the Soviets continued to regard the *Baltika* as something of a ship of state. When Khrushchëv visited New York in 1960 to attend a Plenary Meeting of the United Nations General Assembly (the scene of the infamous shoe incident), he travelled there with the *Baltika* – and enthused in his memoirs how invigorating the sea voyage was.

After the *Mikhail Kalinin* class, in 1964-72, VEB Mathias-Thesen-Werft built the largest newbuilt Soviet passenger vessels of all time, the five-ship *Ivan Franko* (Іван Франко) class, also known as the "author" or "poet" class (as all ships were named after writers from the area of present-day Russia, Ukraine and Georgia). The 176 by 24 metre, 19,900 grt and 750 passenger ships were not built with the Leningrad-London line in mind, but three of them sailed between those ports, calling in Helsinki along the way.

In 1965, two different routes were operated between Leningrad and the UK: the longer Leningrad-Helsinki-Stockholm-Copenhagen-London-Le Havre service operated by the *Nadezhda Krupskaya* and *Estoniya*, and a shorter Leningrad-Helsinki-Gothenburg-London route operated by the *Baltika* and *Ivan Franko*. It is likely that the latter's presence on the route was planned to be temporary from the start, as she belonged to Blasco rather than BMP. That same year, BMP took delivery of their first own *Ivan Franko* class ship, the *Aleksandr Pushkin* (Александр Пушкин). The following spring, the *Aleksandr Pushkin* and *Ivan Franko* initiated a new transatlantic service from Leningrad to Montreal, with intermediate calls in Helsinki, Bremerhaven, London and Quebec although, again, the precise intermediate calls varied over time. Nevertheless, the service did allow passengers also

A postcard view of the ***Mikhail Kalinin*** at Stockholm. Already berthed ahead of her is the Rederi Ab Svea Finland-Sweden ferry ***Svea Jarl***. *(Rami Wirrankoski collection)*

A car being lifted off the ***Mikhail Kalinin*** in Copenhagen, 1962. The arrival of the car-passenger ferry ***England*** two years later likely ended the demand for car transport from the UK to Denmark on the Soviet ships (see Chapter 6). *(Berlingske Tidende/Museet for Søfart CC-BY-NC-SA)*

The ***Finnfellow***, Finnlines' short-lived Finland-UK ferry with limited passenger accommodation, unloading at Felixstowe. The ship's unashamedly functional superstructure served as a model for later Finnish-built icebreakers and early-generation jumbo ferries such as the ***Finnjet***. *(FotoFlite)*

to make a Helsinki-London crossing, though primarily passengers for this leg were directed to the dedicated Leningrad-London route. The Leningrad-Montreal line was one of the rare instances when a transatlantic service has been operated from a Finnish port. It was quickly discovered there was no need for two ships on the route and the service was subsequently run solely by the *Aleksandr Pushkin*.

By 1971 at latest the Soviets' long-haul North European and transatlantic passenger services were made seasonal, operating from April until September. The following year, the call at Helsinki was removed from the Leningrad-Montreal route, with Finland now again served solely by the Leningrad-London route.

The Finnish ferry interlude

The new Soviet ships of the 1950s and 60s, while externally quite attractive, were outdated in terms of design very soon after their delivery. The *Mikhail Kalinin* class had been built just before the advent of car-passenger ferries on long-haul passenger services (as described in the other chapters, car-passenger ferries were introduced on the routes from Denmark, Sweden and Norway to the UK between 1964 and 1966, replacing almost all traditional liners). The Soviets, in contrast, only took delivery of their first car-passenger ferry in 1975 – and never used such ships on the Leningrad-London line. However, 1973 did see the introduction of the first – and only – roro passenger vessel to have sailed between Finland and the UK, the *Finnfellow* of Finnlines.

Owned by Finnish industrial interests, Finnlines had operated cargo services from Finnish to UK ports since the company's foundation in 1947. In 1969, the company – or rather its then-parent Merivienti Oy (literally 'Sea Export Company') – had taken delivery of an exceptional roro vessel, the *Finncarrier*, which was designed to operate independently even in the most difficult ice conditions on the Finnish coast, while carrying 1,600 lane metres of cargo and 36 passengers. The *Finncarrier* and her 1972-built sister *Hans Gutzeit* were placed on the Helsinki-Lübeck route, but the third sister *Finnfellow*, delivered in 1973, entered service on a Helsinki-Kotka-Felixstowe route. The *Hans Gutzeit* and *Finnfellow* were built to a slightly modified design with 48 passenger berths. The *Finnfellow*'s arrival marked the return of Finnish-flagged passenger services to the UK – although admittedly only in limited numbers, with the passenger berths likely reserved solely to cargo drivers.

The end of the line

In the end, the *Finnfellow*'s stint on the UK service proved short. Following the creation of Finncarriers, a joint roro cargo subsidiary of Finnlines and FÅA, in 1976, the *Finnfellow* was transferred to the Helsinki-Lübeck service. After that date, Finncarriers and their partner, the United Baltic Corporation, operated the Finland-UK services with roro freighters, although these continued to have space for up to 12 passengers; on some vessels, such as FÅA's *Arcturus* (3) of 1982, the passenger areas were designed by leading Finnish interior architects of the day and fitted out to a high standard.

As the 1970s progressed, BMP reduced services on the

A late-80s view of the ***Estoniya***, showing the changes made to her aft superstructure when she was converted to a cruise ship. Also note the BMP roro cargo vessel – likely the Finnish-built ***Smolensk*** – sailing parallel to her in the background. *(FotoFlite)*

Leningrad-London routes. Many factors contributed to this: the economic depression following the 1973 oil crisis (while this did not affect the Soviet planned economy as such, their western passengers were effected), increased competition from airplanes, and – perhaps most crucially – the fact the Soviets realised their passenger-only vessels could make more money by cruising (mostly under charter to western tour operators) than in liner traffic. During the decade, both the *Mikhail Kalinin* and the *Estoniya* were converted to cruise ships, the *Nadezhda Krupskaya* was transferred to the Soviet Navy as a troopship and the *Mariya Ulyanova* (2) transferred to the fleet of Fesco. By 1977, only the *Baltika* remained in Soviet Union-UK liner service, sailing on the Leningrad-Helsinki-Copenhagen-London line.

Surprisingly, considering how recent the event is, information on when exactly the Leningrad-Helsinki-London services ceased is conflicting: some sources state this happened at the end of the 1977 summer season, with the *Baltika*, too, converted to full-time cruising, while others claim she made at least occasional line voyages until 1986. Additional research during the making of this book has shed no further light on the subject (quite the opposite, in fact: one of the few contacts the author was able to make in Russia claimed a passenger service continued until 1990, though could provide no further information). It could even be that the services did cease in 1977, but were later restarted (possibly after the cessation of the transatlantic services to Montreal and New York in 1980) and continued until 1986 – but it could equally be that after 1977, all services were cruises and the sources claiming liner voyages continued until 1986 are confusing the two.

What all sources agree on is that the *Baltika* was the last passenger vessel to sail on the Soviet Union-Finland-UK route,

FÅA's 1982 cargo roro ***Arcturus*** (3) was considered the company's "centenary ship" and restored the classic name to the Finland-UK routes. Vuokko Laakso, the leading Finnish ship interior designer of the day, was hired to design her crew and passenger areas. *(Krzysztof Brzoza)*

a rare example of pre-World War II passenger liner design by the time of her scrapping in 1987. She could have continued inservice even longer, had it not been for the Soviet's decision to withdraw all their pre-World War II passenger vessels from service following the sinking of the 1925-vintage *Admiral Nakhimov* (Адмирал Нахимов) in 1986. It is of interest to note that the Soviets continued to hold the *Baltika* in high regard right until the end: she was one of two ships the Soviets chose to use as accommodation vessels during the 1986 Gorbachev-Reagan summit in Reykjavík, Iceland (the other was the 1980-vintage Helsinki-Tallinn ferry *Georg Ots* (Георг Отс) – Gorbachev stayed on the latter, attracting some negative comment from his countrymen for not choosing the *Baltika*).

Apart from the limited passenger accommodation on cargo

The ***Baltika***, seen here during her final season of operation, was the last passenger vessel to sail regularly on the Finland-UK trades and a veritable anachronism by the time she was withdrawn. *(FotoFlite)*

ships, generally only available to freight vehicle drivers, the only practical way of travelling from Finland to the UK after the *Baltika* was withdrawn has been by air; passenger ferry services from Finland connect to ports on the Baltic Sea, requiring overland voyages by road or rail to join ferries bound for the UK. Following the advent of modern jet airplane, the Soviet-operated Finland-UK passenger services were an anachronism as, due to the need to cross both most of the length of the Baltic Sea as well as the North Sea, the route does not offer a "natural" passenger connection in the same way as those from the other Nordic countries did. At the same time, the service run by the *Baltika* was not attractive for cargo, as Finland-UK freight tonnage was replaced by efficient roro ferries already in the early 1970s. Today, the cargo services from ports in southern Finland – arguably the descendants of the passenger-cargo services of FÅA – are in the hands of Finnlines and Mann Lines, but an extensive operation also exists to carry forest industry products from Finland's Gulf of Bothnia ports (as well as Swedish ports on the same gulf) to the UK.

In retrospect, Finland-UK passenger services surviving as long as they did was primarily the result of the Soviet Union operating on a different economic basis from the Northern European shipping companies, which – despite being based on countries with mixed economies rather than free market capitalism – operated by the terms of profit and loss and could not maintain a long-haul passenger service that simply didn't attract enough passengers. Things were different on the shorter routes from the other Nordic countries to the UK, all of which were operared until the 21st century.

Mann Lines' Visentini-type freight roro ***ML Freyja*** is today the only ship dedicated to the link between southern Finland and the UK, operating a nine-day Turku-Bremerhaven-Harwich-Cuxhaven-Paldiski-Turku rotation. *(Krzysztof Brzoza)*

Chapter three

Sweden to Britain: Large and Luxurious

For much of their existence, the Sweden-UK routes were arguably the most important cross-North Sea services, with the biggest and most luxuriously appointed, usually purpose-built, ships operated on them. In common with the services from Norway and Denmark, initially the UK-based Wilson Line dominated the routes, but after World War I the balance shifted in favour of local Swedish operator Svenska Lloyd.

In contrast with the other services, the car-passenger ferry era of the Sweden-UK routes was characterised by competition between the newcomer Tor Line, Svenska Lloyd and the latter's would-be partners but eventual rivals Rederi AB Svea and Ellerman's Wilson Line. In the end, Tor Line triumphed, only to be swallowed up by Denmark's DFDS. The latter company then operated the routes until their closure in 2006.

The Wilson family's lines

The first attempts of a regular service between Sweden and the United Kingdom were made during the Napoleonic Wars, when in 1803 a postal and passenger route was opened by using sailing ships. Despite the obvious unreliability of ship relying on the wind, the route continued even after Napoléon's final defeat. The first attempt of moving to steam power was made in 1834 by George's Steamship Company, which ran a two-ship Gothenburg-Hull service. The larger of their ships, the *Superb*, could transport 54 passengers. Despite a subsidy for the carriage of mail from the British Crown the operation was unprofitable and terminated after just one season.

The next attempt was made in 1840, when the Hull-based Thomas Wilson Sons & Co, better known as the Wilson Line, initiated steamer service linking Gothenburg via Kristiansand in Norway to Hull, the company having operated sailing ships between Gothenburg and Hull from 1825. At this time Sweden and Norway were in a personal union as the United Kingdoms of Sweden and Norway. The Wilsons secured subsidies from both Sweden and Britain, making the two-ship service run with the steamers *Glen Albyn* and *Innisfail* a success. However, in 1842 the Swedish postal services discontinued the subsidy, and the steamer service was withdrawn.

By the end of the decade, trade between Sweden and the UK had grown so much that Wilson Line believed an unsubsidized service linking Gothenburg to Hull via Christiania (present-day Oslo) could be profitable. The service was restarted in 1850 using the steamer *Courier*, but again without success. When Wilson Line again abandoned the route, Thomas Wilson's son John West Wilson, who had migrated to Gothenburg to act as his father's local agent, stepped in and took over the service. In keeping with the family tradition, the ships in John West Wilson's service were painted in the same livery as those of Wilson Line: forest green hull, white superstructure and a red funnel with a black top. John West Wilson's service proved short-lived, but for reasons positive for the development of the route: after the outbreak of the Crimean War in 1853, it was incorporated into the route network of Wilson Line, who now continued to operate the service successfully. Eventually newbuilt cargo-passenger steamers appeared on the route in 1870: the *Rollo* (1) and

Wilson Line's 1870-built ***Rollo*** (1) in port, showing the inwards taper of the hull just below the superstructure, a common feature in ships built during the era. *(Maritime Museum: Hull Museums)*

An oil painting of Wilson's ***Romeo*** of 1881 by R.D. Widdas. Note the Swedish version of the Union Flag of Sweden-Norway flying from the forward mast. *(Maritime Museum: Hull Museums)*

Orlando (1) of 795 passengers, followed by the 836-passenger *Romeo* in 1881 (by this time, all Wilson steamers were given names ending with -o – for reasons unknown, many on the Sweden-UK routes had connections to Italy).

Enter the Swedes

In Gothenburg, there was interest in gaining passenger links to other UK ports than just Hull – especially in a direct route to London. Already in 1855, the local businessman August Leffer had briefly tried to run a Gothenburg-London service. Between 1863 and 1867 (or possibly later), an unknown (likely British) company operated an Edinburgh (Leith)-Kristiansand-Gothenburg-Copenhagen service with the steamers *Gnome* (built 1856, 522 tons) and *Snowdon* (built 1855, 271 tons), but did not achieve long-term success.

John West Wilson returned to passenger shipping in 1865, when Ångfartygs AB Göteborg-London (literally: Steamship Company Gothenburg-London Ltd) was formed under his leadership. The new line successfully operated a two-ship service with the steamers *Prins Oscar* and *Victoria*, transporting both passengers and cargo. Again, John West Wilson chose to paint the ships of his company in the same colours used by his father's firm, despite the fact they were now indirect competitors.

The next entrant into the Sweden-UK trades was the Gothenburg-based Ångfartygs AB Thule (literally Steamship Company Thule, but better known in English as the Thule Line), which was established in 1870 to run a service linking Gothenburg to Edinburgh (Leith). The perhaps somewhat unusual choice of UK port is explained by two factors: on one hand, the newcomer company was afraid to enter direct competition with the established operators to Hull and London, but on the other hand Edinburgh was a practical destination for migrants bound for America, as the overland journey from Edinburgh to the transatlantic steamers departing from Glasgow was short.

The first Thule steamers were the *Frithiof*, *Ingeborg* and *Kung Ring* (all three named after characters in Norse sagas, a theme which would continue with most subsequent Thule vessels). In 1879 they were joined by a new ship built by the Motala shipyard in Gothenburg: the 1,300 grt *Bele*, which is listed as carrying 42 passengers – presumably this figure includes only first- and second-class passengers, not migrants carried in "deck class".

Consolidation took place in 1882, when Ångfartygs AB Thule purchased Ångfartygs AB Göteborg-London. Following the takeover, the *Bele* was moved to the Gothenburg-London service, where she was paired with the brand-new *Thorsten* of 1,700 grt and 55 passengers (again, presumably this figure does not include deck class). The old Göteborg-London

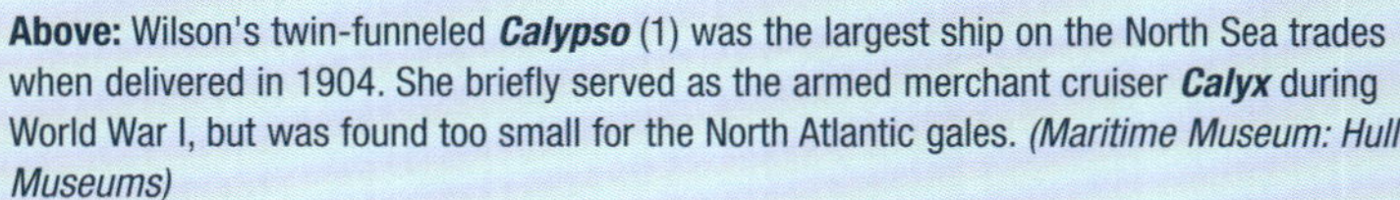

Above: Wilson's twin-funneled ***Calypso*** (1) was the largest ship on the North Sea trades when delivered in 1904. She briefly served as the armed merchant cruiser ***Calyx*** during World War I, but was found too small for the North Atlantic gales. *(Maritime Museum: Hull Museums)*

Left: Wilson's ***Ariosto*** was fitted with refrigeration machinery for the cargo holds and electric lights through-out when delivered in 1890. This impressive oil painting is by E. Gooche. *(Maritime Museum: Hull Museums)*

Middle left: Ångfartygs AB Thule's "self-titeled" ***Thule*** of 1892 shows the typical slightly aft of amidships funnel (and engine) placement of the era. *(Ian Boyle collection)*

Bottom left: Thule's 1883-built ***Thorsten*** sailed on the Sweden-UK routes for over three decades, before sold to Estonian owners in 1920 and scrapped in 1925. *(Ian Boyle collection)*

Below: The 1909-built ***Saga*** *(*1) was Thule's last newbuilt passenger vessel. After she left the Sweden-UK services in 1929, she enjoyed a further career with the Compagnie Générale Transatlantique, until eventually torpedoed in World War II. Her name would be recycled for several subsequent Sweden-UK passenger vessels, as we shall see.. *(Ian Boyle collection)*

company steamers were in turn moved to the Edinburgh service.

Largest on the North Sea

Passenger numbers on the Sweden-UK routes grew at a brisk pace during the remainder of the 19th century and the first decade of the 20th. Resultingly, both Wilson and Thule contracted a series of new ships during this period (an additional reason for investing in new tonnage for Wilson Line was expansion of their Norwegian rivals at the same time, as explained in Chapter 4). Wilson's ships tended to be the largest on the North Sea, while those of Thule were often the largest under the Swedish flag. Both companies developed their own niches: Wilson Line concentrated on the lucrative migrant trades, serving Hull (with a secondary service to Grimsby), while Thule's services to the English and Scottish capitals attracted more affluent passengers.

The race for ever-larger ships was started by Wilson Line, who took delivery in 1889 of the largest passenger steamer on the North Sea, the *Ariosto* of 2,400 grt and 1,133 passengers, for a direct Hull to Gothenburg service, with the intermediate call in Norway abandoned (in favour of a dedicated Hull-Christiania service described in the next chapter). Ångfartygs AB Thule answered by taking delivery of the 2,000 grt and (at least) 75 passenger *Thule* – the largest ship under the Swedish flag – in 1892 for the London line. She was followed in 1898 by the *Balder* of 1,400 grt and 109 passengers for the Edinburgh service. Wilson Line's next new ship was the *Calypso* (1) of 1904, which took the title of the North Sea's largest steamer from her running mate *Ariosto* with her 2,876 grt, carrying 964 passengers. Thule answered in 1909 with the *Saga* (1) for the London line, which was again Sweden's largest at 2,800 grt and 170 passengers. Starting from 1910, Thule's London steamers sailed only as far as Harwich during the summer seasons, decreasing crossing times during the high season.

The last new ship of the era was Wilson Line's *Bayardo* from 1911. Tragically, the 3,600 grt and (at least) 100 passenger ship grounded on the Humber River already in 1912. Although all passengers, cargo and even the interior fittings could be saved, the ship itself broke in two and had to be demolished as a danger to navigation. As a replacement for the lost *Bayardo*, Wilson Line transferred the 1896-built *Spero* (1) of 1,100 grt and (at least) 45 passengers as the *Calypso*'s (1) running mate.

War and changes of ownership

Although Sweden remained neutral during World War I (as is perhaps well known, Sweden's overall policy of neutrality has been highly successful – the country was last at war in 1814), a large-scale war in Europe naturally disturbed shipping between Sweden and the UK. When war broke out in July 1914, Wilson Line stopped all their sailings. Ångfartygs AB Thule, on the other hand, continued services on the Gothenburg-Edinburgh line, using their older ships, throughout the war years. Wilson Line suffered heavy losses – only one of their passenger ships survived, but was not deemed worthy of repair. In 1916 the Wilson family decided to divest themselves of the firm, selling it to Sir John Ellerman, who thus became the biggest ship owner in Britain and one of the richest men – if not **the** richest man – in the country. Ellerman renamed the company Ellerman's Wilson Line, but it continued to be administered separately from his other shipping companies.

In the same year, Ångfartygs AB Thule also got a new owner in the form of the 1868-founded Svenska Lloyd (Swedish Lloyd), who already operated cargo steamers between Sweden and UK. The takeover was a part of Svenska Lloyd's larger strategy of expansion in preparation for projected post-war tonnage shortage, but also inspired by the belief by Svenska Lloyd's leadership – unusual in Sweden during the early part of World War I – that Britain and its allies, rather than Germany, would emerge victorious in the conflict (Herbert Metcalfe, Svenska Lloyd's then-managing director, was British by birth). In addition to buying Ångfartygs AB Thule, between 1915 and 1917 Svenska Lloyd also took over Ångfartygs AB Göteborg-Manchester, Ångfartygs AB Svithiod and Nordiska Rederi AB, becoming the biggest Sweden-UK cargo operator and sole Swedish shipping company to operate passenger sailings between Sweden and the British Isles. Interestingly, with the takeover of Ångfartygs AB Thule Svenska Lloyd abandoned their original funnel colours (a yellow stripe with a blue letter L on a black background) and instead adopted Thule's blue disc with a gold star on white background.

Swedish dominance

With the loss of their passenger fleet, Ellerman's Wilson Line were in no position to compete with Svenska Lloyd in the immediate post-war years – especially as the Swedish company's passenger fleet had survived the war virtually unscathed. After the war, Svenska Lloyd placed the *Thule* and *Balder* on a Gothenburg-Harwich service (the service to London was discontinued), while the *Thorsten* and *Bele* sailed from Gothenburg to Edinburgh. The flagship *Saga* (1) was absent from this schedule as she was under charter to Moore-McCormack Line for their New York-Rio de Janeiro run – an action perhaps dictated by the company's precarious financial position, resulting from an excessive (and expensive) post-war newbuilding programme. Indeed, Svenska Lloyd had to struggle for survival through much of the 1920s. When the *Saga* (1) returned from charter in 1919, she was used to open a new route, linking Gothenburg to Newcastle. To provide a two-ship service, Svenska Lloyd purchased the Australian steamer *Western Australia*, originally the Russian-flagged *Mongolia* of 1901. The 3,000 grt and 572 passenger ship was renamed *Patricia* (1), thus introducing to the passenger fleet Svenska Lloyd's tradition of ship names ending with *-ia*.

The operation of three different lines to the UK was not as lucrative as was hoped, especially as trade with Britain plummeted from exceptionally high levels in 1920 to just a fraction in 1921, and experiencing only slight growth during the rest of the inter-war era. In 1921, the *Bele* was chartered out (and sank during the charter), while the *Thorsten* was sold. Operations on the three routes continued with just four ships

Wilson Line's last purpose-built Sweden-UK passenger steamer, the ***Bayardo*** of 1911, took the accolade of the largest vessel on the routes when delivered, but grounded on the Humber after just eight months in service. Her wreck is seen here prior to destruction by dynamite as a navigational hazard. *(Maritime Museum: Hull Museums)*

until a reorganisation in 1922: the *Saga* (1) and *Patricia* (1) re-opened the Gothenburg-London service, while the *Thule* and *Balder* moved to the Gothenburg-Newcastle line. The routes to Edinburgh and Harwich were closed down.

Ellerman's Wilson Line had been able to rise to the challenge in 1920, when the 1899-built *Italia* was transferred to EWL from the fleet of the sister company Ellerman & Papayanni. The 3,700 grt, 317 passenger ship was renamed *Rollo* (2) and re-opened the Hull-Gothenburg service. During the same year, EWL acquired two other passenger steamers, the *Orlando* (2) and *Calypso* (2) second hand. This pair primarily served on other routes, but occasionally visited the Gothenburg service (they are discussed in more detail in Chapter 4). EWL's primary pre-war business from Sweden, the transport of migrants, had received a competitor during the war, when Svenska Amerika Linien (the Swedish American Line) had initiated direct services from Gothenburg to New York. When the US radically curtailed their intake of immigrants in the early 1920a, EWL could not make the passenger services between Gothenburg and Hull profitable and closed these down (the company's cargo steamers on the route continued to carry a restricted number of passengers, as was common at the time).

Suecia & Britannia: Biggest on the North Sea

While Ellerman's Wilson Line struggled, Svenska Lloyd's strategy of concentrating on more affluent passengers was successful. Indeed, the company's centennial book describes the passenger services as "the only long-term positive development" during the 1920s, and the most resistant to the cycles of economic upturn and depression. A major reason was Britain's growing political, cultural and economic importance in Europe; while Sweden had previously oriented

A postcard view of EWL's ***Calypso*** (2), originally built in 1897 for colonial services between Belgium and Belgian Congo as the ***Bruxellesville***. She served EWL from 1920 until sold for scrap in 1936. *(Ian Boyle collection)*

Although built in Italy for Russian owners, the 1901-built ***Patricia*** (1) acquired by Svenska Lloyd in 1920 was similar to the company's pre-existing ***Saga*** (1) in size and appearance. *(Ian Boyle collection)*

A fine aerial view of the ***Suecia***. She and her sister ***Britannia*** were adaptable vessels, morphing from the originally first-class dominated luxury liners into vessels catering primarily for the tourist class trade during the post-war era. *(FotoFlite)*

A postcard view of the what is likely the ***Suecia*** at Gothenburg. Judging by the cars parked on the quayside, the photo was likely taken in the 1950s. *(Joonas Kortelainen collection)*

An artist's impression of the ***Suecia***'s forward-facing first class covered promenade, with furniture somewhat in Gustavian style. *(Anders Bergenek collection)*

towards Germany, it now begun to turn more towards Britain, with a resulting increase in both tourists and business travellers. It is no surprise that the Gothenburg-London line was the apple of managing director Herbert Metcalfe's eye. Despite this positive development, the *Thule* was sold in 1925 to improve the company's overall ailing performance. With her departure, the Gothenburg-Newcastle route became a single-ship service with the *Balder*.

During the second half of the 1920s, Svenska Lloyd's economies improved enough to contract new ships. With the good result of the Gothenburg-London line and the fact Svenska Lloyd's existing passenger ships were relatively old, the first new investments were a pair of passenger steamers for the UK route. The company initially approached the Swedish authorities for subventions to build the ships at one of Sweden's strunggling shipyards, but when no state aid was forthcoming, the order went instead to the Newcastle builders Swan Hunter, who also helped arrange funding. The contract was signed in 1927.

The ships, which were both the largest and fastest on the North Sea, were delivered in 1929 as the *Suecia* and *Britannia*. They were an unprecedented 4,350 grt, but transported only 248 passengers and very little cargo. No less than 208 passengers were carried in first class, with the remaining 40 in third class. Indeed, a contemporary advertisement stated the ships to be "in a class of their own" when it came to passenger comfort. Their interiors were described as being in "traditional and cozy ship-style." Fittingly, the *Suecia*'s interiors were decorated in historical styles once popular in Sweden, while the *Britannia*'s interiors had a more British character. Herbert Melcalfe had participated in much of the design process, including commissioning mock-up cabins and testing them personally, with modifications made to the final product based on his experiences. On the technical side, the ships were equipped with Parson steam turbines, with three screws giving a service speed of 17,5 knots (resulting in a 35-hour crossing time) and a top speed of 19 knots.

Coinciding with the arrival of the new ships, a new passenger terminal was taken into use at Tilbury Landing Stage, from where passengers could take a direct train connection to the St. Pancras Station in London. Cargo, however, was loaded and unloaded at Millwall Docks.

The new ships replaced the *Saga* (1) and *Patricia* (1) on the Gothenburg-London (Tilbury) line. Instead of being transferred to the Newcastle service, the older pair were sold. The *Balder*, the oldest ship in the fleet, continued on the Newcastle route alone; in 1930 she was radically modernised and renamed *Northumbria*. At least during the winter of 1932-33 she was joined by the steamer *Ingeborg.* Very little information has been available about the latter ship – a 1908-built Svenska Lloyd cargo steamer with that name did exist, but it is possible the ship appearing in the passenger schedules was a different *Ingeborg* under charter from another operator.

Despite the Great Depression, which was made worse in Sweden by the "Kreuger Crash", a further economic downturn that followed the bankruptcy of the Sweden-based international conglomerate Kreuger group in 1933, both passenger numbers and profits continued to be healthy on the Gothenburg-London route and would continue to grow at a good pace through-out the 1930s. In 1935, Svenska Lloyd acquired from the Byron Steamship Company the steamer *Patris II*, built by the same shipyard as the *Suecia* and *Britannia* in 1926. The 3,900 grt and 250 passenger liner was given a substantial refit and renamed *Patricia* (2) for use as a third ship on the Gothenburg-London line. In contrast to the other Svenska Lloyd passenger steamers, the *Patricia* (2) was oil-fired. Experiences from her were so good that in 1937, the *Suecia* and *Britannia* were also converted from coal to oil firing, resulting in lower bunker costs, smaller crews (therefore further decreasing operating costs) and a slightly higher top speed. During the 1938 summer season, services to the London region were further increased with the *Northumbria* sailing to Harwich instead of Newcastle. This apparently did not give the desired result, as the experiment was not repeated.

The ***Suecia***'s first class lounge was decorated in light and airy rococo style. *(Anders Bergenek collection)*

The same space onboard the ***Britannia*** had a more British ambience, with plentiful use of dark wood. A replica of this space, with recycled original furniture, was later assembled onboard the ***Saga*** (3) of 1966, fittingly named the Britannia Room. *(Anders Bergenek collection)*

The ***Britannia***'s first class dining room. *(Anders Bergenek collection)*

The ***Patricia*** (2), acquired second-hand in 1935, served Svenska Lloyd for just five years, but enjoyed a 31-year career with the Swedish Navy under the same name. *(Svensk Sjöfartstidning archive)*

The wartime newbuilding Saga (2)

During the late 1930s, few shipping companies predicted that the world would soon spiral into protracted military

The ***Saga*** (2) was a "white ship" designed for ferry service and off-season cruising. After her decade in Svenska Lloyd service, she was sold first to the Compagnie Générale Transatlantique for Bordeaux-Casablanca liner service as the ***Ville de Bordeaux*** and then to Bulgaria as the cruise ship ***Nessebar***, before scrapped in Yugoslavia, 1975. *(FotoFlite)*

conflict. Like all companies operating on the passenger trades from Scandinavia to the UK, Svenska Lloyd commissioned a new ship on the eve of the war. In their case, the *Saga* (2), an expanded version of the *Suecia* and *Britannia* projected to carry 400 passengers, was contracted in 1939 from the Götaverken yard in Gothenburg (though the hull was subcontracted to the Lindholmen yard). In a break from company tradition, but following precedent set by other North Sea passenger operators, diesel engines were specified. In addition to constantly growing passenger numbers, a contributing factor to the decision to order a new ship was the appearance of Fred. Olsen's new ships *Black Prince* (1) and *Black Watch* (1) for their Oslo-Newcastle route in 1938 and 1939, respectively, as the Fred. Olsen ships were larger and – at least arguably – more luxurious than the *Suecia* and Britannia (for more details on the *Black Prince* (1) and *Black Watch* (1), see Chapter 4), and Oslo was easily reachable from Sweden by rail.

When large-scale war broke out in Europe in September 1939, the *Suecia* and *Britannia* were promptly laid up. The *Patricia* (2) made one more return trip between Gothenburg and London after war broke out, primarily carrying Britons still in Sweden home in one direction, and Swedes from Britain in the other, after which she, too, was laid up.

The *Saga* (2) was launched in 1940 and the incomplete hull was promptly laid up, joining the rest of the fleet. The *Patricia* (2) left the fleet early during the war, first chartered and then sold to the Swedish Navy as a submarine mothership (while Sweden remained neutral during the conflict, the Swedish Armed Forces made preparations in case this would change). Sweden's neutrality did not stop Svenska Lloyd from suffering heavy war loses: a total of 21 ships were lost, including the sinking of the *Northumbria* in an Allied air raid in Norway in 1943.

Like many other Scandinavian shipping companies, Svenska Lloyd were convinced that the future of passenger transport was in the air. Already in 1941, the company had founded an airline subsidiary, Svenska Aero Lloyd, with the intention of operating twice-daily return trips from Gothenburg to London once peace returned. Unfortunately, they could not secure permission to carry passengers from the Swedish authorities, who instead favoured the state-owned AB Aerotransport and the Svensk Interkontinental Lufttrafik AB, owned by the powerful Wallenberg family.

As the war in Europe was drawing to a close, work on the *Saga* (2) recommenced in 1944. After Germany's capitulation, the *Suecia* and *Britannia* were chartered to the Allies as troopships in 1945, primarily sailing between Hull and Cuxhaven. Following refits, the duo re-initiated passenger services on the Gothenburg-London line Spring 1946. They were joined by the new *Saga* (2) in May. Svenska Lloyd were thus in an exceptionally good position to compete on the North Sea passenger trades, as their competitors from Norway and Denmark had suffered heavy war losses, as explained in Chapters 4 and 6 below.

As built, the 6,500 grt *Saga* (2) could carry 400 passengers, but the berths were now spread across four classes: 156 in first, 88 in second and 96 in third class, plus 60 berths in dormitories, designed for use of school groups, scouts etc. Despite having arguably less high-class accommodation from

The ***Patricia*** (3) served with Svenska Lloyd for just six years, but she spent 24 years as a cruise ship for various operators, and a further stint as an accommodation vessel, before finally scrapped in 1997. *(FotoFlite)*

The first-class observation lounge onboard the ***Patricia*** (3). *(Svensk Sjöfartstidning archive)*

The vaguely tropical ambience of what is probably the ***Patricia*** (3)'s writing room was well-suited for her off-season cruising. *(Svensk Sjöfartstidning archive)*

The decor of the ***Patricia*** (3)'s restaurant showed hints of modernism otherwise absent from her interiors. *(Svensk Sjöfartstidning archive)*

The bar at the first class grand staircase of the ***Patricia*** (3), with tables set for coffee service.*(Svensk Sjöfartstidning archive)*

The ***Patricia*** (3) was delivered to Svenska Lloyd in 1951. She is seen here off the English coast, likely on one of her long winter-season cruises. Her premature sale in 1957 also meant the end of cruises aimed at the Swedish market. *(FotoFlite)*

the older fleetmates, the *Saga* (2) had been designed with off-season cruising in mind, and made long cruises from Gothenburg to the Canary Isles during the winter months, primarily aimed at the Swedish market. Her diesel engines gave an 18.5 knot service speed. With the new ship, Svenska Lloyd adopted a white hull colour across their passenger fleet. However, this was very short-lived on the *Suecia* and *Britannia*, which reverted to the original black almost immediately, due to lower maintenance costs – the old black colour had the tendency to "leak" through the white, requiring constant repainting.

Due to scarcity of hotel accommodation in the immediate post-war London, during the off-season the *Suecia* and *Britannia* would spend a week moored at the port of London, acting as floating hotels for the visiting Swedes. These "mini-cruises" were surprisingly popular and were continued until the 1960s, despite the rapid rebuilding of the British capital.

In 1948, a fourth ship briefly joined the Svenska Lloyd fleet, when 1919-built steamer *Ragne* was chartered from the fellow Swedish shipping company Rederi AB Svea to provide extra capacity during the Olympic Games in London. The 1,373 grt *Ragne* had a capacity for 465 passengers and sailed between Gothenburg and Newcastle.

The short-lived Patricia (3)

Passenger numbers onboard Svenska Lloyd's ships rose to new heights during the late 1940s, and quickly exceeded the predictions on which the *Saga* (2) had been commissioned. By 1950, passenger numbers had more than doubled compared to the last complete pre-war year (1938). Bolstered by the impressive growth figures, Svenska Lloyd had commissioned a new, larger passenger liner from Swan Hunter already in 1948 for delivery in 1951. While waiting for the new ship, the *Ragne* was again chartered to provide extra capacity with a Gothenburg-Newcastle service during the 1950 summer season. Furthermore, in 1950 the *Suecia* and *Britannia* were rebuilt, in part to bring their interiors up to the same standards as on the *Saga* (2), but also to increase passenger capacity: after the refit, they carried 202 passengers in first class, 40 in third and a further 60 in a group dormitory set up in one of the former cargo holds, thus giving a total capacity of 302.

The latest newbuilding, eventually named *Patricia* (3), was delivered in 1951. She was essentially an "improved edition" of the *Saga* (2), with a similar layout and exterior design, but larger at 7,800 grt (making her the largest passenger liner on the North Sea), while carrying 408 passengers – but she was powered by steam turbines rather than diesel engines (the *Saga* (2) suffered chronic vibration problems), and had a slightly higher service speed at 19 knots. Like the *Saga* (2), the *Patricia* (3) was designed for off-season cruising, venturing as far as Bermuda during the 1952 winter season. Two cruise ships were too much for the Swedish market, and during the winters 1953-55 the *Patricia* (3) was chartered to an American company for cruises from New York to the Caribbean.

Unfortunately, Svenska Lloyd's predictions on the rise of the airplane came true during the 1950s. Things were not helped by the fact that the competing companies in Norway-UK and Denmark-UK trades were able to introduce new ships in the early 1950s. Svenska Lloyd's passenger numbers started diminishing already in 1952. At first, the company was able to maintain satisfactory loadings, but at a price level that, combined with rising operational expenses (especially crew costs), could not be maintained.

Already in 1955 Svenska Lloyd decided to reduce their passenger fleet. As the newer ships had higher capital costs and were more expensive to operate, the *Saga* (2) and *Patricia* (3) were the ones to leave the fleet. The *Saga* (2) was sold to Compagnie Générale Transatlantique (known as the French Line in English) with delivery in 1956, becoming their *Ville de Bordeaux* for trans-Mediterranean trades. The outbreak of the Suez Crisis during the same year brought further problems, as the *Patricia*'s (3) scheduled Mediterranean cruise season had to be cancelled, cutting further into the profit margins. This, in part, contributed to the sale of the *Patricia* (3) in 1957 to the Hamburg-Amerikanische Paketfahrt AG (HAPAG, known in English as the Hamburg-America Line), becoming their cruise ship *Ariadne* (2) and returning to her old haunts in the Caribbean.

Coinciding with the departure of the newer vessels, the *Suecia* and *Britannia* were refitted to carry 343 passengers each. Reflecting changing passenger patterns, tourist class (that replaced third class) now carried the largest number of passengers. At the same time – and for the first time in the history of Svenska Lloyd – an onboard shop was added. The fleet reduction, combined with a new policy of occasional charter flights to create 'sail and fly' packages, proved to be the right move and the route returned to profit (albeit with slim margins) by the end of the decade. However, at the same time it was clear that "the two charming old ladies" would need replacing soon, and that the replacements would need to be combined cargo and passenger ships, the income from cargo transports carrying the ships through the long winter season when passenger numbers were low. Due to high crew expenses, the new ships' harbour times would need to be minimised – at the time, a cargo liner still spent 50-60% of each year in port, which would simply not be profitable for a passenger liner requiring a large crew.

Enter the car ferry era

The passenger trades between Sweden and Britain were not the sunset business the events of the latter 1950s might have led on. By the mid-1960s, car ferry services between the countries were such an attractive proposition that two different consortiums entered the trades with a total of five newbuilt ships. In a somewhat complex story, Svenska Lloyd was the first to plan a new car-passenger ferry service, but the first to actually operate a car ferry service on the Sweden-UK routes was the newcomer Tor Line.

Realising that cargo would be more important than passengers for a car-passenger ferry service, especially in light of Sweden'sgrowing trade with the UK, Svenska Lloyd sought a partnership with an existing cargo operator on the Sweden-UK routes to help co-finance the move of the service to the car ferry era. The choice fell on one their biggest competitors,

Above: Although concieved notably later than the ships of England-Sweden Line, Tor Line's ***Tor Anglia*** was the first car-passenger ferry in Sweden-UK trades. The photo shows her in Lübeck during her sea trials with a plain blue hull. Later on, a large Tor Line text was added to the hull, an early use of the today-ubiquituos device on trans-North Sea vessels. *(Foto Schilling, Anders Bergenek collection)*

Left: The interiors of the ***Tor Anglia*** were in vibrant and colourful 1960s modernist style, though the black-and-white photos here naturally do not do the colours justice. Seen here is the restaurant, which was advertised as having "the largest Swedish smörgåsbord on the North Sea." *(Svensk Sjöfartstidning archive)*

Middle left: The ***Tor Anglia***'s dance salon. One would suspect the vases with flowers were there for photographic purposes and not commonly used when the ship was in service. *(Svensk Sjöfartstidning archive)*

Bottom left: The forward-facing smoking room of the ***Tor Anglia***, with fashionable Arne Jakobsen Swan chairs, originally designed for the Royal Hotel in Copenhagen, giving a somewhat luxurious touch to the space. *(Svensk Sjöfartstidning archive)*

Below: A Tor Line brochure image of fashionably clothed models posing at the ***Tor Anglia***'s reception. The company were known for the abundant use of attractive young females in advertising. *(Anders Bergenek collection)*

Above: A 1968 aerial view of the ***Saga*** (3) at speed, likely taken somewhere in the Thames Estuary. While the exterior design of the ***Saga*** (3) and her sisters was somewhat old-fashioned for the era, later commentators have given high praise for their looks. *(FotoFlite)*

Left: The bar and lounge complex on the aft part of Saloon deck of the ***Saga*** (3) was divided into four areas with different ambiences. Here is a view from the Restaurant Lounge to the Restaurant Bar. *(Stig Sjötedt Reklamfoto, Joonas Kortelainen collection)*

Middle left: The decor of the Wasa restaurant onboard the ***Saga*** (3) was inspired by the Operakällaren in Stockholm. Although the name recalled the famous warship preserved in Stockholm, the decorations related to the 17th century sailing vessel ***Riksvasa***, the wreck of which dismantled in the 1960s and parts of it were used in the decor of the Wasa restaurant, alongside the metal artwork by Bertil Wallien decipting the ***Riksvasa***'s story. *(Stig Sjötedt Reklamfoto, Joonas Kortelainen collection)*

Bottom left: Arcades both port and starboard connected the spaces on the Saloon deck of the ***Saga*** (3); however, the only way from one side of the ship to the other was via the aft lounge area, or by taking the stairs a deck down and then up again. *(Anders Bergenek collection)*

Below: Another aerial view of the ***Saga*** (3), showing the vast expanses of teak-covered open decks. *(FotoFlite)*

Ellerman's Wilson Line. EWL were interested, despite the fact that by this time they were almost a pure cargo operator and had just one passenger vessel (sailing between Hull and Copenhagen, see Chapter 6, although their Sweden-UK cargo steamers did carry up to 12 passengers). EWL's existing Sweden-UK ships were conventional cargo ships of an increasingly obsolete design needing replacement, which made the idea of collaboration attractive. In 1963, the companies signed an agreement build a pair of ferries, with a capacity for circa 400 passengers, 100 cars and 100 containers for a Gothenburg-Hull route. These were designed to be relatively slow, with the idea being that the ships would spend two nights and a day at sea en-route. Hull was chosen as the British port due its vicinity to the industrial areas of the Midlands, important for cargo – but undoubtedly EWL's involvement was a contributing factor.

Rederi AB Svea, another Swedish shipping company, entered negotiations with EWL and Svenska Lloyd to join as a third partner in this new venture in 1964. Svea were a fellow operator of Sweden-UK cargo vessels and even operated a joint cargo service with EWL between Britain and the east coast of Sweden. In addition to those Svea had a sizeable passenger shipping arm, operating conventional liners and car-passenger ferries from Sweden to Finland (in collaboration with FÅA, who we have met in Chapter 3, and Ångfartygs Ab Bore) and Sweden to Denmark. In a similar arrangement to what Rederi AB Svea had with their Finnish partners, Svenska Lloyd, Svea and EWL established a joint marketing venture, known in English as England-Sweden Line and in Swedish as England-Sverige Linjen (both handily abbreviating to ESL), with each partner contributing one ship. (Some sources claim the initials ESL came from the company names, Ellerman's, Svea and Lloyd, but this was coincidental). The addition of a third ship allowed the continuation of the Gothenburg-London (Tilbury) route alongside the new service to Hull; the public reception to the plan of abandoning London services had been largely negative and therefore Svenska Lloyd were keen to maintain it.

On their services between Sweden and Mediterranean, Svenska Lloyd had been an early adapter to containerised shipping. For the North Sea routes, the company envisioned a passenger vessel with separate decks for containers and private cars, rather than a more conventional ferry arrangement of a double-height cargo deck used both by trucks and private cars. Yet, when the partners approached the Danish naval architects Knud E. Hansen (KEH) to design their ships, KEH initially offered a car-passenger ferry based on the then-under construction Kloster ferry *Sunward*, capable of carrying trucks in addition to private cars. Svea were in favour of going ahead with KEH's suggestion (perhaps due to good experiences with roro ferries from their other operations), but Svenska Lloyd insisted on their original container idea, while EWL wanted a conventional, crane-loaded cargo hold forward of the superstructure. At the same time, Svenska Lloyd's leadership insisted on a more conservative exterior design than KEH's previous output had been.

In the crossfire of conflicting interests, the ESL ships became a mixture of a conventional cargo vessel, container vessel and car-passenger ferry. In the long run, the most problematic aspect was the fact the cargo decks could not carry commercial vehicles. Furthermore, the flatbeds used for loading and unloading the containers were of an expensive bespoke design. While the ships could do a full turn-around within a working day, instead of six days for a conventional cargo vessel of the same capacity, the operation was notably slower than on a pure roro vessel.

In the end, only Svenska Lloyd and Svea commissioned ships of the KEH design. Both signed contracts with the Lindholmen yard in Gothenburg in 1964. EWL opted to take a design produced in-hourse, with the same capacity and cargo arrangements, from the Cammell Laird shipyard in Birkenhead.

As the ESL consortium were designing their ships, two other Swedish shipping companies hitherto specialising in the tanker trades, Rederi AB Transoil and Rex Rederi, learned of the ESL concept and realised it would be relatively simple to build superior car-passenger ferries with full cargo decks and run a profitable competing service. Transoil had been established in 1927 as a subsidiary of the Swedish shipping giant Rederi AB Transatlantic for the tanker trades, but had become an independent company 1952. Rex Rederi, on the other hand, had been founded in Stockholm in 1923. The name Tor Line came from the names of the two companies (**T**rans**o**il and **R**ex), but it should be noted that Tor is also the Swedish spelling of the Norse god known as "Thor" in English.

Tor Line appointed the Swedish naval architect Åke Törnqvist as the project leader for their new ships. He envisioned large and fast ferries that could do a trip from Gothenburg to the UK in a little over 24 hours. Like ESL, Tor Line wanted an UK port close to the industrial areas in the Midlands to make the service attractive for freight. Hull was the preferred port, but they were not interested and the final choice fell on nearby Immingham. A further benefit of sailing to this area was the relatively short distance, meaning the planned crossing time could be achieved with a service speed of 21 knots (maximum speed being 24 knots). Crucially, the ships were designed with car decks with enough clearance to accommodate trucks, allowing for much higher flexibility than ESL's approach.

Once Törnqvist had created the basics of the ships, Knud E. Hansen were commissioned to produce a detailed concept design; however, when Tor Line learned that KEH were also working with ESL, they quickly severed ties and the ships' design was finished in-house. The Lübecker Flender-Werke in West Germany eventually won the contract to build the ships, with deliveries set for 1966 and 1967.

Even before the ships could be delivered, Tor Line was struggling to finance them. In 1965, two new companies were coaxed into investing: the Swedish shipping company Brätt-Gotha (in which Rederi AB Transoil had a large shareholding) and the Koninklijke Nederlandse Stoomboot-Maatschappij (KNSM), a large shipping company based in the Netherlands. As England-Sweden Line's planned ferry services promised heavy competition on the Sweden-UK routes, with KNSM's involvement the idea was born to also operate a triangular

Sweden-UK-Netherlands service, giving the company a less competed leg to stand on. The involvement of Brätt-Gotha brought the Swedish ferry specialist Erik Kekonius into the Tor Line sphere; Kekonius had previously helped the Swedish publishing house Bonnier build their successful Lion Ferry subsidiary.

Originally, the ESL ships were slated for delivery before Tor Line's ships. However, once ESL learned about Tor Line's planned competing service and the full-height cargo decks, they got cold feet and the already under-construction ships were rebuilt to carry a small number of trucks. This delayed their delivery times so that the first company to initiate a car-passenger service between Sweden and the UK was Tor Line.

Tor Line's first ship, the *Tor Anglia,* was delivered in March 1966. At 7,000 grt and with a capacity for 980 passengers (albeit cabin berths for only 404, with seats and couchettes for a further 460) and 300 cars or 450 lane metres of cargo, she was a notable improvement over Svenska Lloyd's aged steamers. The name of the ship reflects the fashion of the era of giving ships Latin (or Latin-derived) names, but at the same time it's likely no accident the *Tor Anglia* shared its name with the popular UK-manufactured Ford Anglia family car – indeed, for those less well versed in Latin, particularly outside Britain, the car model was likely the first association of the name). The *Tor Anglia* initially sailed on the Gothenburg-Immingham-Amsterdam route. Between Sweden and the UK, the crossing time was 26 hours. Especially in the UK-Sweden direction, the oft-quoted faster crossing was actually not that much faster than what was offered by ESL: the *Tor Anglia* sailed from Immingham at midnight, followed by a day at sea, arrival at Gothenburg at two in the morning and disembarkation only at six in the morning. Thus, both companies' schedules required passengers to spend two nights and a day onboard.

The first ESL ship, Svenska Lloyd's *Saga* (3), followed soon after the *Tor Anglia*, initially sailing exclusively on the Gothenburg-Hull route. She was joined by EWL's *Spero* (3) in the late summer, the construction of this ship having been further delayed by strikes at the shipyard (as a stopgap solution, the Sealink passenger steamer *Avalon* was briefly chartered). The *Spero* (3) replaced the conventional EWL cargo ships *Rollo* (3) and *Cicero*. Then, when Svea's *Svea* was delivered in the Autumn, she replaced the *Saga* (3) on the Gothenburg-Hull route, with the latter ship moving to her originally planned Gothenburg-London route, replacing the *Suecia* and *Britannia* The two last-mentioned were sold for further trading in the Mediterranean, but scrapped in 1973. During the 1967 summer season, the three ESL ships rotated between the Hull and London routes, allowing for optimal deployment (normally the *Saga* (3) spent one night every two weeks in London to even out her schedule), but this remained an oddity and usually the Gothenburg-London service was the sole prerogative of the *Saga* (3).

In addition to the *Saga* (3) and *Svea*, Svenska Lloyd commissioned a third, somewhat larger and more passenger-oriented sister, the *Patricia* (4) for a new Southampton-Bilbao service (a logical move as Svenska Lloyd were already an important cargo operator from Spain to Northern Europe). While this route lies outside the scope of this book, it did have an effect on Svenska Lloyd's Gothenburg-London services, as we shall see.

Of the ESL ships, the *Saga* (3) and *Svea* were both 7,900 grt, while the *Spero* (3) was smaller at 6,900 grt. All carried 408 passengers, all with cabin berths, and space for 100 cars on the car deck, 106 containers on a separate cargo deck and circa five trucks (on the *Spero* (3), truck capacity was later radically increased by removing the starboard side car deck and replacing it with a hoistable platform, thus turning the ship into a conventional ferry). For interior design, each owner brought their own style and standard of fitting to the passenger accommodation. A common factor was a high-quality finish, with the product aimed at fairly affluent passengers. The *Saga* (3)'s interiors were designed by Swedish architects Astrid Sampe, Rolf Carlsson and Robert Tillberg in a conservative manner not dissimilar to the then-recent Svenska Amerika Linien cruise ships; the *Svea*'s interiors were more bright and upbeat, the work of Swedish architect Eva Ralf; while the *Spero* (3) received a more robust interior in fashionable British modernist style from the pen of British architect Charles Bose. In keeping with the egalitarian trends in Scandinavia (and ahead of many other operators in the area), the ESL ships were one-class, although as a remnant from the era of class segregation several public rooms were duplicated, with, for example, one lounge fitted to suit the tastes of old first-class passengers and another with simpler fittings suitable to the lower classes. Externally, all three ships were painted in the liveries of their owners, again mirroring the arrangements Svea had with their partners on Sweden-Finland routes. The only concession made to graphic unity was the repainting on the *Spero*'s (3) original dark green hull to light grey (used on ESL's reefers) soon after delivery.

In contrast, the interiors of the *Tor Anglia* (and her to-be-delivered sister *Tor Hollandia*) were vibrant and contemporary, in the stripped-back but colourful modernist style in vogue at the time, created by the Swedish designed Ulf Stenhammar. Like the ESL ships, the Tor ferries were single-class. To attract passengers, Tor Line believed the crossing needed to be an attraction in itself. Thus their ships were designed to offer activities such as dancing, cabaret shows, casino gaming etc – and shops selling goods at tax-free prices. Particular attention was paid to two distinct passenger groups, to whom flying would not be an alternative, for either practical or economic reasons: motorists and young adults. Thus, the onboard facilities, not just the decor, differed somewhat from those of the competition. Furthermore, the Tor Line ships were made instantly recognisable by a blue-hulled livery designed by Åke Törnqvist.

On both ESL routes, crossings were scheduled to take 36 hours. Departures were in the evening, followed by two nights and a day at sea before a morning arrival. Original projections were that the service would break even from the cargo income alone, and all passenger income would be pure profit. However, the arrival of Tor Line's faster service naturally greatly upset these plans. Even so, the three ESL partners were established players in the cargo services between Sweden

Above: The ***Spero*** (3) as delivered with the traditional forest green hull of EWL. The scarcity of photos of her in this livery suggests she was repainted with a grey hull almost immediately. *(Anders Bergenek collection)*

Left: The ***Spero*** (3)'s restaurant was decorated with rosewood panels combined with red carpets and upholstery. Artworks decipted scenes from Hull, Gothenburg and Stockholm – the homes of the three ESL partners. *(Maritime Museum: Hull Museums)*

Middle left: The York Lounge, up on Bridge Deck of the ***Spero*** (3) – the actual bridge was on Navigation Bridge Deck above – offered splendid forward views and was decorated with teak panels, while the carpets were blue and upholstery light brown. *(Anders Bergenek collection)*

Bottom left: : A deck scene from the ***Spero*** (3). *(Anders Bergenek collection)*

Below: An aerial view of the ***Spero*** (3) with the later grey hull. Although not success in Sweden-UK trades, the ship enjoyed a 30-year career in Greek waters until scrapped in 2004. *(Anders Bergenek collection)*

Above: Apart from the livery, Rederi AB Svea's ***Svea*** differed from ***Saga*** (3) only by her funnel, which was slightly lower and had deflector fins mounted aft to help disperse smoke. *(Anders Bergenek collection)*

Left: The Restaurant Bar onboard the ***Svea***. Contrast with the picture of the same space onboard the ***Saga*** (3) on page 56. *(Svensk Sjöfartstidning archive)*

Middle left: On the ***Svea*** (and ***Saga*** (3)), the cafeteria was located forward on the port side, but with no forward views, as these were taken up by an annexe of the restaurant on the starboard side. *(Svensk Sjöfartstidning archive)*

Bottom left: The Restaurant Lounge of the ***Svea***, with aft views and a dance floor. The open partition on the right was originally the only way to cross between port and starboard sides of the Saloon deck on the ***Svea*** and her sisters. *(Svensk Sjöfartstidning archive)*

Below: One of the Saloon Deck arcades onboard the ***Svea***, again similar but not identical to the same space found onboard the ***Saga*** (3). This is one of the few spaces not altered when the ship passed to Svenska Lloyd ownership three years after delivery. *(Svensk Sjöfartstidning archive)*

The ***Tor Hollandia*** seen in her second livery; as built, she was delivered with a plain blue hull and the funnel symbols in the real funnels. Subsequently, the funnel colours were altered to match those of the ***Tor Anglia***, with the funnel symbol in the dummy funnel, likely at the same time as the Tor Line texts were painted on her hull. *(Anders Bergenek collection)*

and the UK, with good pre-existing relations to various customers, and at the time it seemed they could easily not only compete with the newcomers but eventually win the unavoidable war for cargo and passengers (Svenska Lloyd of course also had their pre-existing passenger connections). What they did not take into account was the fact that the immense overcapacity for both passengers and cargo resulting from the arrival of five modern ferries pushed down not only prices of passenger tickets but also freight rates, making it very difficult for any of the companies to break even.

While the *Saga* (3) and her running mates were conservative for the era, Svenska Lloyd's new managing director (appointed 1967) and part-owner Torgeir Christoffersen, who had already participated on the design of the ESL ships in his previous post as vice-managing director, had a much more forward-looking vision of the Sweden-UK routes' future: on the occasion of Svenska Lloyd's centenary in 1969, he envisioned that in the near future, hovercraft five times the size of the SRN4-class would make the crossing from Gothenburg to the Ramsgate hoverport in just ten hours. (Svenska Lloyd owned 50% of the English Channel hovercraft operator Hoverlloyd, who operated SRN4-type craft, with the other half owned by the Svenska Amerika Linien). As we shall see, these and other lofty visions of Svenska Lloyd's future would come to nothing.

During the 1966-67 winter season, the *Tor Anglia* suffered a potentially dangerous accident, when the officer on duty noted her bow visor moving while out at sea. When crew members were dispatched to investigate, they discovered that the majority of the locking pins had failed. With the ship's rear turned to the wind, the crew managed to weld the visor shut temporarily. Once she reached land, the visor was permanently welded shut to prevent future problems on the often tempestuous North Sea. A similar operation was carried out on the under-construction *Tor Hollandia* and thus, although originally designed with drive-through car decks, the latter ship was stern-loading only when in Tor Line service (perhaps sensibly, ESL had opted to design their ships without bow gates from the start).

Before the *Tor Hollandia* had even been delivered, Tor Line had run out of money again. The financial result of 1966 had been disastrous. At the same time there were internal disagreements behind the scenes between Transoil and Rex, which eventually resulted in Rex buying Transoil (and through it, a controlling share in Brätt-Gotha). However, this quick expansion left Rex with insufficient funds to carry on. A saviour arrived in the form of the Swedish shipping giant Salén, who purchased Rex Rederi, through it gaining control of 75% of Tor Line, with KNSM retaining their 25% share.

When the *Tor Hollandia* was delivered in April 1967, ending the flurry of newbuildings for the Sweden-UK routes, she was received by Sven Salén, the head of the Salén shipping companies. The *Tor Hollandia* had a somewhat modified superstructure compared to the *Tor Anglia*, which gave her a larger gross register at 7,400 grt, with a capacity for 980 passengers and 300 cars. There were 472 cabin berths, the increase compared to the *Tor Anglia* being mostly explained by converting three-berth cabins on the older sister to four berths. The cabin decks were also redesigned in order to fit a larger number of cabins with private facilities. Subsequently, the *Tor Anglia*'s three-berth cabins were similarly converted to four berths, thus increasing her cabin capacity to 466 from the original 404. Soon after the delivery of the *Tor Hollandia*, the previously plain blue hull livery was altered with the company name painted on the sides in large white letters; Tor Line were

The former **Svea** transformed into Svenska Lloyd's ***Hispania***, easily identifiable from her sisters thanks to the deflector fins in the fummer. Notice that the cranes on her foredeck, as seen on the picture on page 60, have been removed as a result of conversion of the forward cargo hold to additional cabins. *(FotoFlite)*

The redecorated Restaurant Lounge onboard the ***Hispania***. Compare with the space in its original appearance on page 60. *(Stig Sjötedt Reklamfoto, Joonas Kortelainen collection)*

The restaurant onboard the ***Hispania***, with the decor designed to provide a somewhat Iberian ambience for a ship primarily envisioned for the UK-Spain routes. *(Anders Bergenek collection)*

the first company on the Nordics-UK routes to adopt this now-omnipresent feature.

With the arrival of the new ship, Tor Line's traffic was reorganised into a triangular route: the *Tor Hollandia* ran Gothenburg-Amsterdam-Immingham-Gothenburg, while the *Tor Anglia* operated in the opposite direction. Two departures per week were offered in both directions on all three lines. The two routes to the Netherlands, and Gothenburg-Amsterdam in particular, were important to the company's income, being less competed and relatively attractive to motorist and cargo. The triangle route also had potential as a mini-cruise, which were actively marketed during the low season from 1968. Berth capacity on the the Tor ships was further increased in 1969 refits, when the garages located on A deck were converted into dormitories with circa 200 beds. Thus, the total berth capacity of the *Tor Anglia* rose to 818 and of the *Tor Hollandia* to 888 (note, however, that the *cabin* berth capacity remained unaltered). At the same time the gross register tonnages of both ships grew by circa 400 grt, to 7,400 and 7,800, respectively, due to the fact that, by the measurements of the time, car decks were not included in the tonnage figures.

With the refits, Tor Line were following the example of Svenska Lloyd, who had increased the passenger capacity of the *Saga* (3) in a similar manner in late 1967, when the crane-loadable forward cargo hold had been converted into cabins and several two-berth cabins were converted into four-berth ones. With these measures, the passenger capacity of the ship rose to 486.

Svea and EWL quit the game

It should not come as a surprise that the Gothenburg-UK routes suffered from overcapacity after 1967. In light of later events it is perhaps surprising that initially Svenska Lloyd

The former ***Svea*/*Hispania*** in her "third life" on the Sweden-UK routes as the ***Saga*** (4), seen here in the Gothenburg archipelago. Both her Saloon and A-Decks were extended aftwards (allowing for the fitment of the swimming pool visible on Saloon deck) when she was the ***Hispania***, but with style and dimensions so similar to the original it's difficult to notice any change. *(Anders Bergenek collection)*

seemed to emerge as the winner, despite the combination of longest crossing times and limited capacity for trucks.

If Tor Line was struggling, there were also difficulties within ESL, as especially Svenska Lloyd and Ellerman's Wilson Line had a hard time changing their modes from competition to cooperation. Furthermore, the Gothenburg-London route proved an odd combination with the Gothenburg-Hull service, the latter being much more cargo-oriented. Already in the beginning of 1968 Svenska Lloyd decided to quit the consortium, with the separation taking effect at the end of the summer season in September. Again, Svenska Lloyd operated and marketed the Gothenburg-London route alone. EWL and Svea were left to operate a trunk-ESL in face of heavy competition from Tor Line. Soon after Svenska Lloyd had left ESL, Svea decided to give up passenger services between Sweden and the UK, and in early 1969 the *Svea* was sold – to Svenska Lloyd! She was replaced on the Gothenburg-Hull route by the roro cargo-only ship *Servus*, which continued the joint service with EWL.

Tor Line quickly reacted to the *Svea*'s withdrawal by altering their schedules and abandoning the triangular service: now there were three weekly return trips on the Gothenburg-Immingham route, but only one of the Gothenburg-Amsterdam line. At the same time, crossing times on the service were decreased to 25 hours and harbour turn-around times to just four hours. EWL similarly planned to increase the speed of their Gothenburg-Hull crossings, as the *Spero*'s (3) speed reserves made it possible to make a crossing in 29 hours, which would have allowed the ship to make two return trips per week. A test sailing on the higher speed was successful, but the resulting schedule changes were deemed impractical for cargo and the plans were never put into action. An intermediate call at Kristiansand in Norway was also explored for improving loadings, but it would have meant stepping on the toes of the passenger services Fred. Olsen (see Chapter 4), with whom EWL operated a joint UK-Norway cargo service.

After she was taken over by Svenska Lloyd, the *Svea* was renamed *Hispania.* She briefly sailed on the Gothenburg-London line during a docking of the *Saga* (3), before extensively rebuilt for the service her new name hinted at: a running mate of the *Patricia* (4) on the UK-Spain line. In addition to a superstructure expansion, converting two-berth cabins to four berths and replacing the port side car deck with cabins to give the ship the same passenger capacity as the *Patricia* (4) at 748, the *Hispania*'s three-year-old original interior decor was replaced with the more conventional style favoured by Svenska Lloyd, but with Spanish touches suitable for her new service. The refit increased her gross register tonnage to 8,600.

While the passenger numbers of the Southampton-Bilbao line were good during the high season, it quickly became evident there was not enough demand for two ships around the year. When, at the same time, Svenska Lloyd needed additional cargo capacity on the Gothenburg-London route (due to their new cargo-only vessels being delayed), already in late 1970 the *Hispania* moved back to the North Sea service as the running mate of the *Saga* (3). While the move was cargo-motivated, the introduction of a second passenger vessel also resulted in a radical increase in passenger numbers, mostly at the expense of Tor Line, as the direct service to London was more popular than the one to Immingham amongst the passengers, despite Svenska Lloyd's higher prices. Nonetheless, operating two passenger vessels around the year between Gothenburg and London was projected to become unprofitable, due to constantly rising operating costs, and Svenska Lloyd studied alternative employments for the *Hispania*, such as a long Gothenburg-London-Southampton-Bilbao line, but no practical solution was discovered.

Although combining passengers and cargo was a good idea on paper, reality proved different. UK ports had persistent problems with strikes – London Tilbury's workers being particularly prone to take industrial action. As passengers were not willing to remain in port, waiting for stevedores' strikes to end, the ships often had to sail back to Sweden with unloaded cargo still onboard, creating a domino effect taking multiple crossings to resolve. To get past the problem, both Svenska Lloyd and Tor Line invested in dedicated cargo tonnage during the 1970s. These, naturally, lie outside the scope of this book, but when reading the following part of this chapter it should be remembered that not only Svenska Lloyd and Tor Line but also Rederi AB Svea and Ellerman's Wilson Line invested in new roro cargo tonnage during the rest of the decade, and that the competition in the cargo services was even more cut-throat, and continued for a longer time, than competition in the passenger services, cutting into the profit margins of the remaining passenger operators.

In 1971-72, Svenska Lloyd's freight division suffered acute difficulties and the company needed additional funds to cover the losses. At the same time, the fellow Swedish shipping company Stena Line needed additional tonnage for the duration of the 1972 Summer Olympics in Munich. Svenska Lloyd decided the best option would be to sell the *Saga* (3) to Stena, retaining the *Hispania*, which was more economic to operate due to her higher passenger capacity, to run the UK service.

The *Saga* (3) was sold in early 1972. Afterwards, the *Hispania* was renamed *Saga* (4), now operating the Gothenburg-London service alone. At the same time, EWL were ready to give up on their Gothenburg-Hull service, and entered negotiations to charter the *Spero* (3) to Svenska Lloyd for the Gothenburg-London route for seven years. No agreement was reached – as Svenska Lloyd had just reverted to one-ship operation, it is unlikely the negotiations were serious on their side to start with – and EWL transferred the *Spero* (3) to a new Hull-Zeebrugge service, replacing her with the roro cargo ship *Destro* on the Gothenburg-Hull route. The *Spero*'s (3) Zeebrugge service was another failure, and in early 1973 the ship was laid up and subsequently sold, spelling an end to EWL's passenger services. The radical decrease in competing services naturally benefitted Tor Line, who not only made a good result (thanks to being able to increase prices) but realised that, with growing passenger figures, their existing ships would soon be too small for the needs of the service.

Biggest on the North Sea one last time

Only Svenska Lloyd and Tor Line remained on the Sweden-UK passenger services in 1973, the former operating the *Saga* (4) and the latter the *Tor Anglia* and *Tor Hollandia*. The sale of the *Saga* (3) had not been a long-term solution to Svenska Lloyd's financial difficulties, and the company remained in critical need of more funds. At the same time managing director Torgeir Christoffersen, who had largely been responsible for Svenska Lloyd's dedication to services with car-passenger ferries, decided to retire and sell his shares in the company. Although initial discussions were carried out with Tor Line's owners Salén – a move which would have resulted in a merger of Tor Line and Svenska Lloyd – in the end Christoffersen sold his shares to the competing Swedish shipping giant Broström. In theory, Svenska Lloyd had secured an owner with enough financial muscle to ensure a bright future, especially as Brostöm were already engaged in passenger shipping in the form of the famous Svenska Amerika Linien. Reality proved different: Broström were rapidly losing interest in the passenger business, and were on the brink of financial difficulties themselves. To paraphrase one of Anders Bergenek's articles on the subject, Svenska Lloyd found themselves getting out of the frying pan and into the fire.

In contrast, Tor Line – under the leadership of Christer Salén (who had been appointed managing director in 1971) – had contracted two car-passenger ferries from the Lübecker Flender-Werke in West Germany in 1973 that would bring them undisputed leadership on the North Sea routes. (Dubigeon-Normandie in France and an unnamed Japanese yard had been the other contenders). The new ships would be amongst the largest ferries in the world, far surpassing the existing North Sea tonnage in size, and on top of that they would be faster than the existing duo. Svenska Lloyd's new owners' response to this was to simply keep sailing with the *Saga* (4), despite the ship's deficiencies as a cargo carrier – although it should be noted the ship's passenger capacity was further increased to 784 in a 1974 refit by converting the children's playroom, teen's lounge and one public toilet into cabins.

Ownership changes followed for Tor Line in the beginning of 1975. In a somewhat complex deal, Rederi AB Transatlantic purchased one third of Tor Line's shares, taking over the entire share of KNSM plus a part of Salén's shareholding. At the same time Transatlantic's subsidiary Nike Line, which operated cargo ships between Stockholm and Rotterdam, was merged into Tor Line (this was unprofitable and the service was quickly discontinued). Thus, Tor Line was again a wholly Swedish-owned, with Salén controlling two thirds and Transatlantic one third.

The first of Tor Line's new ships, the *Tor Britannia,* was delivered in 1975, with the sister ship *Tor Scandinavia* following a year later. At 15,700 grt and a capacity for 1,507 passengers, the ships were amongst the largest ferries in the

The ***Tor Scandinavia*** somewhere on the North Sea on a sunny day – you can just make out the sunbathers lounging around the pool. The provision of a swimming pool was perhaps inspired by the existance of an outdoors pool onboard the ***Saga*** (4). *(FotoFlite)*

world and certainly the largest on the North Sea by some margin. As delivered, the *Tor Britannia* had cabin berths for 1,234 passengers, but for the *Tor Scandinavia* two-berth cabins were turned into four-berth ones, increasing the cabin capacity to 1,416. Subsequently, the *Tor Britannia* was similarly modified. In contrast to the older-generation ships, passenger dormitories were now elimited in favour of four-berth economy cabins without private facilities. At the same time, larger luxury cabins were also absent.

On the car deck, there was space for 420 cars or 910 lane metres for cargo, with turn-arounds speeded up by the specification of two ramps aft, spanning almost the ships' entire width. Initial design of the ships was contracted from Knud E. Hansen, but again finished in-house by a team led by Thomas Wigforss (ironically, a former Svenska Lloyd employee). In terms of dimensions the ships became unusually sleek, as a narrow but long hull was ideal for the high speeds the ships were designed for. Some sources also claim the width of the Immingham tidal locks restricted the ships' beam to 23.62 metres, but this seems dubious as the locks are 27.40 metres wide.

In keeping with the trend of the era, cabins were placed forward and public rooms aft. There was also a practical reason for this, as on the *Tor Anglia* and *Tor Hollandia* the large windows of forward-facing lounges were broken in heavy weather on several occasions. On the new ships, forward-facing windows were almost completely eliminated. Public rooms included a cafeteria (a part of which could be converted into a cinema), a combined buffet and à la carte restaurant, dance bar, casino, children's playroom, a shop, a multipurpose room that served as a café during the day and a disco at night, a sauna, and an outdoors swimming pool. While the sauna was on the bottom-most passenger deck and the pool on the

A classic postcard view of the ***Tor Scandinavia*** (closer to the camera) and ***Tor Britannia*** passing out at sea. *(Kalle Id collection)*

The ***Tor Scandinavia***'s restaurant. The two sisters had somewhat different interior decors; on the ***Tor Britannia***, the glass artworks seen here were replaced by metal sculptures. (*Svensk Sjöfartstidning archive)*

Another aerial view of the ***Tor Scandinavia***. Although her livery is identical to what it was when delivered, Esbjerg as the home port reveals the photo was taken in 1982, after the service was taken over by DFDS but before the ship was repainted in DFDS colours. *(FotoFlite)*

top deck, there was a direct elevator connection between the two. All passenger areas were decorated in the typical 1970s modernist style with clean lines and bright colours, designed by leading ferry interior designers of the era: Kay Kørbing from Denmark (restaurants, passageways and cabins) and Vuokko Laakso from Finland (bars). Harry Nilsson, meanwhile, designed the crew areas. There were so many works of art onboard, many personally chosen by Christer Salén, that contemporaries described the ships as floating art exhibitions.

While the ships were painted in Tor Line's now-traditional blue-hulled livery, during construction the Swedish PR agency Arbmans 6 had suggested a radically different treatment: in their vision, the first ship would have been named *Happy Days* and painted rose red, while the second would have been given a light green or turquoise colour scheme and named *Good Times*. Perhaps fortunately, Tor Line did not follow up on this advice.

Behind the scenes, the ships were designed for fast and efficient provisioning to keep turn-around times as short as possible; for example, conventional shelves were eliminated from both the kitchens and the shops, in favour of a palletised system where the readily-loaded shelf pallet would be swapped during the turnaround, instead of needing stock the shelves onboard (thus meaning the shelvers would work on dry land, and be paid lower wages than the onboard crew). For the first time, the navigation equipment was entirely computerized and a new, computer-based booking system was taken into use when the ships arrived. Finally, in keeping with the egalitarian trends in Sweden at the time, all crew cabins were located on the top decks, with all crew members having their own, single-berth cabins with windows (albeit most crew cabins shared the toilet and shower cubicle with their neighbour).

The *Tor Britannia* and *Tor Scandinavia* had been contracted before the first oil crisis in 1973. They were designed for a service speed of 24 knots (with a top speed of 27 knots), making it possible to sail from Gothenburg to Immingham in just 21 hours. However, in the end the ships rarely sailed to Immingham: when the *Tor Britannia* was delivered in May 1975, she opened a new service to Felixstowe, which was much closer to London (with all its attractions for tourists) and could be reached in 24 hours, thanks to the high service speed (although a contributing factor to the move were disputes over harbour fees at Immingham). The new ship replaced the *Tor Anglia*, which was first laid up and then chartered out (to Larvik-Frederikshavns Ferjen) for the summer season, until eventually sold to Trans Tirreno Express in Italy. However, in the autumn the *Tor Hollandia* had found a buyer (becoming the *Ariadne* (3) with Minoan Lines – initially, Tor Line had planned to use her for a new service in the Red Sea!), and Tor Line chartered back the *Tor Anglia* (now under Italian flag and with mostly Italian crew) to sail alongside the *Tor Britannia*. However, due to the different service speeds, the older ships' route was not modified to match the new ship. Until the delivery of the *Tor Scandinavia*, Tor Line's ships' operated two different services and schedules: the *Tor Britannia* sailed twice a week from Gothenburg to Felixstowe and once a week from Gothenburg to Amsterdam, while the *Tor Hollandia*, and later *Tor Anglia*, made a single return trip per week on the three routes they had served previously (Gothenburg-Immingham, Immingham-Amsterdam and Gothenburg-Amsterdam).

The *Tor Anglia* suffered a serious accident at Ijmuiden in March 1976, and Tor Line had to operate with just one ship until the *Tor Scandinavia* was delivered in April. Once repaired, the *Tor Anglia* joined the Trans Tirreno Express as the *Expresso Olbia*. Once both the *Tor Britannia* and *Tor Scandinavia* were in service, they offered three weekly departures from Gothenburg to Felixstowe, one weekly departure from Gothenburg to Immingham and two weekly departures from Gothenburg to Amsterdam. The Immingham-Amsterdam service was discontinued.

The port-side connecting arcade on the restaurant deck of the ***Tor Scandinavia*** with comfortable sofas (upholstered in dark green) to lounge in. *(Svensk Sjöfartstidning archive)*

Café Grillen, located to the left on the arcade picture above. Later on, DFDS converted this space to an à la carte restaurant. *(Svensk Sjöfartstidning archive)*

Pyrrhic victory

In face of the steep new challenge, Svenska Lloyd worked additional sailings into the high season schedules from 1975 onwards. This was no help: with Tor Line now sailing to Felixstowe, Svenska Lloyd lost their primary competitive advantage – a direct service to London – and passenger numbers plummeted. In early 1977, Tor Line's management suggested that Svenska Lloyd withdraw the *Saga* (4) and the companies coordinate their cargo services. Despite an offer of monetary compensation, the managing director of Broström turned this down. A short while later, Svenska Lloyd decided to close their passenger division at the end of the 1977 summer season. Thus both the Gothenburg-London and Southampton-Bilbao services ceased. The *Saga* (4) and *Patricia* (4) were laid up in Gothenburg and put for sale.

In hindsight, Svenska Lloyd's big mistake had been the insistence on a non-standard cargo solution for the *Saga* (3) and the rest of the ESL fleet. Had Svenska Lloyd's ships been conventional car-passenger ferries, the direct service to London would have presented a much steeper challenge to the newcomer Tor Line. Considering the financial difficulties faced by Tor Line during the early years, a stronger competing product from Svenska Lloyd might have resulted in Tor Line collapsing and Svenska Lloyd remaining as the incumbent operator, or forced a merger in terms favourable to Svenska Lloyd. But history played out as it did, and Svenska Lloyd's almost sixty years in passenger shipping were over.

Yet things were not bright for Tor Line. After the *Tor Britannia* and *Tor Scandinavia* had been contracted, the first oil crisis had multiplied the price of fuel, creating a nightmarish situation for a company whose primary business model was speed. At the same time, the pay received by Swedish sailors rose dramatically during the 1970s, so much so that by the end of the decade the Swedish flag was amongst the most expensive in the world. A further issue was the rising value of the West German mark against the Swedish krona after 1973, as the *Tor Britannia* and *Tor Scandinavia*'s build contracts had been made in West German currency and thus the ships had ended up costing more kronor than originally calculated.

After Svenska Lloyd's withdrawal, Tor Line concentrated their UK passenger services to Felixstowe. At the same time, the company felt there was still need for a service to a port in northern England and negotiated with Svenska Lloyd to charter or purchase the *Saga* (4), but no agreement was reached. Instead, the *Saga* (4) was sold to Minoan Lines as the *Knossos*, and enjoyed a long career in the Mediterranean until scrapped in 2011. The *Patricia* (4), meanwhile, was sold to Stena Line, who heightened her cargo deck to allow the carriage of trucks (something that Svenska Lloyd should perhaps have done much earlier) and renamed the ship *Stena Saga* to capitalise on the famous name of her sister ships. Interestingly, the ship still exists at the time of writing as the Malaysian casino cruise ship *Amusement World*.

Tor Line did not give up on the idea of a service to a port in northern England. Before they could act further with the plan, Stena Line made it known in 1977 that they would be chartering the 1967-built *Winston Churchill* (see Chapter 6 for details) from DFDS for summer-only Gothenburg-Newcastle service starting 1978. Tor Line were not keen on competition returning to the Sweden-UK routes and initiated negotiations with Fred. Olsen to open a competing Gothenburg-Newcastle

The ***Winston Churchill*** had been one of DFDS' first-generation car-passenger ferries when delivered for the Esbjerg-Harwich route in 1967. A decade later she had been supplanted by newer tonnage and was freed up for secondary services and charters, like Tor Line's Gothenburg-Newcastle route – in which she remained in DFDS livery as seen here. *(FotoFlite)*

service using the Olsen's ships (Fred. Olsen's North Sea services are discussed in more detail in the next chapter). The threat worked, Stena Line withdrew, and the planned Gothenburg-Newcastle service was run by Tor Line in collaboration with DFDS using the *Winston Churchill*.

While the summer service to Newcastle was successful and became a regular feature – indeed, Tor Line carried a record number of passengers during 1978 – the company's cargo division faced unprecedented competition when the Swedish government, in an attempt to help the country's ailing shipbuilding industry, gave heavy subventions to an upstart cargo operator, Oden Line, to build new roro cargo ships for the North Sea services. Worse still, Oden Line also took over Tor Line's lucrative contract to export Volvo cars. The new, stone-hard competition on the cargo routes, combined with the high operating and capital costs of the passenger services, placed Tor Line in an increasingly difficult financial position.

After the *Winston Churchill*'s second summer season (which ended with the ship grounding outside Gothenburg, resulting in the need for an extensive refit), Tor Line had plans to convert the service to an year-round one, once again in collaboration with Fred. Olsen (with whom Tor had entered a pool agreement on cargo services in the interim), with the route Gothenburg-Kristiansand-Newcastle, this time using the chartered *Espresso Olbia* (formerly Tor Line's own *Tor Anglia*). After the *Expresso Olbia* had been chartered, the Olsens suddenly withdrew, citing too high fuel expenses. The service never happened and the *Espresso Olbia* was laid up in Gothenburg, costing charter fees but generating no income.

Tor Line were known, during their existence as a passenger operator, for their bold marketing moves. Several were made during the second half of the 1970s, including captain Sune Dahlström receiving permission from the Swedish magistrate to perform weddings onboard the *Tor Scandinavia*, cruises aimed specifically at twins, and even a BBC TV series, *Triangle*, filmed onboard the *Tor Scandinavia.* An attempt to reproduce the success of the US TV series *The Love Boat*, *Triangle* failed to recreate the popularity of the original.

Sessan Tor Line

Tor Line's passenger services were heavily seasonal, with profits made during the short summer high season and winters operated at a loss. To help make more money, the *Tor Scandinavia* was chartered out as a floating exposition to The Expo Ship in the Middle East for the winters of 1979 and 1980, but this was not enough to solve Tor Line's mounting financial problems, made worse by the fact Salén, too, were in difficulties and not in a position to financially support Tor Line.

As a solution, Tor Line sought cooperation with another Gothenburg-based ferry operator, Rederi Ab Göteborg-Frederikshavn, better known with the marketing name Sessanlinjen, in which Tor was a minority shareholder. In 1979, the two companies formed a joint venture, Sessan Tor Line. Tor and Sessan's route networks were complimentary, but this also meant that there were essentially no chances of fleet rationalisation – only savings from the joint venture could come from combined administration and marketing. Further negotiations involving Stena Line followed during the same year, with the aim of creating a single Gothenburg-based passenger shipping company, but came to nothing. Stena Line remained a threat to Tor Line for the remainder of the latter company's existence, as Stena had not abandoned their ambitions for a Sweden-UK service. Indeed, Stena's CEO and owner Sten A. Olsson even publicly stated he planned to use one of the jumbo ferries under construction in Poland to start such a service – but in the end, the ships were severely delayed and by the time of their delivery Stena had lost interest in the UK routes.

At the same time as Sessan Tor Line was born, a consolidation process took place in the Sweden-UK cargo sector, where Tor Line gradually swallowed up most of their competitors. In 1978, Tor Line had taken over the remains of Ellerman's Wilson Line's operations (what remained of EWL went bankrupt 1981), while in 1980 Tor Line's and Svenska Lloyd's cargo operations merged to form Tor Lloyd, spelling the end of Svenska Lloyd as an independent company.

Sessan Tor Line officially begun operations in January 1980, with both companies' ships painted with new funnel symbols, combining the funnel logos of both participants, and Sessan Tor Line texts on the sides. However, otherwise the liveries remained unchanged, with the ex-Sessan ships sporting white hulls and ex-Tor ferries blue ones. In addition to the existing Tor duo, the routes of which remained unchanged, the *Winston Churchill* again returned to run a summer service from Gothenburg to Newcastle in 1980. That year, Tor Line even looked into starting a new ferry service in the Caribbean, linking Florida in the United States to the Yucatan Peninsula in Mexico, but nothing came of this.

Disagreements soon arose within Sessan Tor Line. Tor Line favoured a radical fleet reduction to improve profitability, suggesting the sale or redeployment elsewhere of the *Tor Britannia* and *Prinsessan Birgitta* (the withdrawal of the latter would have meant an end to Sessan's loss-making services to Germany), or by selling or chartering out one of Sessan's two large under-construction newbuildings on delivery. Sessan's managing director Ulf Trapp was unwilling to see so many Swedish sailors made redundant and instead reached out to Stena, selling his personal shareholding in Sessanlinjen to

A 1980 view of the ***Tor Britannia*** in Sessan Tor Line livery, with the combined company names on the sides and amalgam funnel colours with Sessan's whimsical royal mermaid on top of Tor's unashamedly modernist wheel on waves. *(Bruce Peter collection)*

The ***Dana Gloria*** (1) joined the Gothenbiurg-Newcastle route from summer 1981, replacing the ***Winston Churchill***. *(FotoFlite)*

After the break-up of Sessan Tor Line in early 1981, the Sessan part of the company name was quickly painted over from the sides of the ***Tor Britannia***, leaving the company name (even more) offset (than the original) from the centerline of the ship and painted in a different typeface from the actual company logo. *(FotoFlite)*

A mid-1980s view of the ***Tor Britannia***, now in the full DFDS livery, likely taken outside Harwich. A picture of her with the DFDS Tor Line markings, which used a different font from those of her sister, can be seen on page 15. *(FotoFlite)*

A postcard of the ***Tor Scandinavia*** during her winter 1982-83 charter as the ***World Wide Expo***. While previous winter charterers had occasionally altered the livery, this was the only time her name officially changed for the duration. *(Ian Boyle collection)*

The ***Prins Hamlet***, seen here on the River Tyne, was the last "summer ship" to operate the Gothenburg-Newcastle route, before fleet reorganisation made additional vessels for the summer seasons unnecessary. *(Hilton T. Davis)*

Stena. A war for the control of Rederi Ab Göteborg-Frederikshavn followed, with both Stena and Tor attempting to buy as many shares as they could. In the end, Stena prevailed and gained a controlling 51% share of Sessan in January 1981. Sessan Tor Line was wound up two months later, and Stena and Sessan subsequently merged. The loss of their partner left Tor Line in an unbearable situation. Seeing no other way out, Salén and Transatlantic reorganised Tor Line with the intention of selling the passenger division.

Following the break with Sessan Linjen, Tor Line operated in 1981 as before, with the *Tor Britannia* and *Tor Scandinavia* sailing from Gothenburg to Felixstowe and Amsterdam, while the summer-only Gothenburg-Newcastle route run jointly with DFDS was now operated by the 1975-built former Silja Line ferry *Dana Gloria* (1, see Chapters 4 and 6) that DFDS had recently acquired from Effoa (formerly Finska Ångfartygs Aktiebolaget, see Chapter 2 for the company's involvement in passenger services to Britain). At the same time, negotiations for the takeover of Tor Line were carried out with DFDS, Stena Line and even the ship's own crews, who proposed the creation of a new, employee-owned operator for the *Tor Britannia* and *Tor Scandinavia*. In the end, DFDS prevailed.

DFDS takes over

The sale of Tor Line's passenger operations to DFDS came to pass in a roundabout way. First, in November 1981, the *Tor Britannia* was sold to DFDS' North American subsidiary Scandinavian World Cruises. The new owners renamed the ship *Scandinavian Star*, with the intention of rebuilding her for four-night cruises from Florida to the Bahamas. Just one month after taking over the *Tor Britannia*, DFDS agreed to buy what remained of Tor Line's passenger operations: the *Tor Scandinavia* and the services she operated. Subsequently,

The ***Tor Britannia*** seen departing Harwich in the "racing stripes" DFDS Seaways livery applied in 1986, which unified the previous complex sub-brands that included not just DFDS Tor Line but also DFDS Danish Ferries and DFDS Prins Ferries. *(FotoFlite)*

DFDS also took over Tor Line's cargo division, and Tor thus ceased to exist as an independent company. The Tor Line name lived on, however, in the DFDS subsidiary DFDS Tor Line until a brand reorganisation in 2010 unified all DFDS shipping operations as DFDS Seaways.

Following the change of ownership in December 1981, the *Tor Scandinavia* was moved to the Danish registry and subsequently repainted in a modified white-hulled DFDS livery with a DFDS Tor Line text on her sides. Otherwise, her service remained unchanged. Meanwhile, the plan of refitting the *Scandinavian Star* proved too expensive and, following a lay-up in Copenhagen, the ship reverted to her original name in 1982. Her interior decor was restored and she re-joined her sister on the routes from Gothenburg to Felixstowe and Amsterdam in March 1982. The following winter, the *Tor Scandinavia* was chartered out as an expo ship one last time, now to the Far East under the temporary name *World Wide Expo*.

The year 1983 brought larger-scale changes to the old Tor Line ships as DFDS rationalised their cross-North Sea network and incorporated the Tor twins better into it: the UK port of the main route to Sweden was moved to Harwich, from which DFDS' ships to Denmark already operated (see Chapter 6). The service from Gothenburg to Amsterdam was abandoned, and instead the *Tor Britannia* and *Tor Scandinavia* now operated from Harwich to both Gothenburg and Esbjerg.

The Gothenburg-Newcastle summer service slotted easily into the DFDS route networr, having been run with DFDS ships to start with. During the 1980s the route was operated by the already-familiar *Dana Gloria* (1) and *Winston Churchill*, then by the *Venus* (3), *Jupiter* (2, both chartered from Fred. Olsen, see Chapter 4) and *Prins Hamlet*. The latter had been built in 1973 by Werft Nobiskug for Prinzen Line's Hamburg-Harwich service as the *Prinz Hamlet* (2). She was 5,829 grt and carried 1,100 passengers as well as 225 cars. DFDS took over the Prinzen Line service in 1981, but the ownership of the *Prinz Hamlet* (2) passed to the company only in 1987, when her name was amended to the Danish spelling *Prins Hamlet*. She spent the summers of 1987 and 1988 sailing from Esbjerg and Gothenburg to Newcastle, before sold on in autumn 1988. The mid-80s also saw DFDS introduce a new white and blue livery, with a new Scandinavian Seaways marketing name following in 1989.

Decline...

In 1989-1990, the services from Gothenburg were gradually reorganised. The *Tor Britannia* and *Tor Scandinavia* no longer sailed on the Esbjerg-Harwich route; instead, the Gothenburg-Amsterdam service was re-opened and operated around the year. In addition, the two ships took over the Gothenburg-Newcastle service during the summer seasons, eliminating the need for additional tonnage summer tonnage, and made Gothenburg-Copenhagen trips in the place of the Newcastle sailings during the rest of the year.

TOR BRITANNIA
TOR SCANDINAVIA
ESBJERG
DFDS TOR

A 1986 view of the ***Tor Scandinavia*** (closer to the camera) and ***Tor Britannia*** passing outside Harwich. The former is still in the old DFDS Tor Line livery, while the latter has already received the new "racing stripes" DFDS Seaways livery. With the livery change, the use of the Tor Line name in passenger services ended. *(FotoFlite)*

The "racing stripes" livery had barely been taken into use, when the company marketing name was amended to Scandinavian Seaways. This December 1988 view of the ***Tor Scandinavia*** shows her painted with the new company name on the sides. *(FotoFlite)*

The arcade of the ***Princess of Scandinavia*** after the 1991-1992 refit. Compare with the original look of the space on page 67. *(Kalle Id)*

The early-90s refit made extensive use of marble cladding, such as in the elevator shaft seen here. Quite a change from the original panelling, which had been flaming orange! *(Kalle Id)*

During the winter of 1991-92 both Tor twins were given radical refits: the public rooms were entirely rebuilt, with new decor by Tillberg Design, new cabins were built in the former upper car deck, and the former couchette area below the car deck was converted to cabins. The cabin berth capacity thus grew to 1,543, but with a drop in car capacity. With the refit, the ships were also renamed in accordance with Scandinavian Seaways' new naming scheme: the *Tor Britannia* became the *Prince of Scandinavia* and the *Tor Scandinavia* the *Princess of Scandinavia*. Ironically, this refit made the ships similar to the England-Sweden Line ships they had outcompeted in the 1970s in that they could only load commercial vehicles in the rear part of the car decks.

The Amsterdam-service proved problematic and it was shortened to IJmuiden on the Dutch end in 1994. This was not enough to make it profitable and the following year the route was, again, closed down. Now, DFDS decided the *Princess of Scandinavia* was enough to handle the passenger services from Gothenburg to Harwich, Newcastle and Copenhagen on an around-the-year basis. The cargo business on the Sweden-UK routes continued to experience healthy growth, further facilitated by Sweden's accession into the European Union in 1995, but no similar growth in passenger numbers was experienced.

The *Prince of Scandinavia* rejoined the route for the 1995 and 1996 summer seasons, but after that she became a reserve vessel, moving between routes and covering for dockings of other vessels – including returning to the Gothenburg-UK services to cover for the *Princess of Scandinavia*'s docking in 1998, when she was refitted with large sponsons welded to her sides in order to improve stability (nescessary due to the new, more stringent safety regulations following the sinking of the Baltic ferry *Estonia* in

1994). Soon afterwards, the Scandinavian Seaways marketing name was abandoned in favour of re-introducing the DFDS Seaways brand.

The end of tax free sales in intra-European Union traffic in summer 1999 caused further changes in the *Princess of Scandinavia*'s services: the routes from Gothenburg to Harwich and Copenhagen were closed down; instead, the ship sailed around to the year from Gothenburg to Newcastle, with an intermediate call at Kristiansand in Norway. As Norway was (and is) not a part of the EU, this guaranteed the continuation of tax free sales onboard. During the winter season, leisurely 24-hour Gothenburg-Kristiansand cruises were made alongside the full Newcastle sailings.

Due to major engine issues, the *Princess of Scandinavia* was rebuilt between September 1999 and April 2000, first at Frederikshavn in Denmark and then St. Nazaire in France. The *Prince of Scandinavia* operated in her stead; this was the latter ship's final stint on the routes she was built for. Afterwards, she operated on various other DFDS routes until sold to Moby Lines for trading in the Mediterranean as the *Moby Drea* in 2003.

...and fall

With the *Princess of Scandinavia* nearing 30 years of age, DFDS begun looking into the future of the Sweden-UK services. Operating an aged vessel designed before the first oil crisis was becoming increasingly expensive, while the arrival of low-cost airlines had a negative effect on the passenger numbers.

Studies showed that a switch to ropax tonnage, as had been done on the Denmark-UK service in 2002, would be profitable, but even larger profits could be made by giving up passenger services and focusing on the existing roro cargo operations under the DFDS Tor Line name. According to Anders Bergenek and Klas Brogen's book *Passagerare till sjöss*, a detailed history of the Swedish passenger ferry industry, DFDS Tor Line was also aversed to passenger services "disrupting" the existing cargo services. A contributing factor may have been the fact the change of the Esbjerg-Harwich and Cuxhaven-Harwich routes to ropax was had proven less successful than had been forecast.

Thus, DFDS decided to close down the Gothenburg-Kristiansand-Newcastle service at the end of the 2006 summer season. The *Princess of Scandinavia* was withdrawn in 31 October 2006 and sold to Moby Lines two days later.

Tracing the past development of the service, the division of the Sweden-UK services to cargo-only vessels complemented

The empty pool deck of the ***Princess of Scandinavia***, photographed while traversing the stormy Skagerak a few weeks before the ship was withdrawn. *(Kalle Id)*

The ***Princess of Scandinavia*** arrives at Newcastle prior to the work been carried out to provide sponsons to her hull. *(Miles Cowsill)*

A 2004 summer view of the ***Princess of Scandinavia*** in her final appearance, with the sponsons welded on in 1998 and DFDS Seaways brand name taken back into use in 1999. By now, the 1976-vintage ship was arguably something of an anachronism on the North Sea, despite the numerous upgrades carried out over the years. *(FotoFlite)*

Another October 2006 view, with the sun setting on the ***Princess of Scandinavia*** in Gothenburg. On 2 November, she became the Moby Otta with Moby Lines. *(Kalle Id)*

Today, the cargo connection between western Sweden and the UK is in the hands of DFDS' Flower class freight roros, of which the ***Gardenia Seaways*** seen here is an example (although she primarily operates on the Vlaardingen-Immingham link). *(DFDS)*

by passenger-oriented ferries did not help the survival of the passenger service. Also problematic were the 1991-92 refits of the (former) *Tor Britannia* and *Tor Scandinavia*, which made them more passenger-oriented and complementary to, but increasingly superfluous for, the main cargo service. Had the vessels been replaced by ropax tonnage in the 1990s, when the type started appearing elsewhere in European waters, the subsequent development of the passenger services would have likely been different. However, the then-recent investment in rebuilding the existing vessels, combined with DFDS passenger division's cruise ferry focus made such an investment path seem undesirable – eventually spelling the end of the services.

After the withdrawal of the *Princess of Scandinavia*, DFDS remains the dominant force in shipping from Sweden's west coast to the UK (thanks in large part to the 1980s acquisition of Tor Line as described above), with roro cargo vessels linking the logistics hubs in Gothenburg and Immingham six times a week, keeping the trade vital to both countries' economies flowing. While these ships have a capacity for a maximum of 12 passengers, they do not carry any as the port of Immingham has not been approved for passenger services by the UK Border Force. Thus, there are currently no means for passengers to make a direct sea crossing from Sweden to the UK.

DFDS did not abandon passenger services from the Scandinavian Peninsula with the closure of the Sweden-UK routes, however: they acquired the Norway-UK services of Fjord Line at the same time as the Gothenburg-Newcastle route was closed. The next chapter looks at the history of the Norway-UK routes.

Chapter four

Norway to Britain: Competition and Innovation

The ***Eldorado*** (2) of Wilson Line was purpose-built for the lines linking Hull to Bergen and Trondheim in 1886, replacing a one-year-older sister ship of the same name that had been sold to Greece. She was the first Wilson ship equipped with electric lights through-out and served the company until 1911. *(Maritime Museum: Hull Museums)*

The services linking Norway to Britain differed from those linking other Nordic countries in several ways. While in the other Nordic countries, services to the British Isles were quickly concentrated in just one port – often on just one line operated by a single company – Norway enjoyed two competing services: the (relatively) short one from Bergen and the surrounding ports, and the longer services from Oslo and other ports in southern Norway. This is explained by Norway's mountainous geography, which meant that overland connections were – and in places still are – slow and at times even dangerous; yet the division also reflects the fierce traditional rivalry between Oslo and Bergen.

The focus shifted to cooperation in the car ferry era, in the form of the innovative combined car ferry-reefer-cruise ships jointly owned by Det Bergenske Dampskibsselskab and Fred. Olsen. These were the mainstays of the Norway-UK routes from 1966 until the early 1990s. After these ships, services reverted to being operated by conventional ferries acquired second-hand. Eventually, Bergen won over Oslo. The remaining Bergen-Stavanger-Newcastle route passed under ownership of DFDS Seaways in 2006, but was closed down in 2008.

British companies initiate passenger services

The early decades of the Norway-UK passenger services are unusually well documented in existing literature. While

numerous companies, both from Norway and Britain, attempted services during the mid- and late 1800s, only the Wilson Line of Hull was able to achieve long-term success.

The first, very brief, scheduled regular passenger link between Norway and Britain was by the UK-based Saint George Steam Packer Company. During the summer season of 1839, the steamers *Sirius* (1) and *Vulture*, sailing on a route connecting London to Saint Petersburg via Gothenburg and Copenhagen, added a call in Kristiansand to their route, after receiving compensation from the Norwegian government for the carriage of mail to both Denmark and the UK. However, this service ceased after the single summer season. The *Sirius* (1) was likely the 1837-built steamer that had been the first to cross the North Atlantic relying solely on steam power the year before her stint on the London-Saint Petersburg service.

The next company to try their luck – again with support from the Norwegian state – was Wilson Line, who opened a Hull-Kristiansand-Gothenburg service in 1840 using the steamers *Glen Albyn* and *Innisfail*. However, already in 1842 the service was closed down when the Swedish and Norwegian authorities refused to raise the subsidy for carrying mail. Services were restored in 1852, when an intermediate call at Christiania (as present-day Oslo was known until 1897) was added on the Hull-Gothenburg route operated by the *Scandinavian*. Shortly afterwards, Det Søndenfjelds-Norske Dampskibsselskab (freely translated as "The Southern

Norwegian Steamship Company") opened a competing service by placing the brand new steamer *Ganger Rolf* on the Christiania-Hull service, with intermediate calls in Arendal and Kristiansand. Heavy competition led to a ten-year joint service agreement between Wilson Line and Søndenfjeldske in 1856, but competition flared again once the agreement ran out. Søndenfjeldske, with its smaller resources, could not compete and withdrew from the UK services. They remained an important operator on other routes from Norway until 1970.

Competition for the Wilsons soon returned, however: in 1863, the steamers *Gnome* (built 1856, 522 tons) and *Snowdon* (built 1855, 271 tons) initiated an Edinburgh (Leith)-Kristiansand-Gothenburg-Copenhagen service. Information about this service is scarce: it is unknown which company exactly operated it, and when the service ceased, though it appears to have been run at least until 1867. A further competing service from southern Norway was run by the Henderson Brothers, with the help of a postal subsidy, between 1870 and 1872 with the 1866-built *Scotia* sailing on the route Christiania-Kristiansand-Edinburgh (Leith).

Starting from the 1860s, services from UK ports to Western Norway – Stavanger, Bergen and Trondheim (the latter written 'Drontheim' in English at the time, following German rather than Norwegian spelling) attracted numerous companies to try their luck. Most of these were British firms; the Norwegian companies concentrated their efforts in passenger steamer connections to Norway's biggest trade partner and Europe's rising star, Germany. The Norwegian historian Lauritz Pettersen Jr. summed up the situation bluntly in his book on the early history of the Bergen-Newcastle service: "In England there was little to no demand for exports from Bergen [and] England could offer very little that the Bergen businessmen could not buy from Germany and the Continent."

In 1865, the Fedden Brothers advertised a passenger service from Newcastle to Bergen and Trondheim with the steamer *Nordland*, which offered "very superior accommodation for about 60 first-class passengers." However, it is unknown if the advertised sailings ever actually took place. The same year, a new service between Trondheim and Newcastle, calling en-route at Christiansund, Molde and Aalesund, was initiated by a steamer named either *The Queen* or *Tyne Queen*, primarily for the export of pyrites from Ytterøya near Trondheim, with coal is return cargo, but also carrying passengers. A second steamer, the *Hilda*, joined the service the same year. This service was taken over by the Allan Line in 1869, who turned it into a feeder service for their transatlantic liners. The *Hilda* sunk in 1870, and Allan Line abandoned the route two years later.

Wilson Line expanded to the west coast of Norway in 1867, when the company opened a new line from Hull to Stavanger and Bergen. The following year, a regular service from Newcastle to Stavanger and Bergen was opened by the British company Borries Craig & Co, using the chartered Norwegian steamer *Saga*, which was joined in 1870 by another Norwegian ship, the *Odin*. Also in 1870, the postal contract between Trondheim and Newcastle was reported to belong to the Montreal Steamship Co., operating a bi-weekly service with the steamer *Norway* (1). Trondheim also attracted the attention of Wilson Line, who expanded their Hull-Bergen service to that city in 1871. Around the same time, the 1857-established Trondheim-based shipping company Det Nordenfjeldske Dampskibsselskab (NFDS, freely translated as "The Northern Steamship Company") had ambitions to start a Trondheim-UK service of their own, but the presence of so many competing companies discouraged them for the time being.

Also in 1871, the newly-established Det Norsk-Amerikanske Dampskibsselskab (literally "The Norwegian-American Steamship Company", but known in English as the Norse American Line) started offering passenger sailing from Newcastle to Bergen and Christiania. This first attempt to run a Scandinavian transatlantic company relied on migrants: in an era when migration from Europe to North America was common, Norwegians were particularly eager to do so – compared to the population, Norwegians ranked at number one when it came to seeking a new life across the Atlantic. Most Det Norsk-Amerikanske Dampskibsselskab's sailings continued from the Norwegian ports to North America, but the company appears to have also ran occasional dedicated North Sea sailings. Time was not yet ripe for a Norwegian transatlantic line and services ceased in 1877. The other Norway-UK services listed here met with similar fate – apart from Wilson Line, who became the dominant operator on services between Norway and the UK.

Although all companies listed above carried passengers, and the imortance of migrants should not be forgotten, the main rationale of the services – especially those to Bergen and Trondheim – was cargo: Norway exported pyrite and copper ore to the UK, and imported refined goods, such as textiles. Initially, most passengers made a one-way voyage, emigrating to North America. However, in the 1870s the Norwegian fjords became a popular tourist destination for the first time, especially after Oscar II, the King of Sweden and Norway, toured the fjords following his coronation in 1872. Thus, tourists were carried in increasing numbers, particularly on the services to Bergen and Trondheim.

Despite the increasing tourist potential of western Norway, Wilson Line concentrated their newest and largest ships on the line to Christiania. In 1870, the 795-passenger duo *Rollo* (1) and *Orlando* (1) were completed and placed on the Hull-Christiania-Gothenburg line. These were followed in 1881 by the larger, 1,840 gross register ton (grt) and 863 passenger *Romeo*.

Two long-term Norwegian competitors to Wilson Line in passenger services emerged in 1880, when Østlandske Lloyd commenced services from Larvik (a town south of Oslo) to Newcastle, and P.G. Halvorsen started a weekly service from Bergen to Newcastle. Initially, both companies concentrated more on freight, but as the years progressed, the carriage of passengers increased in importance. In the subsequent years, several other Norwegian companies initiated services to UK ports, both from western and southern Norway. At the time, Wilson Line did not see the companies sailing to Newcastle as major threats, as they did not directly compete with Wilson's services to Hull. Wilson Line even entered an agreement with Østlandske Lloyd, with both companies agreeing to stay out of each others' ports.

Lines from Bergen and Trondheim

The true pioneer of Norwegian-flagged services from Western Norway to the UK was the Bergen businessman Peter Gabriel Halvorsen. He operated a fleet of cargo ships, exporting pyrites from Norway to the Continent and importing coal from the UK. In 1880, Halvorsen initiated limited passenger services between Bergen and Newcastle with the 709 grt cargo ship *Johan Svedrup*. In 1882, the *Johan Svedrup* was joined by the 893 grt *Norge*, which could carry 100 passengers. The acquisition of a second ship allowed weekly departures from both ports.

Additional sailings by a Norwegian company started in 1881, when the 1851-established Det Bergenske Dampskibsselskab (BDS) opened a summer-only tourist service from Edinburgh (Leith) to Trondheim via Bergen. A similar tourist service from Bergen and Stavanger to Edinburgh was operated by Det Stavangerske Dampskibsselskab in 1886. Wilson Line's response to these new developments was to build in 1885 the 434-passenger, 935 grt *Eldorado* (1) for the line to Bergen – however, after just one year in service the ship was sold to Greece. Her place was taken by a larger *Eldorado* (2), which had the same passenger capacity but a larger gross tonnage figure at 1,382. Another newbuilding for the Trondheim line, the *Salmo* (1) was delivered in 1887. She could carry 542 passengers in her 721 grt hull. A further newbuilding, the *Juno*, of 1,080 grt, 50 first class passengers and an unspecified number of second class and steerage, was delivered in 1889.

Wilson Line's dominance was broken in 1890, when the Norwegian authorities begun to subsidise the carriage of mail from western Norwegian ports to the UK. This came to be in no small part thanks to personal efforts by P. G. Halvorsen. State support was granted for two services: a twice-weekly Bergen-Stavanger-Newcastle link, operated by P. G. Halvorsen, and a weekly service from Trondheim to Newcastle via Bergen and various smaller Norwegian coastal towns, operated as a joint service by BDS and NFDS, marketed in the UK as B & N Line. For BDS and NFDS, this collaboration was a logical continuation of their joint services along the Norwegian coast, as well as from Norwegian ports to Hamburg.

Halvorsen and NFDS commissioned new vessels for the subsidized services, while BDS initially relied on their existing tonnage. Halvorsen's new ship was the impressively sized 1,555 grt Britannia, that could carry at least 180 passengers. Supposedly, the *Britannia* had been designed by Halvorsen himself, but if so, it was not a ship to be proud of: not only had she been expensive to build, she was also fuel-hungry and reportedly vibrated so heavily that passengers were seasick in all weathers. NFDS' newbuilding was the smaller but more successful 1,084 grt *Ragnvald Jarl*. BDS' initial main ship on the service was the 1883-built, 989 grt and 270 passenger *Mercur* (ex-*Kong Dag*) acquired second-hand, though she was occasionally supplanted by the 972 grt and 399 passenger *Neptun* built in 1890 for the routes to Germany (as is perhaps evident from above, BDS tended to choose names of stars and planets for their ships, while NFDS primarily opted for Norwegian historical figures).

In response to the competition, Wilson Line raised the stakes by lowering prices, opening their own Bergen-Hamburg service, and taking delivery of a new ship in 1890: the 1,328 grt and 362 passenger *Tasso* for the Hull-Trondheim line. Wilson Line's strategy was successful: already 1891 the four companies reached an agreement, by the terms of which the Wilsons abandoned their Bergen-Hamburg line, and all operators agreed on joint prices on the Norway-UK routes. Even with the abandonment of the Hamburg line this was a victory for the Wilsons, who retained their position as the biggest operator on the routes between western Norway and Britain.

The ink had barely dried on the agreement when P.G. Halvorsen's *Norge* sank. This was the final blow for the already struggling company, which was declared bankrupt shortly afterwards. With Halvorsen out of the picture, BDS assumed responsibility for the direct Bergen-Newcastle service, which was initially operated by the aforementioned *Mercur*, but already during the same year she was joined by the newbuilt *Mira* (966 grt and 396 passengers). In 1894 a third ship was added in the form of the *Venus* (1), a 1,067 grt and 104 passenger steamer, the contract for which had been taken over in mid-construction. The *Vega* (1), a sister ship to the *Venus* (1), followed in 1895, at which point the *Mercur* was moved to other services. The *Mira* was moved away from the Bergen-Newcastle line in 1903, which briefly reverted to a two-ship service. However, already in 1905 a third ship was restored, in the form of the newbuilt 1,322 grt and 230-passenger *Irma.* She had been conceived for the mostly coastal route linking Bergen to Hamburg, and reportedly gave a lively ride on the line across the North Sea to the UK.

Later in 1905, the United Kingdoms of Sweden and Norway, which had been established in 1814, was dissolved following a Norwegian plebiscite overwhelmingly (99.95 percent) in favour of independence. Already in the same autumn Carl, a Danish prince, was crowned the King of Norway, taking the name Haakon VII. When NFDS took delivery of their new, 1,347 brt and 532 passenger flagship for the Trondheim-Bergen-Newcastle line in 1907, it was named *Haakon VII* in honour of the new king. NFDS' centennial history, published in 1957, described the *Haakon VII* as "not only Norway's largest but also its most elegant passenger ship."

The opening of a rail line between Kristiania (as Christiania had been restyled in 1897) and Bergen in 1909 meant that the Bergen-Newcastle route now became the main mail route between Norway and Britain, and could now attract passengers from further afield – not just from Norway but also from Sweden as, due to the shorter crossing time, the service was competitive for passengers for whom speed was of the essence. On the other hand, the Norwegian independence had not been well received in all circles in Sweden and this may

Above: Wilson Line's ***Tasso*** was delivered in 1890 for the Hull-Trondheim line. She was subsequently lengthened in 1901, but her career with Wilson was cut short by a 1911 collision with the HAPAG steamer ***President Lincoln*** in the Straits of Dover. She was sold after repairs and sailed primarily for Greek owners until foundered in 1920. *(Maritime Museum: Hull Museums)*

Left: NFDS' ***Ragnvald Jarl*** served on the Trondheim-Newcastle route from 1890 until 1907 and again in 1914-1917. She was sold for further trading in Spain in 1919, and subsequently scrapped in Spain in the late 1920s. *(Ambrose Greenway collection)*

Middle left: BDS's ***Neptun*** was built in 1890 for the services from Norway's coast to Hamburg, but occasionally sailed on the Trondheim-Bergen-Newcastle route. *(Ambrose Greenway collection)*

Bottom left: P.G. Halvorsen's ***Britannia*** was externally attractive, but an utter failure in terms of functionality and the prime cause in Halvorsen's bankruptcy. She is seen here in a later life as the Brazilian armed merchant cruiser ***Andrada***. *(Ambrose Greenway collection)*n

Below: A port scene with the ***Ragnvald Jarl*** closest to the camera, carrying the black hull commonly used in liner services – at the time, Norwegian operators commonly repainted their ships white for summer cruise services to the fjords. *(Ambrose Greenway collection)*

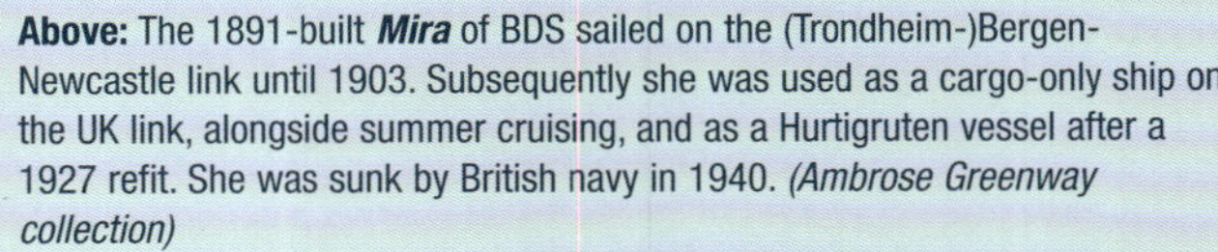

Above: The 1891-built ***Mira*** of BDS sailed on the (Trondheim-)Bergen-Newcastle link until 1903. Subsequently she was used as a cargo-only ship on the UK link, alongside summer cruising, and as a Hurtigruten vessel after a 1927 refit. She was sunk by British navy in 1940. *(Ambrose Greenway collection)*

Left: The ***Venus*** (1), delivered in 1893, spent almost her entire career on the Bergen-Newcastle service. In preparation for the delivery of the new ***Venus*** (2) in 1931 she was renamed ***Sylvia*** and and became a reserve ship, only to be scrapped two years later. *(Ambrose Greenway collection)*

Middle left: When delivered, NFDS' ***Haakon VII*** was the flagship of the Norwegian merchant fleet both in terms of size and comfort – though the latter arguably only by a small margin when compared to her running mate, the ***Irma*** of BDS. *(Anders Beer Wilse, Norsk Folkemuseum)*

Bottom left: : The ***Haakon VII*** sailed on the routes to the UK until 1921, after which she was briefly laid up. In 1922 she was reactivated for the Hurtigruten and became a popular ship on the service – but partially sunk in 1929 and, after the damage was found too expensive to repair, she was scrapped. *(Postcard, Rami Wirrankoski collection)*

Below: The 1889-built ***Scotland*** (1) of Færder Dampskibsselskab, photographed here during her brief career under Fred. Olsen ownership. *(Ambrose Greenway collection)*

have had a detrimental effect in Swedes' willingness to sail on Norwegian ships. Nonetheless, sailing from Bergen was made more appealing in 1913, when the Norway ships' terminal in Newcastle was moved from the Albert Edward Dock in North Shields to Newcastle Quayside, right in the center of the city.

The hitherto warm relationship between NFDS and BDS begun to cool after the delivery of the *Haakon VII.* The key disagreements were the services to the UK and BDS' dominant position on it. Finally, a solution was reached in 1914, when BDS agreed to withdraw from the services to Trondheim. After this, the Bergen-Stavanger-Newcastle line was operated by BDS' *Irma, Vega* (1) and *Venus* (1), while the Trondheim-Bergen-Newcastle route was run by NFDS' *Ragnvald Jarl* and *Haakon VII*. With NFDS' ships also sailing via Bergen, daily departures were offered from Bergen and Newcastle.

Lines from the Kristianiafjord

Østlandske Lloyd had been established in 1867 to operate coastal services in Southern Norway. As noted above, the company started a passenger service from Larvik to Newcastle in 1880. Initially, this was operated with second-hand cargo steamers modified to carry a small number of passengers. Another Norwegian company, Færder Dampskibsselskab, started a route from Christiania to the Scottish town of Grangemouth in 1886 with the 1875-built *Færder* of 1,484 grt and circa 100 passengers.

As had happened on other routes, the competitors attempted to outdo each other with a steady stream of newbuildings. The race was started by Færder in 1889 with the *Scotland* (1) of 889 grt and at least 90 passengers. The next year, both Wilson and Østlandske Lloyd responded, Østlandske with their first purpose-built vesseld, the *Sterling* (1). Wilson's ship was the *Montebello* of 1,735 grt and 700 passengers, which was placed on a new, dedicated service to Christiania from Hull via Kristiansand (instead of continuing from Christiania to Gothenburg). On this route, the *Montebello* was partnered with the smaller, 72-passenger *Angelo* of 1,272 grt, which dated from 1874. Færder followed their competitors by taking delivery of a sister ship to the *Scotland* (1), the *Norway* (2), in 1891.

The next newbuildings appeared around the turn of the century. Wilson Line took delivery, in 1899, of the North Sea's largest liner, the 2,376 grt *Ariosto*, which could carry 1,133 passengers. She was placed on the Hull-Kristiania-Gothenburg -line (Christiania having been renamed to Kristiania in 1897). Østlandske Lloyd responded by acquiring, in 1902, the 1886-built *Graceful* of 1,047 grt and 112 passengers, which was renamed *Sovereign* (1).

The increased pressure from Wilson Line and Østlandske Lloyd left Færder Dampskibsselskab struggling, and a new owner was sought for the Kristiania-Grangemouth line. In 1903, the company and its fleet were sold to Fred. Olsen & Co., the long-established Hvitsten-based cargo shipping company. The new owners immediately contracted a new, 1,104 grt ship for the Kristiania-Grangemouth service, which was delivered in 1904 as the *Scotland* (2). The first *Scotland* was sold to make way for her new namesake. Wilson Line's response was the *Oslo*, delivered in 1906, which was 2,296 grt and could carry 879 passengers. She replaced the *Angelo* on the Kristiania-Hull line. The choice of name perhaps reflected the increased Norwegian nationalism surrounding the country's independence, as Oslo had been Kristiania's original name until 1624, when the city was relocated following a major fire and renamed after the then-ruling king of Denmark and Norway.

With the influx of new vessels, Østlandske Lloyd were also beginning to struggle with their North Sea passenger services.

The damesalong (ladies' lounge) onboard the ***Haakon VII***. *(Anders Beer Wilse)*

The lesesalong (reading room) onboard the ***Haakon VII***. Notice the then-fashionable floral-pattern wallpapers. *(Anders Beer Wilse)*

In 1906, Fred. Olsen & Co. acquired Østlandske Lloyd's routes and ships sailing from Larvik to Newcastle and Antwerp. The new owners quickly reorganised the services: the Norwegian port was moved from Larvik to Kristiania, and three new vessels were contracted; of the existing ships, only the Newcastle line's 1886-built *Sovereign* (1) was to be retained. In 1907, she was partnered with the new 1,323 grt *Sterling* (2). Wilson Line responded by replacing both of their ships on the Kristiania-Hull route in 1909-1910. The first to arrive was the *Aaro* of 2,603 grt, that carried 738 passengers, which replaced the *Montebello* (the origin of the name *Aaro* is unknown; it is a

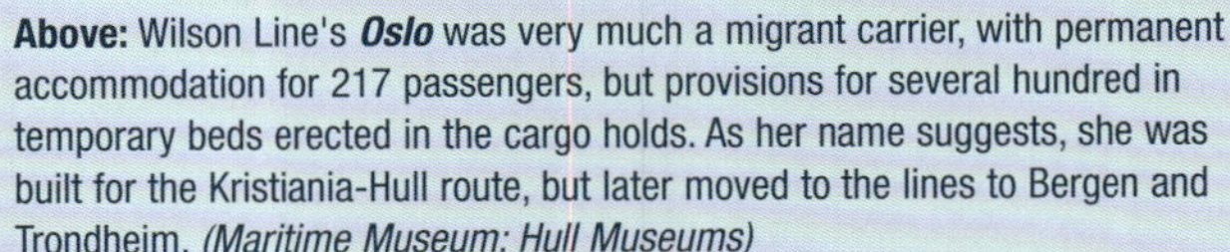

Above: Wilson Line's ***Oslo*** was very much a migrant carrier, with permanent accommodation for 217 passengers, but provisions for several hundred in temporary beds erected in the cargo holds. As her name suggests, she was built for the Kristiania-Hull route, but later moved to the lines to Bergen and Trondheim. *(Maritime Museum: Hull Museums)*

Left: Østlandske Lloyd's ***Sovereign*** (1) was a well-travelled ship, having been delivered for South African coastal trades in 1886 and also sailing on British coastal trades before Østlandske bought her in 1902. This undated view shows her the Østlandske funnel colours, the only image of the Østlandske livery discovered when making this book. *(Ambrose Greenway collection)*

Middle left: Østlandske's 1890-built ***Sterling*** (1) was sold almost immediately after Fred. Olsen took over the Østlandske operation in 1906. None-the-less, she briefly sailed in Fred. Olsen colours, as seen here. She later sailed for Danish, Swedish and Icelandic owners, until wrecked in 1922. *(Ambrose Greenway collection)*

Bottom left: Wilson Line's unusually named ***Aaro*** of 1909 was the company's first ship to be equipped with a wireless telegraph. Like almost all of Wilson Line's passenger vessels of the era, she was lost in World War I, torpedoed by German submarines on the North Sea in 1916. *(Maritime Museum: Hull Museums)*

Below: A somewhat fanciful painting postcard of Wilson Line's last Kristiania-route newbuilding ***Eskimo*** in the Fjords. The artist has made the ship look taller and moved the superstructure towards the bow. The ***Eskimo*** was Wilson's sole ship to survive World War I, but she was not seen worth restoring. Yet, after being sold to French owners in 1921, she saw eight years of further service before scrapped. *(Ian Boyle collection)*

Finnish male given name but bears no relevance to Norway. Possibly it is a misspelling of either Åros, a village on the Oslofjord, or the Danish island Aarø). She was followed by the 3,326 grt *Eskimo*; although notably larger than the *Oslo*, which she replaced, she carried only 568 passengers. On being replaced by the *Eskimo*, the *Oslo* moved to the service from Hull to Bergen and Trondheim.

With these new ships, Wilson Line remained the dominant passenger operator on lines from southern Norway – but not without a strong challenge from Fred. Olsen, who took delivery in 1910 of the new 1,447 grt *Norway* (3), which replaced her older namesake on the Kristinia-Grangemouth route. Tragedy struck already the following year, when the 1904-built *Scotland* (2) sank. Fortunately, a replacement was already under construction; this was the *Norway* (3)'s sister, which was delivered as the *Scotland* (3) in 1912. The same year, Fred. Olsen also took delivery of a new ship for the Kristiania-Newcastle route; this was the *Bessheim* of 1,781 grt and at least 80 passengers, which replaced the *Sovereign* (1). Fred. Olsen's cargo vessels had already been known for having names beginning with a B for some time, and with the *Bessheim* this expanded to the company's passenger ships (Bessheim is a relatively well-known mountain lodge in southern Norway). The *Bessheim* was also the company's fastest ship, and with the *Sterling* (2) she offered weekly departures from both ports.

The Bergen line becomes BDS' monopoly

When the First World War broke out in 1914, BDS and NFDS suspended services due to high insurance fees, but the Norwegian authorities quickly agreed to compensate for any war losses, and services recommenced. Although Norway officially remained neutral during the conflict, the line between Newcastle and Bergen was of utmost importance for communications between the Britain, France and Russia. During the first two war years, BDS and NFDS made good profits on the route to Britain, as Wilson Line had (naturally) suspended services.

BDS took delivery in 1915 of the new *Jupiter* (1) from the Lindholmen shipyard in Gothenburg for the Bergen-Newcastle line. At 2,625 grt she was a large ship for the era, but her passenger capacity was relatively small at 300. Germany's unrestricted submarine warfare interrupted services by Norwegian shipping companies in 1917 – but not before BDS' 1895-built *Vega* (1) had been lost. The following year the British authorities chartered the *Jupiter* (1) for a service between Bergen and Aberdeen in Scotland.

As noted above in Chapter 3, Wilson Line was sold during the war to Sir John Ellerman, and the company was renamed Ellerman's Wilson Line (EWL). It suffered heavy losses during the conflict: half the fleet was lost and the only passenger vessel to survive was the *Eskimo*, which was not deemed worthy of repair. Thus EWL were without passenger-carrying vessels when the war ended. In contrast, all (independent) Nordic countries had remained neutral during the conflict, suffered minimal losses and increased their market share during the war years. After the war, EWL decided not to continue services to Bergen, instead concentrating solely on the route to Kristiania.

BDS and NFDS re-initiated the Bergen-Newcastle line in 1918; the extension to Trondheim was discontinued. The route was operated by BDS' *Venus* (1), *Irma, Iris* and *Jupiter* (1), sailing alongside NFDS' *Haakon VII*. While the other ships were familiar on the route from earlier, the *Iris* was a 1901-built steamer of 1,213 grt, which had been acquired by BDS in 1907 for the Bergen-Rotterdam line. She carried 102 passengers.

A brief economic boom followed the end of the war, during

The career of 1910-built **Norway** (2) only lasted for seven years. *(Ambrose Greenway collection)*

The **Norway** (2)'s sister ship **Scotland** (3) was built in 1912 to replace the sunken **Scotland** (2). The **Scotland** (3) was another short-lived ship, being wrecked in 1916. *(Ambrose Greenway collection)*

which BDS contracted a new ship for the services to the UK: the 1920-built *Leda* (1), a near-sister to the *Jupiter* (1), but fitted with steam turbines instead of triple expansion engines. Apart from different power plants, the two ships were identical in size and capacities. During the same year, the the 1883-built *Mercur*, already familiar from the UK routes, was rebuilt with engines taken from the 1900-built Hurtigrute *Astraea* (which had sunk in 1910). She too was used on the Bergen-Newcastle route.

The new ship arrived at an inopportune time, as the post-

The ***Jupiter*** (1) of 1915 was – unusually – ordered from the Lindholmen yard in Gothenburg. After a lengthy career with BDS, lasting until 1955 with several stints of the Bergen-Newcastle route she was originally built for, she was sold to Greek owners and re-emerged as a successful cruise ship after a refit. *(A. Duncan, Rami Wirrankoski collection)*

BDS' ***Iris*** had originally been built as the ***Ingerid*** for a Dutch company's services to Norway. BDS purchased her in 1907 and she briefly sailed on the UK service after World War II. *(Ambrose Greenway collection)*

The ***Leda*** (1) was a British-built semi-sister to the ***Jupiter*** (1), with a different power plant. Externally, she also differed by the smaller superstructure windows. *(A. Duncan, Rami Wirrankoski collection)*

war boom had ended already in 1920. NFDS had expanded heavily during the short boom and faced acute financial difficulties. In 1921, the company decided to withdraw the *Haakon VII* from the Bergen-Newcastle service (she was instead moved to the Hurtigruten coastal service). The intention was that NFDS' absence from the services to the UK would be temporary, but this was not to be. The Bergen-Newcastle line thus became BDS' monopoly. The withdrawal of the *Haakon VII* was not enough alone to solve the problem of overcapacity, especially as the Norwegian economy was slow to recover and experienced a further depression in 1926-27; for the rest of the decade, the Bergen-Newcastle service was operated with just the *Venus* (1), *Jupiter* (1) and *Leda* (1).

The 1930s newbuilds Venus and Vega

In 1929, Svenska Lloyd – who operated between Gothenburg and London, as discussed in Chapter 3 – took delivery of a new pair of ships, the *Suecia* and *Britannia*, which were the largest and best-appointed on the North Sea. BDS felt that, in order to compete, they too needed a new ship, and the Norwegian authorities were willing to increase the subsidy paid for mail carriage to facilitate this. In 1931, the new *Venus* (2) was delivered by the Helsingør Skibsværft og Maskinbyggeri in Helsingør (Elsinore), Denmark. At 5,406 grt she was the largest ship on the North Sea, with a speed of 20 knots she was the fastest, and carrying just 277 passengers in high-quality accommodation, she was also held to be the most luxurious. With the high service speed, the *Venus* (2) could make the crossing from Bergen to Newcastle in just 21 hours, six hours less than her older fleetmates. However, her hull form, being optimised for speed, was found to be less than ideal for the stormy North Sea and the ship was known

A fine view of the ***Venus*** (2) out at sea, displaying her angular profile that was somewhat out of touch with the increasing trend for streamlined superstructures at the time. The fact she is flagged overall suggests this photo may be from her maiden voyage. *(Ambrose Greenway collection)*

through-out her career as being a heavy roller. For the first time in the BDS fleet, the *Venus* (2) was fitted with diesel engines (by Burmeister & Wain), and she was the fastest diesel-powered ship in the world at the time of her delivery. King Christian X of Denmark, who toured the ship when she was completed, is said to have found just one fault: she was not Danish-owned. Due to the larger capacity and higher speed, the *Venus* (2) replaced both the *Jupiter* (1) and the *Venus* (1) on the Newcastle line. The former was transferred to the Bergen-Rotterdam service, although occasionally returning to the Newcastle route, while the latter was scrapped.

Although the *Venus* (2) was delivered just as the Great Depression's effect hit Europe, the BDS passenger business continued as normal – in the context of the two previous depressions that had effected Norway in the 1920s, "de harde trettiåra" (roughly "the hard thirties"), as the 1930s depression was known in Norway, the worldwide economic downturn was perhaps simply business as usual. Still, it is telling that services continued for many years with the *Venus* (2) partnered to older, smaller and slower vessels.

By the mid-1930s, it was clear that the 1920-built *Leda* (1) could no longer cope with the growing passenger numbers: during 1936 summer season, both of BDS' cruise ships, *Meteor* (1; built 1904, 3,717 grt and 250 passengers) and *Stella Polaris* (built 1927, 5,208 grt and 200 passengers) were used on the Norway-UK trades, the former sailing from Bergen to Newcastle and the latter to Harwich. Thus, planning for an equal running mate for the *Venus* (2) begun in earnest. Helsingør Skibsværft og Maskinbyggeri again made the lowest bid, but the Norwegian State requested that BDS instead contract the new ship from Italy, in order to balance the bilateral trade account between the two countries. As the State was willing to compensate BDS for the higher price

The ***Venus*** (2) in the floating dock at her builders in Helsingør in foggy weather. Unfortunately, the reason for her drydock visit was not recorded in the materials available. *(Museet for Søfart (CC-BY-NC-SA))*

asked by the Italians, a deal was quickly struck with Cantieri Riuniti dell'Adriatico in Trieste for a ship eventually named *Vega* (3). Delivered in 1938, the *Vega* (3) at 7,287 grt was even larger than the *Venus* (2), with a larger passenger capacity at 465, and was also one knot faster. Power was again by diesel engines, but this time these were built by Sulzer rather than B&W. The interior decor was by the renowned Italian architect Gustavo Pulitzer-Finali and, according to contemporaries, equalled the transatlantic liners of the era. On delivery, the *Vega* (3) replaced the *Leda* (1), which moved to the Bergen-Rotterdam line alongside the *Jupiter* (1). Together, the *Venus* (2) and *Vega* (3) could offer five departures per week from Bergen and Newcastle.

In 1940, BDS suspended the Bergen-Newcastle route, again due to skyrocketing insurance costs caused by the war raging in Europe. When, in the same year, Germany occupied

Above: In contrast with the angular ***Venus*** (2), her 1938-built running mate ***Vega*** (3) – likely seen here on her maiden departure from Bergen – had a fashionably streamlined superstructure, making her look somewhat like a miniature version of Italy's transatlantic flagships ***Rex*** and ***Conte di Savoia***. *(Museet for Søfart (CC-BY-NC-SA))*

Left: The first class lounge of the ***Vega*** (3) was given something of a garden ambience by Gustavo Pulitzer-Finali with the use rattan in the furniture. *(Norsk Maritimt Museum)*

Middle left: : An aft view of the ***Vega*** (3) at sea, flagged overall – possibly for the occasion of her maiden voyage. *(Ambrose Greenway collection)*

Bottom left: Elsewhere, Gustavo Pulitzer-Finali's work on the ***Vega*** (3) was more in the style of Italian modernism, but the second-class lounge was dominated by wooden furniture that gives an impression of almost "wild west" style when viewed through 21st-century eyes. The Pulitzer-Finali coordinated interiors of the ***Conte di Savoia*** had also featured such combinations of different eras in the interior decor. *(Norsk Maritimt Museum)*

Below: BDS' instantly recognisable yacht-like cruise ship ***Stella Polaris*** was an occasional visitor on the Norway-UK routes when extra capacity was needed. After a remarkable 42-year career as a cruise ship, she became a hotel ship in Japan, and sank in 2006 while en-route to Sweden for further use as a floating hotel. *(A. Duncan, Rami Wirrankoski collection)*

Norway, both the *Venus* (2) and *Vega* (3) ended in German hands and were lost in Allied bombings. The *Vega* (3) was a complete loss and had to be scrapped, but the *Venus* (2) was salvaged, of which more below.

The Oslo line becomes Fred. Olsen's monopoly

As on the services to Bergen, those to Kristiania also ceased at the beginning of World War I, with Wilson Line's ship stopping sailing due to the threat of enemy action and Fred. Olsen's ships laid up due to high insurance costs. As soon as insurance was rearranged, Fred. Olsen's ships resumed sailings, but not without wartime incidents: the *Scotland* (2) was wrecked on Firth of Forth in 1916 and, during the same year, the *Bessheim* grounded on the Tyne, but could fortunately be refloated and repaired. Another loss followed in 1917, when the *Norway* (2) was lost to German action.

With both Grangemouth ships lost, the decision was taken not to restore services to that port; instead, passenger sailings to the UK were concentrated to the Kristiania-Newcastle line, operated by the *Sterling* (2) and *Bessheim*. However, the *Sterling* (2) was lost on the Norwegian coast in early 1922, fortunately without loss of life. As a replacement, Fred. Olsen quickly commissioned a sister ship to the ten-year old *Bessheim*, which was delivered in 1923 as the *Blenheim* (1), named after a palace in Oxfordshire. Together, the two ships maintained a weekly service in both directions, increased to twice-weekly during the summer high season. This set the pattern for most of the inter-war era.

As noted, Ellerman's Wilson Line lost their entire passenger fleet during the First World War. The only ship to survive was the *Eskimo*, which was returned to EWL in 1919, but she had been heavily rebuilt by the German navy and EWL did not see her worth refitting; she was, however, sold on for further trading in 1921. Instead, the company acquired three second-hand liners to re-initiate passenger services in 1920: the 317-passenger *Rollo* (2), 696-passenger *Orlando* (2) and the 140-passenger *Calypso (2)*, which were used to restart services from Hull to Kristiania. The same ships also sailed on EWL's lines to Gothenburg, Danzig and even to India; resultingly, the service frequency on the Hull-Kristiania line was low. Starting in the mid-1920s, the Hull-Oslo (the city having reverted to its original name in 1925) service was operated only during the summer season, usually using the *Calypso,* but occasionally also the larger *City of Paris* and *City of Nagpur* under charter from EWL's sister company Ellerman Lines. Finally, EWL bowed out of passenger services to Norway in 1936, leaving the Oslo-UK service solely in the hands of Fred. Olsen.

Following EWL's withdrawal, and in order to compete with the more modern ships of BDS and Svenska Lloyd, Fred. Olsen commissioned two new passenger vessels from the Aker shipyard in Oslo, which the Olsen family themselves owned. These were delivered in 1938 and 1939, receiving the names *Black Prince* (1) and *Black Watch* (1). At 5,035 gross register tons, the pair are sometimes erroneously claimed to be the biggest yet built in Norway. Power was by Burmeister & Wain diesel engines, but due to the distance from Newcastle to Oslo being notably longer than that to Bergen, the Olsen ships could not compete with those of BDS in terms of speed (a Newcastle-Oslo run was scheduled to take 32 hours); instead, high-class accommodation was specified for the 250 passengers carried in two classes, 185 in first class and 65 in second (some sources give 290 as the total number). The interior decor was by the Norwegian architects Arnstein Arnberg and Andre Peters, were modernist in style but with a distinctly Norwegian feel. The layout was also highly regarded, with the maritime historian Bruce Peter describing it as being "particularly inventive". The fact the ships were diesel-powered was also externally visible, as Fred. Olsen painted

The 1904-built ***Orlando*** (2) was one of Ellerman Wilson Line's 1920 acquisitions to rebuild their passenger fleet. Her career with EWL – like that of the ***Rollo*** (2) acquired at the same time – was short: both were laid up in 1928 and subsequently scrapped. *(Maritime Museum: Hull Museums)*

Fred. Olsen's first passenger newbuilding after World War I was arguably the most anachronistic of all discussed in this book: the ***Blenheim*** (1), delivered in 1923, was a sister ship to the ***Bessheim*** delivered 11 years earlier! *(Ambrose Greenway collection)*

their diesel-engined ships' funnels yellow, instead of black with a red band on the steamers. Motor vessels were not a novelty in the Olsens' fleet, as the first motor vessel had been completed already in 1926 for the Oslo-Antwerp line. An interesting external detail on the *Black Prince* (1) and *Black Watch* (1) were their bows, which were decorated with figureheads – the Olsen's having reintroduced this tradition on their 1936-built reefer *Bayard* (1). The *Black Prince* (1)'s figurehead, designed by Emil Lie, showed her namesake, the 14th-century "black prince" Edward of Woodstock in full armour, while the *Black Watch* (1)'s showed a soldier of the

Above: The ***Black Watch*** (1) and her sister were highly regarded for both their exterior and interior design, but World War II would see both ships' careers cut short. The ***Black Watch*** (1) only saw nine months of commercial service. She survived most of the war, only to be bombed by the British four days before Germany capitulated. Note the figurehead schulpture by Ørnulf Bast. *(Bruce Peter collection)*

Left: The first class lounge onboard the ***Black Watch*** (1). *(Norsk Maritimt Museum)*

Middle left: The first class restaurant onboard the ***Black Prince*** (1). Notice the embroideries on the chair backs – a reference to Norwegian arts and crafts that were also used in the decor of other Fred. Olsen vessels. *(Norsk Maritimt Museum)*

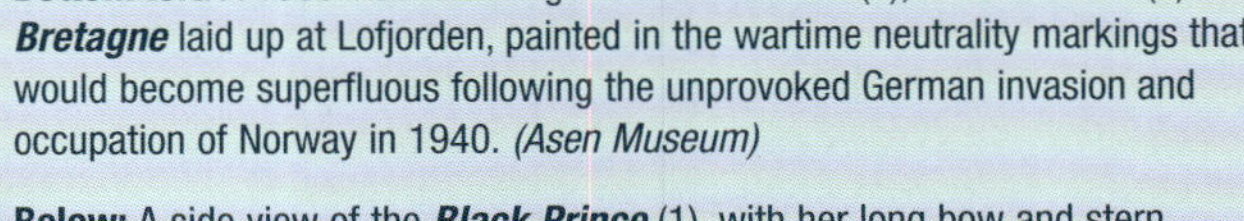

Bottom left: A 1939 view showing the ***Black Watch*** (1), ***Black Prince*** (1) and ***Bretagne*** laid up at Lofjorden, painted in the wartime neutrality markings that would become superfluous following the unprovoked German invasion and occupation of Norway in 1940. *(Asen Museum)*

Below: A side view of the ***Black Prince*** (1), with her long bow and stern making her almost classically beautiful, despite the high superstructure and relatively low funnel. *(Museet for Søfart (CC-BY-NC-SA))*

Scottish Black Watch regiment, designed by Ørnulf Bast.

Unfortunately, the careers of the two attractive liners were cut short by World War II. Both were withdrawn and laid up at the beginning of the conflict in 1939, falling into German hands on the occupation of Norway. The *Black Prince* (1) was destroyed by a fire in Danzig in 1941, and later used by the Luftwaffe for target practice, while the *Black Watch* (1) was lost in Allied bombings just four days before Germany capitulated.

Rebuilding: BDS

If BDS had survived the First World War relatively unscathed, the second treated them less well: circa 60 percent of the fleet was lost. The Bergen-Newcastle line was re-opened in July 1945 with the *Lyra* of 1912, a 1,474 grt ship carrying 175 passengers. A few months later the *Lyra* was joined by a newbuilt ship, the *Astrea*, that BDS came to own by a roundabout way: the ship had been contracted by Finska Ångfartygs Aktiebolaget (FÅA) for the Turku-Copenhagen-Hull run from the Crichton-Vulcan shipyard in Turku (see Chapter 2). However, by the time she was completed in 1941, war had already broken out and the *Astrea* was laid up. In 1944 the ship was sold to FÅA's partners on the Finland-Sweden services, Stockholms Rederi AB Svea (possibly to stop her from being turned over to the Soviet Union as a war reparation). Svea then sold the ship on to BDS in 1945; as BDS had a similar naming convention as FÅA, there was no need to rename the ship. The *Astrea*'s gross register tonnage was 3,190 and, after a refit, she carried 140 passengers. In 1946, the *Lyra* was then replaced by the already familiar *Jupiter* (1). For the 1947 summer season additional capacity was needed, and due to a lack of other options this was again provided by BDS' 1927-built luxury cruise ship *Stella Polaris*. Due to the participation of British forces in the liberation of Norway from German occupation, and housing the Norwegian government in exile and royal family in London, Britain enjoyed high levels of goodwill in Norway, making it an attractive travel destination for Norwegians.

As noted above, the pre-war *Venus* (2) had been severely damaged in Allied bombings, but in the material scarcity of the immediate post-war era, she was considered worth repairing. The repairs were carried out over the course of several years at the Helsingør and Aarhus shipyards; due to material shortages damaged hull plates were flattened and reused rather than replaced. The superstructure and funnels were rebuilt in a different form, and the bow was heightened. When the *Venus* (2) returned to the Bergen-Newcastle route in 1948, her gross register tonnage was 6,269 and the passenger capacity 415. As the trans-North Sea services were, by this time, highly seasonal, the *Venus* (2) was used on a new service during the winter seasons, linking Southampton to Madeira and the Canary Isles. Return trips on this route could also be booked as cruises, making BDS one of the many North European ferry operators to look into cruising as an off-season employment for their ships in the post-war years.

The trio of war survivors was unbalanced in terms of speed and capacity. When passenger numbers begun to rise in the latter 1940s, BDS decided to commission a newbuilt ship from Swan Hunter to replace both the *Jupiter* (1) and *Astrea*. The *Leda* (2) was delivered in 1953, but unusually final outfitting was carried out in Bergen after delivery. The new ship was 6,670 grt and carried 494 passengers in two classes, as well as 65 cars lifted onboard via crane. Although the *Leda* (2) was to be the *Venus* (2)'s running mate, her passenger facilities were designed with a different approach. Whereas the *Venus* (2) was a high-class ship suitable for off-season cruising, with the *Leda* (2) BDS stressed – in keeping with the rising Nordic egalitarian trend – a ship that people from all income classes could travel with, and particular attention was paid to the

The ***Astrea***, designed for Finland-UK services (see Chapter 2), entered service on the Bergen-Newcastle link in 1945. Following the end of her BDS career in 1967 she was sold to Skipafelagið Føroyar as the ***Tjaldur*** (3), but engine problems forced her scrapping in 1969. *(Rami Wirrankoski collection)*

The 1912-built ***Lyra*** had been acquired by BDS second-hand in 1925 for Bergen-Faroes-Iceland services. In the post-war era, she sailed on the Bergen-Newcastle route. *(Ambrose Greenway collection)*

second-class accommodation. Furthermore, the *Leda* (2) was designed to sail around the year on the Bergen-Newcastle line; thus there was no need for the *Venus* (2)'s cruise-like features. Building a new year-round ship was made more attractive by the growing popularity of winter sports, which led to tourists arriving in Norway also during the winter season. In keeping with a brief post-war trend, the *Leda* (2) was fitted with steam turbines rather than diesel engines; with a maximum service speed of 22 knots (some claim she could reach 27 knots), she was the fastest ship on the North Sea and made a still-unbroken record for a Newcastle-Stavanger crossing in 1954: 16 hours and 57 minutes quay to quay. If specification of

A 1955 aerial view of the ***Venus*** (2), showing her radically altered profile when compared to the original (as seen on page 87) – it would be easy to mistake her for an entirely new ship, rather than a rebuilt 1931 vessel. *(FotoFlite)*

The first class lounge of the **Venus** (2) as it appeared after the post-war rebuilding, with the new interiors designed by the Danish architect Palle Suenson. *(Norsk Maritimt Museum)*

The first class restaurant of the ***Venus*** (2) after the post-war rebuilding. Here, again, the new Scandinavian modernist interior design was Palle Suenson, rather than by a Norwegian architect. *(Norsk Maritimt Museum)*

The ***Meteor*** (2) was built as a belated replacement to the Stella Polaris and, like her, was also used on the Bergen-Newcastle route to provide extra capacity. After her BDS career, the ***Meteor*** continued cruising with Epirotiki Lines as the ***Neptune*** from 1972 until 1994. She was eventually scrapped in 2002. *(Berlingske Tidende, Museet for Søfart (CC-BY-NC-SA))*

Another aerial view of the ***Venus*** (2), showing for extensive outer deck areas that were no doubt appriciated during her winter cruise/ferry services to Madeira and the Canary Isles – although it is somewhat strange that no swimming pool was provided. *(FotoFlite)*

steam turbines was something of a retrograde step, the *Leda* (2) was the first ship on the North Sea to be fitted with fin stabilisers; these so impressed the contemporaries that Bo Rosén wrote in *Stora Boken om Fartyg* (published in Finnish as *Laivojen kirja*, the first maritime book owned by the author) that “seasickness is unknown onboard the *Leda*”. Inspired by the success of the *Leda*, the *Venus* was also equipped with stabilisers which reduced, but certainly not eliminated, her lively movements in anything but the smoothest seas.

In the early 1950s, BDS also took delivery of two

Top: A evocative view of the ***Leda*** (2) in port. She would be the last BDS vessel to carry to company's stark – but attractive – black-hulled and -funneled liner livery on the North Sea trades. *(Bruce Peter collection)*

Above left: The first class restaurant of the ***Leda*** (2). Elsewhere, she had – for the first time on a North Sea ferry – a self-serve restaurant for second class passengers. *(Bruce Peter collection)*

Above right: The first class lounge of the ***Leda*** (2), decorated in very similar style to that onboard the ***Venus*** (2). *(Bruce Peter collection)*

Below: The ***Leda*** (2) and ***Venus*** (2) passing somewhere on the Norwegian coast, showing their very different lines; there was no attempt of a unified "company look" here. *(Ambrose Greenway collection)*

newbuildings for the Hurtigruten coastal service from Helsingør Skibsværft og Maskinbyggeri: the *Nordlys* of 1951 and the *Polarlys* of 1952 (both circa 2610 grt and 450 passengers). Of these at least the *Nordlys* was occasional used on the Bergen-Newcastle route. The two -lyses were followed in 1955 by an "expanded edition", the *Meteor* (2) of 2,856 grt and 200 passengers. Primarily, the *Meteor* (2) was envisioned as a cruise ship, but she was also designed for use as a reserve ship and in this function she sailed on the Bergen-Newcastle line during the dockings of the *Leda* (2) at least in 1955 and 1956. Even the *Jupiter* (1) and *Astrea* occasionally returned on the Newcastle route during the *Leda* (2)'s absence.

Rebuilding: Fred. Olsen

Fred. Olsen & Co's losses in the Second World War were heavy: 28 ships of the 57-strong fleet were lost. Only three passenger ships – the *Brabant* of 1926, the *Bali* of 1928 and the *Bretagne* of 1937 – survived. The *Bretagne*, a 3,285 grt ship carrying 148 passengers, was placed on the Oslo-Newcastle line in 1945; before the war she had sailed to Antwerp. The next year, she was joined by the *Bali* (1,428 grt and 100 passengers), which had been given a large-scale refit to make her more suitable for passenger services; even so, she was clearly temporary solution.

The burnt-out hulk of the ***Black Prince*** (1) being towed to Antwerp for her abortive rebuilding. A second attempt to restore her as a cargo vessel also failed. *(Museet for Søfart (CC-BY-NC-SA))*

The ***Bretagne*** sailed on the Oslo-Newcastle line 1945-1953. Sold by Fred. Olsen in 1958, she would go on to have a career on the Mediterranean until laid up in 1967. She was scrapped in 1974. *(Bruce Peter collection)*

As a long-term replacement, Fred. Olsen had hopes that the wreck of the *Black Prince* (1) could be repaired. The ship was towed to Antwerp in 1947 for planned rebuilding, but was found to be in too poor condition and was sold (she was scrapped in in 1951 after a second failed restoration attempt). Instead, the company ordered two new ships for the Oslo-Newcastle run from the Aker yard in Oslo (due to full orderbooks the hulls were subcontracted to the John I. Thornycroft & Co's yard at Southampton). The new *Blenheim* (2) and *Braemar* (1) were delivered in 1951 and 1952, respectively; the 4,766 grt sisters carried 247 passengers (101 in first class, 100 in tourist class and the rest in group dormitories), both making a single return crossing from Oslo to Newcastle per week. In addition to carrying passengers, there were four crane-loaded cargo holds, including one specifically designed to carry 40 cars. The interior design was again entrusted to Arnstein Arneberg; according to The Motor Ship "very few passengers ships of [this] size are decorated so artistically and attractively". The ships' unusual exterior had been devised in wind tunnel tests. The pair's names, again, referred to Britain, albeit in somewhat obscure manner: Blenheim Palace was the birthplace of Sir Winston Churchill, while the Braemar village neighbours the British Royal family's Scottish palace in Balmoral. With the arrival of the new pair, the *Bali* was withdrawn from service and the *Bretagne* returned to the Oslo-Antwerp route.

The innovative multipurpose ships

The two pairs of modern liners – BDS' *Venus* (2) and *Leda* (2), plus Fred. Olsen's *Blenheim* (2) and *Braemar* (1) – fulfilled the demands of passenger services of the 1950s nicely, but by the early 1960s it was clear that the future of passenger shipping between Scandinavian ports and the UK would belong to the car-passenger ferries. Such specialised vessels were expensive to build and, at the same time, both BDS and Fred. Olsen were facing problems with the seasonality on the North Sea services: there were plenty of passengers (and, potentially, passenger cars) during the summer seasons, but few during the winters, while Norway's mountainous geography meant trucks, which could be trusted to fill the car decks in the off-season on other routes, were of lesser importance (particularly on the routes to Bergen). To deal with the challenges, Fred. Olsen's managing director Fredrik Olsen (the third person of that name to lead the company) and his opposite number at BDS, Erik Waaler, decided on collaboration to bring the Norway-UK services into the car ferry era. (Although, as noted below in Chapter 6, Fred. Olsen initially negotiated with DFDS, but approached BDS instead when disagreements arose with DFDS).

The companies devised a unique solution to deal with their dilemma: ships that would sail as car-passenger ferries between Norway and Britain during the summer seasons, but would morph into combined cruise ships and reefers (refrigerated cargo ships) for services between the Canary Isles and Northern Europe for the winters. BDS were, of course, already running a passenger service to the Canaries during the winters with the *Venus* (2), while Fred. Olsen had an existing reefer service to carry fruit and vegetables from the Canaries to Northern Europe (the Olsen family also owned land in the Canary Isles, and would later on become involved

Top: The ***Blenheim*** (2) and her sister had a yacht-like profile with a wind tunnel sculpted superstructure, which helped somewhat obscure the fact they were very conventional passenger-cargo steamers. After her 1969 fire (discussed below) the ***Blenheim*** (2) was converted to a car carrier. *(Ferry Publications Library)*

Top left: Arnstein Arneberg decorated the dining rooms on the ***Blenheim*** (2) and ***Braemar*** (1) in very similar style to the same rooms on the ***Black Prince*** (1) and ***Black Watch*** (1) – even the the embroideries on the chair backs have been repeated! *(Ian Boyle collection)*

Top right: Although not always evident from the black and white photos that still dominated at the time, the interiors of the ***Blenheim*** (2) and ***Braemar*** (1) used bold combinations of wood veneers and strong colours. The first class bar of the ***Braemar*** (1) combined dark woods with shades of mint and dark green. *(Bernt Arild Torstrup collection)*

Below: At the very end of her career, in 1965, the ***Venus*** (2) was repainted in BDS' cruise colours, all white with yellow funnels. The plan may have been to use her for full-time cruiseing after the arrival of the Bergen-Newcastle ship in 1966, but this never happened. After further ferry service, mostly on the Bergen-Rotterdam route, she was scrapped in 1968. *(Ambrose Greenway)*

Above: The ***Jupiter*** (2) transformed the Bergen-Newcastle route into the roll on-roll off ferry era. This postcard view shows her in Cuxhaven, West Germany displaying her decidedly non-BDS livery: only the BDS flag in the funnel – which surely wasn't as well-known as the regular three stripes funnel colours – differentiates from the Fred. Olsen look. *(Joonas Kortelainen collection)*

Left: Another postcard view of the ***Jupiter*** (2). This same photo was also sold as a postcard of the ***Venus*** (3), with the name retouched in the bow. The shape of the figurehead gave away the identity of the ship, however. *(Kalle Id collection)*

Middle left: The first class dining room of the ***Jupiter*** (2) was in the simple but elegant modernist style. In keeping with the fashion of the era, green plants were used as a part of the decor.*(Tor Eriksen)*

Bottom left: The second class cafeteria on the ***Jupiter*** (2) was surprisingly similarly furnished to the first class dining room, right down to the use of plants at the end of the tables – of course, as the ships were single-class when cruising in the winters, a similar standard of quality was nescessary across both classes. *(Tor Eriksen)*

Below: The ***Jupiter*** (2)'s second class lounge, which became the Neptune lounge when the ship was converted to single class even in ferry service, also favoured clean-lined modernism over opulence. Note that plants are again used as a part of the decor in the background. *(Tor Eriksen)*

A superb aerial view of the ***Black Prince*** (2) at speed. The profile of these ships, with the superstructure massed forward and the funnel slightly fore of midships, give in itself an impression of speed, but the application of the Fred. Olsen livery, with the upper parts of the superstructure painted yellow, made them appear even sleeker. *(FotoFlite)*

in intra-Canaries ferry services). The design of the new ships was primarily by Fred. Olsen's technical director John Johnsen, and they were contracted from the Lübecker Flender-Werke in West Germany.

The first combination vessel was jointly owned by Fred. Olsen and BDS, and received two names: during the summers, she was BDS' *Jupiter* (2), sailing between Bergen and Newcastle; during the winters she morphed in Fred. Olsen's *Black Watch* (2), sailing from London (Tilbury) to Madeira and the Canary Isles. BDS abandoned their existing Southampton-Madeira winter service in favour of Fred. Olsen. In North Sea ferry service, the 9,499 grt ship carried 587 passengers, and 184 cars on a stern-loading car deck. The gross tonnage figure made her the largest ferry in the world. The ship entered service as the *Jupiter* (2) for the 1966 summer season between Bergen and Newcastle, replacing the *Venus* (2), which moved to the Bergen-Rotterdam route. Early renderings had showed the *Jupiter* (2) in the BDS "cruise colours" – a yellow funnel with three white stripes and a white hull – and BDS may have considered making this the livery of their entire passenger fleet, as the *Venus* (2) had been painted in those colours in 1965. However, on delivery the *Jupiter* (2) was painted in Fred. Olsen's colours with a yellow funnel and upper superstructure combined with a grey hull; in addition to the name, the only concession to BDS' identity was painting the BDS house flag in the funnel in place of Fred. Olsen's during the summer service.

The second multipurpose ship followed in the autumn of 1966. This was the *Black Prince* (2), which was solely owned by Fred. Olsen. She entered service on the London-Canaries winter route, on which both ships carried just 350 passengers, with only the better-appointed cabins sold. Numerous novel solutions were made to effect a transformation from ferry to cruise use: what had been a sitting lounge in ferry service was revealed to be a pool area in cruise use, while the pool itself had been used as a storage area for the ships shop. To make the ships appeal to cruise clientele, their interiors were designed by the Oslo-based Barstad & Skjævland, who had previously worked on Norske Amerikalinje's (Norwegian America Line's) luxury cruise ships, the style of which was carried over to the *Jupiter* (2)/*Black Watch* (2) and *Black Prince* (2).

A postcard view of the ***Black Prince*** (2) loading in Kristiansand; as the flags in the foreground indicate, Fred. Olsen connected the port to the UK and the Netherlands. On the left, the Skagerak Expressen ferry ***Christian IV*** departs for Denmark; Skagerak Expressen were also taken over by the Olsens in 1968. *(Joonas Kortelainen collection)*

The *Black Prince* (2) entered ferry service between Norway and the UK for the 1967 summer season – but rather than replacing the existing vessels on the Oslo-Newcastle route,

BLENHEIM
BLENHEIM

The success of the ***Jupiter*** (2)/***Black Watch*** (2) and ***Black Prince*** (2) prompted Fred. Olsen to commission an enlarged and improved version of of them in the form of the ***Blenheim*** (3), delivered in 1970. Alas, her delivery was delayed and in service she was never quite as successful as her older sisters. *(FotoFlite)*

she opened new services from Kristiansand to Harwich and Amsterdam. In addition to the *Blenheim* (2) and *Braemar* (1) remaining in service, BDS also retained the *Leda* (2) on the Bergen-Newcastle line around the year – and even the *Venus* (2) occasionally returned to the UK routes before she was sold for scrap at the end of the 1968 summer season. The retention of the older vessels, while unusual compared to the operators sailing from Sweden and Denmark to the UK, made economic sense: it not only allowed the continuation of year-round services to the UK, but also allowed using the newer vessels, that had higher capital expenses, on more profitable services during the winters. This approach is perhaps testified by the fact that when the *Blenheim* (2) was lost in a fire in 1968 (all passenger and crew, as well as most of the cargo, were saved, thanks to the arrival on scene by the Gothenburg-Hull ferry *Spero* (3), discussed in Chapter 3, and other vessels), no replacement was sought and the *Braemar* (1) continued on the Oslo-Kristiansand-Newcastle passenger service alone. It is also telling that on the crossing when the fire broke out, there were only 89 passengers onboard the *Blenheim* (2).

The third multipurpose vessel Blenheim (3)

The *Black Watch* (2) and *Black Prince* (2) were so popular that in 1968 Fred. Olsen ordered a third example. Instead of returning to Lübecker Flender-Werke, the new, larger ship was contracted from the Upper Clyde Shipbuilders in Scotland. The reason was the British Government's open-handed subsidies to the country's shipyards – but, due to terms of the subsidy, she had to be registered in the UK, rather than Norway as was the norm for Fred. Olsen's ships.

Contracting the ship from the UK proved a mistake. At the time, British shipbuilding was riddled with industrial strife – made worse by the fact that each individual trade has its own trade union and demarkation disputes between unions were common. A strike by workers in one trade would have a domino effect, slowing or stalling all work. The yard originally promised delivery for the 10,420 grt, 1,107-passenger and 300-car *Blenheim* (3) in February 1970. In preparation for the new ship, Fred. Olsen had sold 50% of the *Black Prince* (2) to BDS, with the agreement that she would sail alongside the *Jupiter* (2) on the Bergen-Newcastle line as the *Venus* (3) during the 1970 summer season. However, the *Blenheim* (3) was delayed by six months, missing the 1970 summer season entirely. The best replacement available on such short notice was the West German-owned 1969-built *Vikingfjord* of 3,777 grt, 1,000 passengers and 156 cars. In addition to being smaller than the *Blenheim* (3), the *Vikingfjord* was also somewhat slower, with a service speed of 21 knots instead of 23. As bookings had already been accepted for the *Blenheim* (3)'s full capacity, Fred. Olsen had to turn down cars and fly passengers to their destination instead (fortunately, Fred. Olsen were one of the owners of Scandinavian Airlines System so arranging flights for would-be ferry passengers was relatively simple).

The *Blenheim* (3) was finally delivered in the beginning of September 1970, entering service on the London-Madeira-Canaries service. At the same time, the *Black Prince* (2) opened a new winter service from Rotterdam to Madeira and the Canaries. In addition to the fruit trade, she was used to transport German-built cars to the Canaries. As on the older semi-sisters, the *Blenheim* (3)'s interiors were designed by Barstad & Skjævland. Unlike them, she sailed in summer ferry service as a single-class ship. Unfortunately, the *Blenheim* (3)'s troubles were not limited to her delayed delivery: in service her twin Crossley Pielstick diesel engines proved unreliable and she struggled to maintain the specified 23-knot service speed (the *Jupiter* (2)/*Black Watch* (2) and *Venus* (3)/*Black Prince* (2) did not reportedly suffer from similar problems, despite their engines being of the same make). Furthermore, her British crew was much more eager to go on strike than those of the Norwegian-flagged vessels, making the *Blenheim* (3) the "problem child" of the Fred. Olsen fleet.

Fred. Olsen-Bergen Line

Unusually in the Scandinavian context, traditional passenger liners continued in service between Norway and the UK until the mid-1970s. In addition to such (arguably) outdated vessels, a quite different vessel also appeared on the routes: during a drydocking of the *Leda* (2) in Autumn 1973, the brand new luxury cruise ship *Royal Viking Sea* (20,081 grt and 536 passengers) sailed as her replacement; this unusual arrangement was made possible by the fact that BDS were one of the owners of Royal Viking Line. Time, however, was running out on the *Leda* (2) and her fuel-hungry steam turbines, the expense of which could not be justified in the post-oil crisis era. She was withdrawn at the end of the 1974 summer season and laid up. To maintain winter service on the Bergen-Newcastle line, BDS chartered the 1964-built DFDS ferry *England* (2; 8,221 grt, 566 passengers and 120 cars) for the 1974-75 winter season (for more details on the ship, see Chapter 6). When no buyer was found for the *Leda* (2), she was chartered out as an accommodation vessel on several occasions until sold in 1979. Eventually she was converted into a cruise ship in the mid-1980s.

In Autumn 1975, BDS and Fred. Olsen initiated closer cooperation in North Sea passenger services when Fred. Olsen-Bergen Line (for brevity, the abbreviation FOBL is used here) was established as a joint marketing venture for the Bergen-Newcastle, Oslo-Kristiansand-Newcastle and Kristiansand-Harwich services. A new service from Bergen to Cuxhaven was also initiated, replacing the previous Kristiansand-Amsterdam link. The visual identity of FOBL was, again, based on the Fred. Olsen colours; the only addition was painting the three white bands of BDS on the funnels alongside the Fred. Olsen house flag.

The formation of FOBL spelled the end of the Fred. Olsen career of the *Braemar* (1), which was withdrawn and sold at the end of the 1975 summer season. After her withdrawal, the Oslo-Kristiansand-Newcastle route was also operated with the three multipurpose ferries. Some sources erroneously claim the *Braemar* (1) was the last "traditional liner" on the North Sea but, as we have seen in Chapter 2, the Soviet Union continued to use non-roro tonnage on the Leningrad-London route at least until 1977. Nor did the "traditional liners" entirely

Above: The ***Blenheim*** (3) was an elongated version of the older multipurpose ships and her funnel was placed further forward, which gave an even racier look. She was never as successful as her sisters, however, withdrawn from the North Sea already in 1981. She spent her subsequent career on casino cruises from Florida to the Bahamas, and was scrapped following a fire in 1996. *(FotoFlite)*

Left: The Saga Lounge onboard the ***Blenheim*** (3). On the third multipurpose ship, Barstad & Skjævland favoured more extensive use of dark wood veneers than on the older semi-sisters, such as the rosewood with brass inlays seen here. *(Tor Eriksen, John Bryant collection)*

Middle left: The Viking Room continued the ***Blenheim*** (3)'s dark wood theme, but in delightful contrast with light-coloured modernist furniture. The extensive use of houseplants as a part of the decor was carried on from the older near sisters. *(Tor Eriksen, John Bryant collection)*

Bottom left: A builder's photo of the ***Blenheim*** (3) on the slipway at Upper Clyde Shipbuilders. While otherwise still in grey undercoat, the figurehead has already been fully painted. *(Paul Strathdee collection)*

Below: The ***Vikingfjord***, seen here with Fred. Olsen funnel colours, was a problematic last-minute replacement. She was something of a prototype for the "Papeburger" series later produced by the same shipyard, and, although unsuccessful in her North European careers, had a long career as a Mediterranean ferry. *(Joonas Kortelainen collection)*

The ***Venus*** (3) outside Bergen, showing the combined Fred. Olsen-Bergen Line colours – Fred. Olsen colours with BDS' three white stripes added to the funnel. The ***Venus*** (3) and ***Jupiter*** (2) continued to carry these colours even when they were chartered to DFDS in the first half of the 1980s – this photo is from 1983. *(Krzysztof Brzoza collection)*

Fred. Olsen's ***Borgen*** was FOBL's winter ship for 1975-76, but proved ill-suited for the service. She did, however, enjoy a long career on the Skagerrak routes for both Fred. Olsen and later Color Line – she was jumboised by the former in 1982. A further Red Sea career followed from 2005, until she was scrapped in 2011. *(Postcard, Harald Oanes collection)*

A postcard of DFDS' ***England*** retouched with BDS funnel colours. While she did carry these funnel colours during the BDS charter, the blue stripe on the hull was absent in reality. *(Joonas Kortelainen collection)*

disappear from Norway-UK routes: BDS and NFDS occasionally ran their Hurtigruten passenger liners *Nordstjernen* and *Harald Jarl* from Bergen and Trondheim, respectively, to Lerwick and Aberdeen, but these were shopping cruises for Norwegian passengers, not line voyages.

With the *Jupiter* (2), *Venus* (3) and *Blenheim* (3) all heading to the Canaries for the winters (the two first-mentioned continued to revert to their BDS names for the summers even after the formation of FOBL) and the *Braemar* (1) withdrawn, FOBL needed an additional ship to maintain services during the winters; for this use, Fred. Olsen offered the almost brand-new *Borgen*, which had been delivered in June 1975 for the Olsens' Kristiansand-Hirtshals -service. As there was no need for her on that service during the winters, she took over FOBL's routes to Newcastle (the other routes continued to be summer-only). The 5,330 grt, 335 passenger and 240 car *Borgen* had a foursquare appearance, in keeping with the latest trends in ferry design but in contrast with the rest of the FOBL fleet. Although fitted with a full-height cargo deck and therefore well suited for the winter operations when cargo was the primary concern, in practice the *Borgen* proved ill-suited for the long North Sea routes, earning the less than flattering nickname Sorgen ("Sorrow").

Thus, it is no surprise that, for the 1976-77 winter season, Fred. Olsen brought in a different ship, the 1973-built *Bolero*. She was, with a gross tonnage figure of 11,344, FOBL's largest ship, carrying 975 passengers and 270 cars. Originally, she had been designed for a similar dual use as the other FOBL ships, sailing in ferry service between Canada and the USA during the summers and Caribbean cruising during the winters. The *Bolero* remained in service for the 1977 summer season and the following winter, but she was simply too large and was chartered to Stena Line in the beginning of April

1978. To cover for the remaining month of the winter season (the multipurpose ships returned in the beginning of May), FOBL chartered the 1969-built DFDS ferry *Dana Sirena* (1; ex-*Aalborghus*), which was notably smaller at 7,988 grt, 691 passengers and 120 cars. She returned for the 1978-79 winter season. A further chartered ship was sought for the next winter season, but no suitable vessel was found and thus – uniquely in the Scandinavian context – winter services ceased. As noted above in Chapter 3, negotiations had been carried out between Fred. Olsen and Tor Line for a joint year-round service linking Gothenburg to Newcastle via Kristiansand, using the chartered ferry *Expresso Olbia*. Although Tor Line had already secured a charter of the ship, the plan was abandoned, reportedly due to high fuel costs.

With FOBL's winter service ceased, an unlikely operator spotted the chance of restoring Norway-UK winter sailings: the UK-based Townsend Thoresen, better known for their ferry routes across the English channel, who operated a Kristiansand-Edinburgh (Leith) route between October and December 1979 with two weekly return trips. The service was primarily aimed at Norwegians wanting to do their Christmas shopping in Edinburgh. The first three return sailings were operated by the 1975-built *Viking Valiant* (6,387 grt, 1,200 passengers and 275 cars), after which the service was taken over by the smaller, 1965-built *Viking III* (3,824 grt, 940 passengers and 180 cars). Although she had only 300 cabin berths, the *Viking III* was no stranger to the North Sea services, having spent many winter seasons under charter on Prinzenlinie's Bremerhaven-Harwich route. The Kristiansand-Edinburgh service was not a great success and it was not revivied after December 1979.

The ***Bolero*** took over the mantle of FOBL's winter ship from the Borgen. Although well-appointed for ferry services and cruising, she was simply too big for the services at the time. However, she would return to the Norway-UK services on the several occasions in the next decade. *(Ken Lubi)*

The chartered DFDS ferry ***Dana Sirena*** (1) was FOBL's last attempt to provide a winter service. She is seen here on the Tyne in September 1978 with FOBL funnel markings. *(Ken Lubi)*

Despite the fact Townsend Thoresen's Kristiansand-Edinburgh route ran for a little over two months, two different ships were used, with the bulk of the service operated by the 1965-built ***Viking III*** seen here. Despite her age, the ship still exists at the time of writing as the Adriatic ferry ***Red Star I*** – suitably, painted with a bright red hull. *(FotoFlite)*

The former Baltic ferry ***Braemar*** (2) was Fred. Olsen's triumphant return to full-time Norway-UK services. She also introduced a new livery for the company's ferry operations. After leaving the Olsen fleet in 1990, she returned to the Baltic for almost two decades. Following a stint as an accommodation vessel, she today sails in the Mediterranean for Baleària. *(FotoFlite)*

The ***Bolero*** in the livery she carried during her 1984 and 1986-87 stints on the Kristiansand-Harwich route (albeit seen here receiving some TLC on her funnels). *(FotoFlite)*

The public rooms onboard the ***Braemar*** (2) were all named after former Fred. Olsen vessels; seen here is the Bandeirante buffet restaurant. For the most part, Fred. Olsen did not change the ship's just five-year old original decor, which was by the premiere Finnish maritime interior designer Vuokko Laakso. *(Harald Oanes collection)*

A decade of changes

Towards the end of the 1970s, BDS was in deepening financial troubles. The US-based consultants McKinsey & Company had been hired in 1976 to formulate a future strategy, which recommended a drastic reduction of passenger services. One of McKinsey's employees, Torstein Hagen, was hired as BDS' new CEO to turn the strategy into reality. In 1979, BDS sold their four ships on the Hurtigruten (*Midnatsol, Nordlys, Polarlys* and *Nordstjernen*) to Troms Fylkes Dampskibsselskab (TFDS), but this was not enough to save the ailing company. At the end of the 1981 summer season, BDS withdrew from Fred. Olsen-Bergen Line and sold their shares of the *Jupiter* (2) and *Venus* (3) to Nor-Cargo, bringing an end to their involvement in Norway-UK passenger shipping. Arguably, the strategy was flawed from the start: subsequent owners managed to make the services BDS sold profitable, usually with the same tonnage BDS had used; in the end, the reduction of services brought with it BDS' demise.

Fred. Olsen were left seeking other partners for the service, coming up the idea of of "SAS of the seas", a large consortium of ferry operators, but no-one was interested. At the same time, the Danish shipping giant DFDS was actively expanding their passenger operations. In Autumn 1981, DFDS, Fred. Olsen and Nor-Cargo signed a deal whereby DFDS took over the lines from Bergen and Oslo to Newcastle for the next three years, chartering the *Jupiter* (2) and *Venus* (3) for the summer months and marketing the service under the Fred. Olsen-Bergen Line name. The Kristiansand-Harwich and Bergen-Cuxhaven lines were not a part of the deal and was closed down. The *Blenheim* (3) was sold outright to DFDS, for use in Miami-Bahamas cruise/ferry service. A contributing factor to her sale were the inflamed relations with her British crew; Fred. Olsen had previously attempted to move her under the Norwegian flag, but strikes had made them give up the idea. Tellingly, upon learning of the sale to DFDS (and the resulting reflagging to the Bahamas), the *Blenheim* (3)'s crew promptly went on strike. With her sale, use of the once-dominant British flag on the Scandinavia-UK routes ended.

By the end of 1981 DFDS controlled all Scandinavia-UK ferry services (as well as those linking West Germany to the UK). During the summer of 1982, the *Jupiter* (2) and *Venus* (3) were joined by DFDS' own *England* (2), already familiar from above, which sailed on the Oslo-Newcastle line. DFDS' dominance on these routes proved short-lived, however, as Fred. Olsen quickly began having second thoughts. Already in summer 1984 the *Bolero* re-commenced Fred. Olsen's UK sailings with a weekly return trip from Kristiansand to Harwich. As with the Olsens' Norway-Denmark services, the UK route was now marketed under the Fred. Olsen Line name.

When the original charter deal of the *Jupiter* (2) and *Venus* (3) ran out in autumn 1984, DFDS chartered the *Jupiter* (2) for one more season, operating to Norway only on the Oslo-Newcastle line. The *Venus* (3), on the other hand, sailed in summer 1985 for a new company, Norway Line, who chartered the ship from Fred. Olsen and Nor-Cargo. While the Bergen-Newcastle route had made a notable loss for DFDS, Norway Line managed to turn it profitable already during the first summer.

Also in 1985, Fred. Olsen upgraded their Norway-UK ship to the biggest yet seen on these routes. When the struggling Finnish shipping company Rederi Ab Sally wanted to sell their Helsinki-Stockholm ferry *Viking Song*, with delivery in spring 1985, Fred. Olsen were quick on the mark and purchased the ship, renaming her *Braemar* (2). She was given a refit at Blohm & Voss in Hamburg, which included enlarging the originally single-storey night club to an impressive double height winter garden, and improvements to her car deck arrangements. Following the refit, the *Braemar* (2)'s gross tonnage was 14,623, passenger capacity 2,000 and car capacity 500. According to Richard Plummer of Ships Monthly, the *Braemar* (2) had "the highest quality accommodation yet seen on a North Sea service." She was also the newest ship on the Scandinavia-UK routes.

The *Braemar* (2) was placed on service from Oslo to Harwich via Kristiansand, but already in Autumn 1985 Kristiansand was replaced by Hirtshals in Denmark, with the ship also making Oslo-Hirtshals return trips in between the Harwich sailings. This also marked the return of year-round passenger services between Norway and the UK. The success of the Olsens' new route was such that a second ship was projected to be needed already in 1986. Thus the *Bolero* was brought in for a summer Kristiansand-Harwich service in 1986 and 1987. However, demand proved insufficient and the service was discontinued after the second summer season.

During the 1986 summer season, Norway Line continued to operate the Bergen-Newcastle route with the *Venus* (3). DFDS continued to charter the *Jupiter* (2) but used the ship on the routes from Esbjerg and Gothenburg to Newcastle, having abandoned services to Norway entirely. At the end of the 1986 summer season, the joint ownership agreement between Fred. Olsen (who still ran the ships to the Canaries during the winters) and Nor-Cargo ended. The companies solved the problem elegantly: Nor-Cargo bought out Fred. Olsen's share in the *Jupiter* (2)/*Black Watch* (2), while the Olsens correspondingly bought Nor-Cargo's share in the *Venus* (3)/*Black Prince* (2). Nor-Cargo immediately resold the former vessel to Norway Line; it now assumed the name *Jupiter* (2) permanently, taking over the Bergen-Newcastle route. The other ship permanently assumed the name *Black Prince* (2) and was radically rebuilt as a full-time cruise ship at the Wärtsilä Marine shipyard in Turku, Finland. Rather than initiate around-the-year services, Norway Line continued Fred. Olsen's old practice of off-season cruising for the UK market

The ***Braemar*** (2)'s originally single-level night club on Deck 8 was expanded two two-storey tropical garden before she entered Fred. Olsen service. Standing on the stairs is the future Fred. Olsen CEO Anette S. Olsen. *(Harald Oanes collection)*

The reception of the ***Braemar*** (2) on Deck 6 was accessed via escalator from the gangway on Deck 4. *(Harald Oanes collection)*

with the *Jupiter* (2), which was now competing on this market with her previous fleetmate.

A new operator planned Norway-UK services in 1987: the UK ferry company Sealink, at the time owned by the American shipping giant Sea Containers, was reported to be interested in opening a service from Newcastle "to Scandinavia." While the actual port, let alone country, considered was not revealed, the Car Ferry Info magazine held Norway as the likely destination (despite the fact Sealink had previously publicly stated their interest in a service to Denmark). At the time, Sealink was understood to have an option to purchase the 1974-built TT-Line ferry *Peter Pan* (1; renamed *Robin Hood* in

With the acquisition of the ***Jupiter*** (2), Norway Line devised proper a livery of their own, having previously simply used the Fred. Olsen livery with their own flag on the funnel. Notice that the figurehead has been removed from the bow, remaining property of the Olsens. *(Postcard, Ian Boyle collection)*

1986) once the new *Peter Pan* (2) would be delivered in 1987. As noted below in Chapter 6, the *Peter Pan* (1) and her sister had served as the models for DFDS' Denmark-UK ferry *Dana Anglia*, and thus would have made a fine Norway-UK ferry. However, Sealink never purchased the ship, nor opened routes to Scandinavia with any other vessel.

Norway Line passed under new ownership in late 1987, when the Sandefjord-based A/S Kosmos purchased the stock majority. Kosmos had a pre-existing interest in passenger shipping: Jahre Line sailing between Oslo and Kiel. They had also purchased the remaining operations of BDS. The new owners did not, however, use the chance to revert to the classic Bergen Line name, or merge their two existing ferry operations under one brand.

Despite her popularity, Fred. Olsen's *Braemar* (2) had trouble maintaining the tight schedule of the long service from Oslo to Harwich, and in Autumn 1989 her UK port was moved to Newcastle for a shorter crossing. For the 1990 summer season, Fred. Olsen Line further expanded their presence on the UK routes: the *Bolero* returned once again, opening a new Molde-Ålesund-Måløy-Bergen-Newcastle service competing directly with Norway Line. A reasoning for the route was the fact that, due to Norway's mountainous geography, ships still remain the main way of moving goods (and in many cases people) between various coastal settlements. Providing a service not only to Bergen but various coastal towns north of it eliminated the need to transship goods from these ports from the coastal vessels to the UK-bound ferry in Bergen – but also meant fewer crossing to Britain than what Norway Line were able to offer.

In face of the increased competition, Norway Line purchased a replacement for the *Jupiter* (2) in spring 1990 from Stena Line: the 1974-built ferry *Tarek L.* (originally *Prinsessan Birgitta*). The 13,286 grt ship, that could carry 1,230 passengers and 300 cars, was renamed *Venus* (4), given a thorough refit and took over the Bergen-Stavanger-Newcastle service. At the same time, a new service from Bergen and Stavanger to Amsterdam was opened. The *Jupiter* (2) was placed for sale, but when no buyer materialised, she sailed alongside the *Venus* (4) on the service to Amsterdam, as well as as on a new route to Esbjerg. Eventually, the *Jupiter* (2) was sold at the end of the 1990 summer season. With her sale, Norway Line's off-season cruising activities ceased. Afterwards, the *Venus* (4) operated to both Newcastle and Amsterdam, also during the winters; the latter route was perhaps hoped to give the company more breathing room in face of the heavy competition on the routes to the UK.

Enter Color Line

Behind the scenes, things were happening at Kosmos that would have repercussions on the Norway-UK services. The

The ***Jupiter*** (2) departing Turku, Finland after a shipyard visit in May 1988 to take up the summer service between Bergen and Newcastle. The Kosmos funnel colours have replaced those of Norway Line; the Kosmos colours were also painted on the funnels of the otherwise separate sister company Jahre Line around the same time. *(Krzysztof Brzoza)*

I.M. Skaugen shipping company had gained ownership of Kosmos, and Skaugen's owners, Morits and Brynjulf Skaugen, decided to break up the company: the non-ferry operations were directly taken over by I.M. Skaugen, while Jahre Line and Norway Line were merged and became a new Skaugen subsidiary Color Line in late 1990. Initially, the only change for the UK services was repainting the *Venus* (4) in the new blue-hulled colours of Color Line.

As Color Line was formed, the Olsen family were beginning to lose faith in the future of their ferry services from Norway. In Autumn 1990, the *Braemar* (2) was chartered to the Soviet Union's Baltiyskoye Morskoye Parokhodstvo (as noted in Chapter 2, they had in the past operated services from Finland, Sweden and Denmark to the UK) and the Oslo-Hirtshals-Newcastle line was closed, thus ending Oslo's direct link with the UK. At the end of the year, the remaining Fred. Olsen ferry operation out of Norway (the Molde-Newcastle, Kristiansand-Hirtshals and Oslo-Hirtshals lines and the ships sailing on them) were sold to Color Line. The new owner immediately rationalised the UK services, moving the *Bolero* to the Norway-Denmark routes (she was, however, renamed *Jupiter* (3), perhaps signifying the possibility of moving the ship back to the UK services at a later date, but this never happened). By the end of 1990 the *Venus* (4), sailing on the Bergen-Newcastle line, was the only passenger vessel connecting Norway to the UK. Until Autumn 1991, she continued service on the Bergen-Amsterdam route alongside Bergen-Newcastle sailings.

With such a radical reduction, the *Venus* (4) was quickly found to be too small. While Color Line were in need of a larger replacement, DFDS were looking for a ship of the *Venus'* (4) dimensions for their routes linking Denmark and the UK. While the companies were competitors on the short cruise market from Oslo, in this situation they found common ground: in Autumn 1994, Color Line bought the *King of Scandinavia* (1) from DFDS, with the *Venus* (4) used as part payment. The *King of Scandinavia* (1) had been built in 1975 as the *Wellamo* for Finska Ångfartygs Aktiebolaget, and as the *Dana Gloria* (1) she had sailed on both Sweden-UK and Denmark-UK routes (see Chapters 3 and 6, respectively). Now the 20,581 grt ship was renamed *Color Viking* for the Bergen-Newcastle line. She could carry 1,200 passengers and 320 cars.

The era of Fjord Line and DFDS

For Color Line, the years 1994-1999 were marked by a protracted attempt of a merger with the competing Norway-Denmark operator Larvik Skandi Line (LSL). Eventually, in Autumn 1998, LSL and its owner, Nils Olav Sunde, gained a majority share in Color Line. The new owners wanted to concentrate on the routes from Southern Norway to Denmark and Sweden. When, at the same time, the 1993-established Fjord Line were looking to expand their operations, an agreement was reached by which Fjord Line purchased Color Line's Bergen-Newcastle route, including the terminals, staff and the *Color Viking* for 338 million Norwegian krone. Fjord Line were eager to draw from the long traditions of the Bergen-Newcastle line: the *Color Viking* was renamed *Jupiter* (4) and repainted with a black hull, like the BDS liners of old – albeit with less elegant funnel colours, initially white and later mint green as the dominant hue.

As is probably well-known to readers, tax-free sales on ferry services within the European Union ended in July 1999. Norway, however, was and is not a part of the Union (although, to gain access to the Common Market, much Norwegian legislation conforms to that of the EU, but the Norwegians have no say in formulation of EU laws). Thus, the Bergen-Newcastle route was unaffected – but the attraction of continued tax-free sales resulted in the return of passenger

The ***Bolero*** received the new-style Fred. Olsen livery at the very end of her career with the company. She is seen here on the River Tyne during her final stint on Norway services in summer 1990. *(Hilton T. Davis)*

The ***Venus*** (4), originally the ***Prinsessan Birgitta*** built in 1974 for Sessanlinjen, was Norway Line's response to increased competition. Previously, she had enjoyed a lengthy Scandinavian career for Sessanlinjen and Stena Line, but after 1987 she was surplus to their needs. After a series of charters she had been sold to Norway Line in late 1989. *(Hilton T. Davis)*

services from southern Norway to Britain, as it was possible to continue tax-free sales on intra-EU services by adding an intermediate call in a Norwegian port. As described above in Chapter 3, DFDS took advantage of this and altered the route of the *Princess of Scandinavia* (ex-*Tor Scandinavia*), which had previously sailed from Gothenburg to Newcastle and Harwich, to Gothenburg-Kristiansand-Newcastle.

At first, the takeover of the Bergen-Newcastle route proved a burden for Fjord Line. It also coincided with a complex control battle between Fjord Line's owner Bergen-Nordhordland Rutelag (BNR) and the competing Norwegian

A fine view of people spectating as the ***Venus*** (4) sails on the Tyne in summer 1993, now as a Color Line ship. With the withdrawal of both Fred. Olsen ships from Norway-UK services in 1990, the ***Venus*** (4) was soon found too small to cope with the passenger and cargo demand and Color Line set out to find a replacement. *(Ambrose Greenway)*

Another view of the ***Venus*** (4) on the Tyne. Her later career as a DFDS ship, including Denmark-UK service, is covered in Chapter 6. *(Hilton T. Davis)*

The ***Color Viking*** had previously sailed on the routes from Denmark and Sweden to the UK for DFDS (see Chapters 3 and 6). She is seen here on the Tyne in May 1997. *(Ken Lubi)*

domestic ferry operator Hardanger Sunnhordlandske Dampskipsselskap (HSD). This protracted conflict was resolved in 2001, when HSD took over all of BNR's domestic Norwegian operations, while BNR was reduced to operating international ferry connections under the Fjord Line name. However, even in this new arrangement HSD retained a 35 percent share in BNR.

Meanwhile, Color Line (which had in 1999 become fully controlled by Nils Olav Sunde and Larvik Skandi Line) started having second thoughts about giving up the UK service. In 2002, Color Line acquired HSD's 35 percent share in BNR, with the goal of merging Color Line and Fjord Line. The Norwegian competition authorities objected, and Color Line was forced to sell their shares in BNR. This resulted in another complex arrangement where Troms Fylkes Dampskibsselskap (TFDS) took over Fjord Line in its entirety, while BNR went into voluntary liquidation.

For TFDS, Fjord Line's routes to Newcastle and Hanstholm (Denmark) were a logical continuation of the Hurtigruten coastal service, which they operated together with Ofotens og Vesteraalens Dampskibsselskap. The new owners invested in a new ship, the *Spirit of Tasmania* (ex-*Peter Pan* (2) of 1986) in 2003. She was given the somewhat uninspired name *Fjord Norway* and placed on the Bergen-Hanstholm line. The 31,356 grt *Fjord Norway* could carry 1,700 passengers and 550 cars. The investment proved ill-timed, however, as increased competition from budget airlines turned the previously good profits to loss in 2004. The results for 2005 were even worse, with the added obstacle of Color Line opening a competing Bergen-Denmark service. To improve their financial situation, Fjord Line sold the *Jupiter* (4) in Autumn 2005 and the *Fjord Norway* took over the Bergen-Newcastle line. Later in the same year, TFDS sold their share of Fjord Line to new

A fine aft view of the ***Color Viking*** on the Tyne in May 1998, shortly before she and her route were sold to Fjord Line. The ship had been lengthened during her DFDS career in 1988-89, while the sponsons aft were added some time after the Estonia disaster in 1994, the aftermath of which imposed more stringent stability regulations on ferries. *(Marko Stampehl)*

investors for a symbolic price of one krone.

Meanwhile, DFDS decided to close down their Gothenburg-Kristiansand-Newcastle link in Autumn 2006 (as explained in Chapter 3). While DFDS felt there was no future for Sweden-UK passenger services, they had different ideas for Norway-UK routes. At the same time, Fjord Line were teetering on the brink of bankruptcy, so when DFDS approached with an offer to buy the *Fjord Norway* and the Bergen-Newcastle line, Fjord Line eagerly accepted. DFDS' reasoning behind the acquisition was not only route traffic between Norway and the UK (and hopes of at least some of the passengers on the previous Gothenburg-Kristiasand-Newcastle route switching to Bergen-Newcastle), but also selling return trips as short cruises – DFDS were already doing a good job selling "minicruises" to Norwegians on the Oslo-Copenhagen route and to Britons on the Newcastle-IJmuiden line. In Autumn 2006, the *Fjord Norway* was repainted in DFDS colours and renamed *Princess of Norway* (possibly, the name was a reference to the popular Princess Mette-Marit, the wife of Norway's Crown Prince Haakon). After the sale of the Norway-UK operations, Fjord Line rebounded under new ownership and are today a major ferry operator on ferry routes linking Norway to Denmark and Sweden – but these, naturally, lie outside the scope of this book.

The former ***Color Viking*** as the ***Jupiter*** (4) in her first Fjord Line livery, with the black hull – recalling the BDS livery of old – making an uneasy combination with the Fjord Line funnel colours. Note the lack of the company name on the hull, an almost unique feature on a ferry in North European service at the time. *(Hilton T. Davis)*

The ***Jupiter*** (4) in Stavanger, summer 2000, displaying her second Fjord Line livery. After her North Sea career she became a Vietnamese cruise ship, but sunk in 2017 after a lengthy layup. *(Marko Stampehl)*

The end (part 1)

Despite her Norway-referencing name, the *Princess of Norway* was transferred to DFDS' Newcastle-IJmuiden service in 2007, sailing alongside her sister ship *King of Scandinavia* (3). In return, the Bergen-Newcastle line received the 1981-built *Queen of Scandinavia* (originally the *Finlandia* of Silja Line) from the Newcastle-IJmuiden line. The 33,575 grt, 2,000 passenger and 350 car *Queen of Scandinavia* was not an ideal

The ***Fjord Norway*** originally the TT-Line ferry ***Peter Pan*** (2), was acquired from the Australian TT-Line in 2002 and took over the Bergen-Newcastle route in 2005. Her presence proved to be Fjord Line's last hurrah on the route. She is seen here in Hanstholm during her stint on Norway-Denmark services in April 2003. *(Marko Stampehl)*

choice for the line as, being designed for the shallower waters of the northern Baltic Sea, she tended to roll heavily on the North Sea waves – but at the same time, she had impressive passenger facilities well-suited for the minicruise product.

Contrary to expectations, DFDS could not make the Bergen-Newcastle passenger service profitable. In May 2008, the company announced the upcoming closure of the route. On 1 September, the *Queen of Scandinavia* arrived in Newcastle on the last crossing from Bergen. After 158 years, passenger services between Norway and the United Kingdom ended.

After the closure of the Bergen-Newcastle-Stavanger route, DFDS have continued to operate cargo between Norway and the UK, but sailing only from the southern Norwegian ports of Brevik, Fredrikstad and Halden, with the roro cargo services to the ports in Western Norway left in the hands of the Norway-based Sea-Cargo. Although both companies' operate ships with a theoretical maximum passenger capacity of 12, neither carry passengers.

The former ***Fjord Norway*** moored at North Shields as DFDS' Princess of Norway. She remains in the DFDS fleet at the time of writing as the ***Princess Seaways***, the attempt to swap her to a newer ship with Moby Lines in 2019 having been blocked by Moby's funders. *(Marko Stampehl)*

The end (part 2)

The passenger link between Britain and Norway was restored briefly in April 2010, when all air traffic in Europe was suspended due to the Eyjafjallajökull volcano erupting in Iceland. With the budget airlines – that had proven so fatal to numerous long-haul ferry services – out of the picture, numerous travellers were left stranded. To bring them home, ferries were roped in to provide transportation.

The Norwegian training ship *Gann*, originally the Ofotens Dampskibsselskap -owned Hurtigrute *Narvik* of 1982, made a return trip from Stavanger to Newcastle on 16-18 April. The 6,257 grt *Gann* could carry 306 passengers in all-cabin accommodation, plus an additional 104 passengers without cabins. After the *Gann*, the 2002-built Northlink Ferries vessel *Hamnavoe* made a trip with the itinerary Stromness-Bergen-Aberdeen between 19 and 21 April. Her crossings must have been particularly interesting, as the 8,780 grt *Hamnavoe* was a day ferry and, although she could carry 600 passengers in total, only 36 cabin berths were provided. In both cases it is unknown to the author how many passengers were actually carried. Nonetheless, the *Hamnavoe*'s Bergen-Aberdeen crossing was the last passenger sailing between Norway and the UK to date but, as will be explained in the final chapter, there have been several attempts to restore the service, but none have been successful.

Above: The ***Queen of Scandinavia*** had enjoyed a long DFDS career before taking over the Bergen-Newcastle route in 2007. She is seen here in Newcastle during her last week of operation on the Norway service; despite high hopes, DFDS could not turn the fortunes of the Norway-UK service around. *(Miles Cowsill)*

Left: The Coffee & Co. cafeteria photographed during the ***Queen of Scandinavia***'s later life as St. Peter Line's ***Princess Maria***, till unchanged from her DFDS days. *(Kalle Id)*

Middle left: The penultimate ship to provide a Norway-UK liner service was the Norwegian training ship ***Gann***, originally the ODS Hurtigruten ***Narvik***, which made a Stavanger-Newcastle return trip after the eruption of the Eyjafjallajökull volcano in April 2010. She is seen here on a cruise visit to Tallinn in July 2014. *(Kalle Id)*

Bottom left: The ***SC Connector*** is one of Sea-Cargo's roro freighters connecting various western Norwegian ports to Immigham, Rotterdam and Esbjerg. The company also run a dedicated Norway-Aberdeen freight link. *(Hannes van Rijn, John Bryant collection)*

Below: In addition to call at Brevik by the Gothenburg-Immingham freighters (see page 76), DFDS operate from Fredrikstad and Halden to Zeebrugge and Immingham using the chartered Finnish-flagged roro freighter ***Transporter,*** seen here at Fredrikstad shortly after entering DFDS service in 2019. *(Simona Mitmann)*

Chapter five

Iceland and Faroe Islands to Britain: Lifeline By-Product

Iceland, until 1944 a part of Denmark and since then an independent nation, and the Faroe Islands, a self-governing part of Denmark, are grouped together in this book as the UK routes from both island groups were usually operated by the same vessels. The development of these services were unique in the Nordic context: a link to the UK was not the main purpose of the connection, but rather an intermediate call in British ports was included as an added bonus to the primary service: a link to Denmark. Due to this status of the UK service as a part of the lifeline services to the (ex-)"motherland", this chapter also discusses the direct Denmark-Faroes/Iceland services where they had a clear effect in the UK services.

Another notable difference from most other services linking the Nordic countries to the UK is that while DFDS played a vital role in the early decades of the routes, but subsequently withdrew and during the car ferry era it was local companies, particularly from the Faroe Islands, that dominated the scene.

First scheduled passenger services

Until the mid-1850s, shipping to and from the Faroe Islands and Iceland was a royal monopoly, with irregular calls and no dedicated passenger service to speak of. When the Royal Trade Company's sole vessel dedicated to the islands, the schooner *Søløven*, sank in 1857, a new solution was required. In 1858 the Danish ship owner C.P.A. Koch initiated scheduled service from Copenhagen to the Faroes and Iceland, via Edinburgh (Leith) using the passenger-cargo steamer *Arcturus* (1) acquired second-hand.

In 1867, Koch's company merged with three other Danish shipping companies to form Det Forenede Dampskibsselskab (literally "The United Steamship Company"), or DFDS for short. In 1870, the DFDS service to the islands ceased as they again became a state monopoly, but in 1876 DFDS were allowed to join the fray, now operating alongside the state-owned *Diana*. After the state withdrew in 1880, DFDS would be the only company offering scheduled services to Iceland and the Faroes until 1898.

The DFDS era

In 1882, DFDS took delivery of their first ship purpose built for serving Iceland and the Faroes: the *Laura* of 1,068 grt and 120 passengers, built by the Burmeister & Wain shipyard. It seems that with her arrival, regular services linking Iceland and the Faroe Islands to the UK also begun, as DFDS' fleet history lists the ship having sailed on a Copenhagen-Edinburgh-Faroes-Iceland route from the start. In both the Faroe Islands and Iceland, the steamer called in multiple ports. However, according to an article on Faroes-UK passenger services by Andras Mortensen in the book *North Sea Passenger Lines,* the UK calls only begun in 1897, when DFDS received permission from the Danish Crown to operate 18 return trips per year from Copenhagen via Edinburgh to the Faroe Islands.

Regardless of when the services were actually initiated, DFDS needed additional tonnage to fulfill the requirements of the 1897 contract, and in 1898 the company purchased the identical freighters *Vardø* and *Vadsø*, which were rebuilt into passenger-cargo steamers and renamed *Skálholt* and *Hólar*, after the two bishoprics in Iceland (while DFDS' fleet history uses the Danish spelling, Skalholt and Holar, respectively, the names were painted in the Icelandic form in the ships themselves, as can be seen from the accompanying photos). Both operated on the long route from Copenhagen via Edinburgh to the Faroes and Iceland, alongside Icelandic coastal trades. The *Skálholt* and *Hólar* were both 565 gross tons and with capacity for 116 passengers (16 first class and 100 deck).

Despite their agreement with the Danish crown, a competitor appeared for DFDS' services in 1898, when the Sweden-based Skånska Ångfartygs AB placed their 1879-built *Vesta* (1,122 grt, 92 passengers) on a Copenhagen-Edinburgh-Faroes-Iceland service. The competition proved short-lived, as DFDS bought the ship, as well as a second Skånska Ångfartygs steamer, the *Ceres* of 1883 (1,166 grt and 117 passengers) already the following year. Both ships continued to the be used on the Iceland/Faroes services after the takeover by DFDS.

In 1904, a fifth ship was added to the services in the form of the 1898-built *Vega* (2) purchased from the Wasa-Nordsjö Ångbåts Aktiebolaget in Finland, in whose fleet the ship had been used on the Finland-UK services (see Chapter 2). The 795 grt and 353 passenger ship was renamed *Tjaldur*, after the Faroese name for the Eurasian oystercatcher (in Danish, the bird is known as the strandskade).

A reason for so many passenger ships in what was essentially a Danish internal life-line service by a commercial operator, and indeed a contributing factor for the inclusion of the call in Edinburgh, were the romanticist trends that affected travel preferences (also discussed in Chapter 1). Romanticism held rugged nature and the medieval era – including the Vikings – in high regard, and Iceland offered both the rugged nature and what was considered to be the best surviving example of "original" or "pure" Norse culture. Thus, Iceland was something

Above: A reproduction of an impressive painting by an unknown artist of DFDS' first purpose-built ship for the Denmark-UK-Faroes-Iceland trades, the ***Laura*** of 1882, at speed. The use of wind to supplement the steam propulsion of the ship was still common at this time. *(DFDS, Joonas Kortelainen collection)*

Left: The ***Skálholt*** was a fairly small ship for service on the often stormy North Atlantic, but her small size made her very good for use on the Icelandic coastal trades. *(Museet for Søfart (CC-BY-NC-SA))*

Middle left: The ***Skálholt***'s sister ship ***Hólar*** being inspected after a grounding at the quay of the tiny Icelandic hamlet Djúpavík in 1901. *(A. Rosendahl collection, Museet for Søfart (CC-BY-NC-SA))*

Bottom left: While quite similar in exterior appearance to the ***Laura***, the ***Ceres*** had been built at the Kockums Mekaniska Verkstad in Malmö, Sweden – fitting for a Swedish-owned ship. She is seen here in Copenhagen in DFDS colours. *(Museet for Søfart (CC-BY-NC-SA))*

Below: The other ex-Skånska Angbfartygs AB DFDS Iceland ship, the ***Vesta*** of 1879, photographed at Seyðisfjörður in Iceland. The fact she is flagged overall suggests this may be from her first call in the port. *(Museet for Søfart (CC-BY-NC-SA))*

Above: The ***Tjaldur*** (1) of DFDS was originally the Wasa-Nordsjö Ångbats AB Finland-UK liner ***Vega*** (2), see page 25. After 30 years under in DFDS service, she was laid up, but sold for further trading to Greece in 1939. She was eventually torpedoed by the Royal Navy in 1942. *(Sjöhistoriska Museet, Stockholm/Suomen laivahistoriallinen yhdistys)*

Left: As the name suggests, the ***Botnia*** had originally been concieved for DFDS' Denmark-Finland route; however, this had been abandoned in 1905, leaving the ship free for other services. *(Museet for Søfart (CC-BY-NC-SA))*

Middle left: The ***Island*** was the second DFDS ship purpose-built for the services to Iceland and the Faroes. She spent her entire career on these routes, until wrecked in 1937 on the Scottish coast. *(Museet for Søfart (CC-BY-NC-SA))*

Bottom left: The 1890-vintage ***Nidaros***, seen here with World War I -era neutrality markings, visited the Denmark-UK-Faroes-Island route in 1920. *(Museet for Søfart (CC-BY-NC-SA))*

Below: The first-class lounge onboard the ***Island***. *(Museet for Søfart (CC-BY-NC-SA))*

of an ultimate travel destination for wealthy travellers in tune with the romanticist ideas, both from Britain and elsewhere.

Competition on the routes to Iceland and the Faroe Islands (albeit not on routes to UK ports) did not remain gone for long. In 1903, a new Icelandic shipping company, Gufuskipafélagið Thore (roughly 'Steamship Company Thore'), started cargo and passenger services between Reykjavík and Copenhagen. Thore also operated on the Icelandic coastal trades in competition with DFDS. Further competition on the long-haul routes arrived in 1908, when Det Bergenske Dampskibsselskab (BDS, who also ran Norway-UK services and are discussed in detail in Chapter 4) began serving the Faroes from both Norway and Denmark. Competition further stiffened on the UK routes in 1909, when Thore were contracted by the Icelandic parliament (Alþingi, which had been (re-)established in 1874) to offer four yearly return trips from Reykjavík to Edinburgh (Leith), albeit only for cargo. The appearance of competition naturally cut in DFDS' profit margins on the Faroes and Iceland routes.

DFDS' long-serving *Laura* was lost outside Skagarstrand in Iceland in March 1910; while all passengers and crew were evacuated, the ship could not be salvaged. During her 28 years serving on the route, the *Laura* had made 204 return trips between Copenhagen and Iceland. Luckily, DFDS already had a suitable replacement: the 1901-built *Botnia*, which was undergoing a refit in Copenhagen when the *Laura* sank. The *Botnia*, 1,206 grt and with a capacity for 171 passengers following her refit, started services from Copenhagen via Edinburgh to Iceland and the Faroes almost immediately following the loss of the *Laura*. In spring 1912, a brand-new ship was also seen on the Iceland trade, when the *Bergenshus* (1,017 grt and 76 passengers) made a return trip to Iceland and the Faroes. However, this was a one-off and afterwards the ship joined the Stettin-Copenhagen-Norway routes.

It seems that Gufuskipafélagið Thore ceased trading during World War I, but this did not mean decreased competition for DFDS on the routes to Iceland, as the new Icelandic shipping company Eimskipafélag Íslands (freely translating as the "Icelandic Steamship Company", but better known under the shortened name Eimskip) was founded in 1914 and started operations in 1915, including on routes linking Iceland to Denmark.

Despite (or perhaps because of) the increased competition, DFDS invested in their own services to Iceland and the Faroes even during the First World War. While the *Skálholt* was withdrawn in 1914, two newer ships were placed on the Iceland services in 1915: the 1912-built *Christianssund* of 1,017

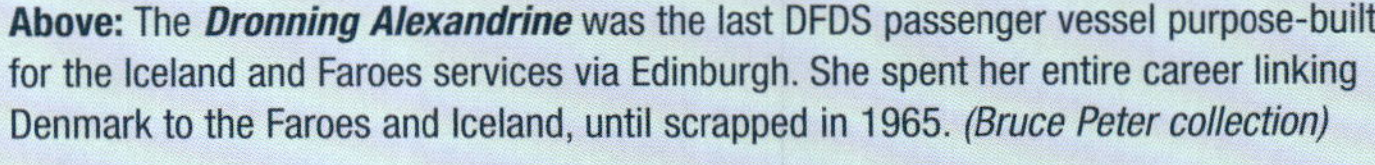

Above: The ***Dronning Alexandrine*** was the last DFDS passenger vessel purpose-built for the Iceland and Faroes services via Edinburgh. She spent her entire career linking Denmark to the Faroes and Iceland, until scrapped in 1965. *(Bruce Peter collection)*

Left: Despite her royal name – perhaps chosen to inspire national unity in the independence-seeking Icelanders – the ***Dronning Alexandrine*** had a somewhat workmanlike exterior appearance.*(Museet for Søfart (CC-BY-NC-SA))*

Middle left: Eimskip's ***Brúarfoss*** attracts a large crowd on her maiden call in Reykjavík, 1927. After World War II, she briefly sailed on the Iceland-UK-Denmark route. *(Magnús Ólafsson, Sjóminjasafnið í Reykjavík)*

Bottom left: Eimskip's sole passenger newbuilding for the UK services, the ***Gullfoss*** of 1950, at port, with a car being lifted on or off the ship. Notice also the company bow symbol, a swastika representing Thor's hammer. *(A. Ernest Glen, Bruce Peter collection)*

Below: The launch day of the ***Gullfoss*** at the Burmeister & Wain shipyard in Copenhagen. *(Museet for Søfart (CC-BY-NC-SA))*

grt and 76 passengers (a sister ship to the *Bergenshus* mentioned above) and the brand-new, purpose-built *Island* ("Iceland", roughly pronounced "ees-land", not like the English word "island") of 1,774 grt and 155 passengers. However, when the *Christianssund* was lost in 1916, no replacement was brought in, and the long service from Copenhagen to Iceland via Edinburgh and Faroe ports was maintained by the *Island*, *Botnia* and *Tjaldur* (1).

The year 1917 would see heavy losses for DFDS' Iceland and Faroes fleet: while the *Hólar* was withdrawn from service in a planned manner, both the *Vesta* and *Ceres* were war losses when under charter to the Icelandic local government. As things were, the services would change in the post-war era and no replacements were acquired.

The decline of DFDS services

The formal relationship between Iceland and Denmark changed in 1918: after a long process of the Icelanders attempting to wrestle either more autonomy or complete independence (a major political divide was whether expanded autonomy or full independence was the ultimate goal for Iceland), Denmark finally agreed that Iceland would become an independent state in a personal union with Denmark, with only the person of the King and foreign policy shared with the former mother country. However – somewhat contradicting the shared foreign policy – Iceland would remain neutral in all conflicts between nations and would maintain no armed forces. This treaty had a set time limit – 25 years – after which Iceland could become fully independent if the Icelanders so wished.

Effecting the passenger trades from Britain to Iceland and Faroes in the inter-war era were changing cultural trends. The remnants of romanticism gave way for an era which embraced technological development, urbanism and other results on human ingenuity, rather than rejecting them. Thus, the desirability of Iceland as a tourist destination plummeted and, as we shall see, the number of passenger vessels sailing via British ports also declined.

Post-war, the *Botnia* sailed to Iceland and the Faroes via Bergen rather than Edinburgh between 1918 and 1920, before returning to the old route alongside the *Tjaldur* (1) and *Island*. During 1920, the 1890-built *Nidaros* (1,024 grt and 144 passengers; Nidaros was the medieval name of Trondheim) also sailed on the service via Edinburgh, but that was only for the one season. In 1921, occasional sailings with the *Island* were extended from Iceland to Greenland, which, like Iceland and Faroes, was (and still is) a part of Denmark.

In 1922, the *Tjaldur* (1) was withdrawn from the services to Iceland and the Faroes. In her place, the 1915-built *Sleipner*, ex-*Trondhjem* (1), was placed on the service linking Denmark via the UK to the Faroes, but she did not sail to Iceland. Named after the eight-legged stallion in Norse mythology, the *Sleipner* was 1,076 grt and could carry 59 passengers. The name Tjaldur almost immediately returned to the Faroes services, as the 1919-established Skipafelagið Føroyar (roughly "Faroes Shipping Company", or SF for short) named their second-hand passenger steamer purchased from the Østasiatisk Kompagni in Denmark *Tjaldur* (2). The *Tjaldur* (2) started a direct service to Copenhagen from the Faroes, something which the locals had demanded for some time but which DFDS had been unwilling to provide. The choice of name undoubtedly caused confusion, as in 1926 DFDS' *Tjaldur* (1) returned to the Copenhagen-Edinburgh-Faroes-Iceland route and thus there were two *Tjaldur*s sailing between the Faroes and Copenhagen.

DFDS brought in one more newbuilding for the Faroes and Iceland routes in 1927, when the *Dronning Alexandrine* (named after the Queen of Denmark) of 1,854 grt and 153 passengers was delivered. The services to were reorganised the following year; now, the *Dronning Alexandrine* and *Sleipner* operated the long Copenhagen-Edinburgh-Tórshavn-Vestmanna-Reykjavik line (this is the first precise port list discovered during the process of making this book). The sources at disposal didn't specify whether Vestmanna refers to the town of that name in the Faroe Islands, or the islands with the same name off the Icelandic coast (Vestmannayear, occasionally anglicized as the Westman Isles). With the arrival of the new ship, the *Botnia* and *Island* operated an otherwise identical service, but terminated at Edinburgh in the south(!). The *Tjaldur* (1) was (again) withdrawn from the Iceland/Faroes services, this time permanently. During the same year, SF initiated a Faroes-UK service of their own, albeit carrying only cargo, with the *Havhestur* (Faroese for northern fulmar). The smaller company could not compete against DFDS and the service was closed in 1933.

The following years marked a decline of DFDS' services to Iceland and the Faroes, undoubtedly in part due to heavy expansion by Eimskip (even if Eimskip did not compete with them in the passenger services to the UK). The long-serving *Botnia* was withdrawn in 1934 and scrapped. Next year, she was replaced by another old timer, the 1896-built *Primula* (1,524 grt and 257 passengers, see Chapter 6 for her earlier career). 1936 saw a massive reduction of services, when both the *Primula* and the *Sleipner* were withdrawn; the former was laid up while the latter moved to the routes linking Copenhagen to Poland. At the same time, the *Dronning Alexandrine* stopped calling at Edinburgh, sailing instead directly from Copenhagen to Tórshavn. In 1937 the *Island* was wrecked off the Scottish coast. While passengers, cargo and the post carried could be saved, the ship herself was a complete loss. When DFDS brought in no replacement and the route of the sole remaining Iceland ship *Dronning Alexandrine* was not altered, this meant the end of the UK link from Iceland and the Faroes.

Soon afterwards, World War II halted scheduled passenger services from Iceland and the Faroe Islands entirely. While both Iceland and Faroes were away from the main theatres of the conflict, they were both occupied by British forces in 1940 to stop them from falling in German hands after Germany had occupied the main parts of Denmark. The responsibility for occupation of Iceland was transferred to the United States in 1941. Essentially, both island groups were independent states during the occupations and, subsequently, both Iceland and the Faroes held independence referendums: Iceland in 1944, overwhelmingly in favour of independence; and the Faroe Islands in 1946, very narrowly in favour of independence (Winston Churchill had refused to any attempts of changing the

Faroe Islands' constitutional position during the occupation). While the Icelandic referendum resulted in full independence already during 1944, the inconclusive nature of the Faroes referendum (voter turnout was only 67 percent, of which 51 percent had supported independence) and subsequent election victory of parties against independence resulted in the Faroe Islands remaining a part of Denmark, albeit with autonomy granted 1948. In both Iceland and the Faroes, the British occupation had been fairly popular, and here, too, Britain continued to enjoy high levels of goodwill after the war.

The last traditional steamer services

After World War II, an Iceland-UK passenger link was restored when Eimskip placed their 1927-built combined passenger and cargo ship *Brúarfoss* of 1,579 grt on an Iceland-UK-Denmark service. When built, the *Brúarfoss* had been Eimskip's first reefer (a ship fitted with refrigerated cargo holds). She was, however, a temporary solution from the start: in 1950, Eimskip took delivery of the purpose-built passenger steamer *Gullfoss* (Eimskip ships were, and are, named after waterfalls, or foss in Icelandic, of Iceland. Gullfoss is one of the best known waterfalls in Iceland and had also been the name of Eimskip's first vessel). Iceland's new flagship was 3,858 grt and carried 209 passengers; her main purpose was to provide a link from Reykjavik to Copenhagen, but she also called in Edinburgh (Leith) along the way. It is perhaps of interest to note that the *Gullfoss* never called at the Faroe Islands en route. (The *Brúarfoss*, meanwhile, remained in the Eimskip fleet until 1957, when she was sold for further trading).

The passenger link from Faroes to the UK was restored only in 1952, when DFDS placed their 1923-built *Trondhjem* (2) of 1,398 grt on a new Copenhagen-Aalborg-Edinburgh-Tórshavn-Trongisvágur route. However, as the *Trondhjem* (2) carried only 24 passengers, this was hardly a large-scale revival – especially as the ship alternated between this and other DFDS routes. Already in 1955 the *Trondhjem* (2) ceased serving the Faroes, and DFDS' involvement in the Faroes-UK services ended again. The company continued to carry passengers between the Faroes and Denmark, an involvement that did not seem to be affected by the opening of the first airport on the Faroe Islands in 1963.

Passenger numbers between Iceland and the UK were effected by what was called the Cod Wars by the British press: a series of conflicts in 1958-1976 resulting from Iceland repeated unilateral expansion of the national fishing waters. The conflicts perhaps explain why the *Gullfoss*' calls in Edinbugh became less frequent from the second half of the 1960s. In the end, the *Gullfoss* was withdrawn from service in 1973 and not replaced (the following year the Cod Wars reached their height and Britain broke diplomatic relations with Iceland). Competition from airplanes had rendered this traditional passenger service unprofitable, and as there was very little demand for roro cargo between Iceland and the rest of the world, a car-passenger ferry connection was not viable. As far as can be ascertained, 1973 was the last time Eimskip operated passenger ships in international service (though they do operate intra-Icelandic passenger vessels to this day).

Almost at the same time, though with no effect on Iceland-UK routes, DFDS re-initiated a Faroes-UK-Denmark service in 1972 and thus restored the Faroes' link to the UK after an absence of 17 years. The *Kronprins Frederik*, built in 1945 for the Denmark-UK services, had previously operated a long-haul service from Copenhagen to Reykjavik via Tórshavn, Klagsvig and Trongisvágur in the Faroe Islands. Following the sale of DFDS' dedicated Esbjerg-Newcastle summer ferry *Prinsessen*, the *Kronprins Frederik* operated a new summer-only Esbjerg-Newcastle-Tórshavn service in 1972-74 (both vessels are discussed in more detail in Chapter 6). In the latter year, the *Kronprins Frederik* was replaced by the car ferry *England* (2), and at the same time the service was broken in two, separating Esbjerg-Newcastle and Esbjerg-Tórshavn – again eliminating the Faroes-UK link. The arrival of the *England* (2) also meant that the Faroe Islands finally moved to the car ferry era – an exceptionally late development when compared to the rest of northern Europe, and symptomatic of the small islands' status as not important enough for new tonnage, the services relying instead on older ships cascaded from other routes.

Three different companies to Britain

Strandfaraskip Landsins, the company owned by the Faroese local government in charge of public transport on the islands, including local ferries, acquired their first car ferry in 1975 from Mols-Linien (at the time a subsidiary of DFDS). This was the 1969-built *Morten Mols* of 2,430 grt, 800 passengers and 135 cars, which was renamed *Smyril* ("merlin"). Although acquired with local services in mind, and indeed having been designed exclusively for short crossings, the *Smyril* was also used on long-haul services from the Faroe Islands to Iceland, Norway, Denmark and the UK (the port of Aberdeen). The routes linking to other countries were run only during the summer season, interspersed with the local Faroese ferry services, so sailing frequences on the Tórshavn-Aberdeen route were not high – but still, this was a restoration of the Faroes-UK link. The crossings proved popular and as the years progressed, it became clear the *Smyril* could not cope with the demand.

The year 1983 saw two new shipping companies attempt services from Iceland and the Faroes to Britain. The first was the Icelandic company Farskip, which chartered the car-passenger ferry *Rogalin* (originally the Silja Line ferry *Aallotar* of 1972) from Polferries and renamed her *Edda*, after the 13th century Norse sagas. The 7,801 grt, 1,000 passenger and 170 car ferry sailed on a Bremerhaven-Newcastle-Reykjavik -route during the 1983 summer season, making one return trip per week. This was not a success, with only 15,000 passengers carried during the season, and the experiment was not repeated.

Smyril Line, a Faroese newcomer, fared notably better. The company had been established in 1982 to provide ferry connections on a regular basis to Denmark, Norway and Iceland on Faroese keels, instead of the occasional connections of the *Smyril* (DFDS continued to operate an Esbjerg-Tórshavn summer service, now with the *Winston Churchill*). The company purchased the 1973-built TT-Saga

Above: The brand-new ***Gullfoss*** photographed at sea on her builder's trials, as testified by the fact she is flying the Danish, rather than the Icelandic, flag. In total, the ***Gullfoss*** made 442 return trips from Reykjavik; after her Eimskip career, she was sold for further trading in the Red Sea, but was lost in a fire in 1976. *(Museet for Søfart (CC-BY-NC-SA))*

Left: An early-50s view of the ***Gullfoss*** in the port of Tórshavn, with the ***Tjaldur*** (2) of Skipafelagið Føroyar arriving. In 1953, the ***Tjaldur*** (2) was replaced by a brand-new ships of the same name – but like her successor, she never connected to the UK. *(Museet for Søfart (CC-BY-NC-SA))*

Middle left: The ***Trondhjem*** (2) had a 40-year long career with DFDS, from 1923 until her scrapping in 1963. In addition to her brief service to Iceland and the Faroes via the UK, she was primarily engaged on the various Denmark-UK routes in the post-war era. *(Museet for Søfart (CC-BY-NC-SA))*

Bottom left: A winter view of the ***Kronprins Frederik*** somewhere in the Faroe Islands or Iceland. Although originally built for the Esbjerg-Harwich route – as explained in the next chapter – she spend her twilight years with DFDS connecting to the Faroe Islands. *(Joonas Kortelainen collection)*

Below: The ***Smyril*** seen at Drelnes, the Faroe Islands, 1995. She continued in Strandfaraskip Landsins service until 2005, when she was replaced by a new ship with the same name. The old ***Smyril*** briefly got a new lease of life as a ferry in the Caribbean and later in Africa, until laid up in 2010 and subsequently scrapped. *(Jenny Williamson)*

Top & above: Despite being designed for the relatively sheltered Malmö-Travemünde route, the ***Norröna*** (1) coped well with the stormy seas of the North Sea and North Atlantic. *(FotoFlite)*

The short-lived ***Edda*** of Farskip on the River Tyne, June 1983. Owned by Polska Zegluga Baltycka (Polferries), she remained under the Polish flag, despite her Iceland-influenced name and funnel colours. *(Ken Lubi)*

Line ferry *Gustav Vasa*, which was renamed *Norröna*. The 7,257 grt, 1,040 passenger and 250 car ferry sailed from Tórshavn to Seydisfördur (Iceland), Bergen (Norway), Hanstholm (Denmark) and Scrabster on the Scottish mainland. Despite a relatively low occupancy rate (just over 50%) during the 1983 summer season, the service was deemed a success. For the 1984 summer season, the calls at Scrabster were abandoned in favour of the ship making an intermediate call at Lerwick on the Shetland Islands on the crossings from Tórshavn to Bergen (and vice versa). Later the Lerwick call was moved to the Tórshavn-Hanstholm crossing instead. For passengers bound to the British mainland, connections were available from Lerwick on P&O Scottish Ferries' services to Aberdeen and Scrabster, and both companies sold through tickets to the other's ships. Like the *Smyril*'s international services, the *Norröna* only sailed during the summer months; during the winters she was either laid up or chartered to other operators. While she was designed for the much calmer waters of the southern Baltic Sea, the *Norröna* (1) proved surprisingly well-suited for services on the North Atlantic.

After a decade of successful service, Smyril Line discontinued the calls in Lerwick in 1993. A contributing factor was the fact that DFDS had given up on their Denmark-Faroes services at the end of the 1992 summer season, which meant the *Norröna* now got a lot of additional business on this route. While this meant the end of Iceland's direct UK link, the Faroes retained theirs as Strandfaraskip Landsins' *Smyril* continued occasional summer service from Tórshavn to Aberdeen until 1996.

Norrönas old and new, 1999-2008

The link from the Faroes and Iceland to Britain did not remain broken for long. Smyril Line expanded their services in the last years of the 1990s: first, winter service between the Faroe Islands and Denmark was initiated in 1998, and starting from the 1999 summer season the intermediate calls at Lerwick were re-instated.

At the same time it was becoming evident that the *Norröna* (1) was getting too small for needs of the growing traffic and Smyril Line decided to commission a newbuilding. While it may seem surprising that a company with just one ship would opt for a newbuilt ship, there was a pressing reason to do so: the dimensions of the Tórshavn harbour meant the ship's length was restricted to just 165 metres, making a bespoke design with a relatively short and wide hull nescessary to get the capacity required. Knud E. Hansen maritime architects were contracted to provide the concept design (they had, in fact, also designed the original *Norröna*).

The new ship, eventually named *Norröna* (2) after her predecessor, was contracted from the Flensburger Schiffbau yard in Flensburg, Germany, but due to the heavy workload at the yard it was subcontracted to the Flender Werft in Lübeck. The ship was delivered in April 2003. Gross tonnage was 35,966, passenger capacity 1,482 with 1,343 cabin berths, while car capacity was 634 with 1,870 lane metres for cargo. The interiors were designed by the Swedish interior architects Figura, perhaps best known for their work with Stena Line. Unusually for the era, public rooms on the *Norröna* (2) were placed aft, with cabins forward. Whereas, in the 1970s and 80s, such arrangements had been favoured in order to make the cabins quieter (placing them furthest from the engines), on the *Norröna* (2) this was done in order to have relatively large windows in the public rooms: due to the frequently stormy North Atlantic weather, fenestration in the forward part of the ship was kept minimal, whereas in the aft part the windows could be larger without fear of on-coming waves smashing them in.

With the delivery of the *Norröna* (2), her older namesake was renamed *Norröna I*, laid up and placed for sale. No buyer emerged, however, which turned out to be a good thing: in January 2004, the *Norröna* (2) collided with a quay in Tórshavn harbour, receiving a ten-metre long gash on her side. Reparations at Blohm+Voss in Hamburg took almost two months, during which time the *Norröna I* was pressed back in service as a replacement. After the *Norröna* (2) returned to service in March, the *Norröna I* was again laid up and finally found a buyer soon afterwards,becoming the missionary ship *Logos Hope*.

Although the *Norröna* (2) was partially funded by the Shetland Islands Council and the Shetland Development Trust was a minority shareholder in Smyril Line, the company wanted to stop the calls at Lerwick in 2006. The reasons were Smyril Line's mounting financial difficulties, caused by the high cost of the *Norröna* (2). A detailed analysis of the company route structure and expenses revealed that only five percent of all passengers embarked or disembarked in Lerwick. Combined with the relatively high harbour costs at Lerwick this meant the calls at the Shetland Islands made a loss. A contributing factor was the change of the operator on the Shetland-Scottish mainland routes in 2002: the new operator Northlink did not

As built, the ***Norröna*** (2) had a large area dedicated to shopping, with the lobby between the shops seen here. *(Per Jensen)*

Following the long-established trend of Scandinavian ferries, the ***Norröna*** (2) has both a buffet and an à la carte restaurant, the latter seen here as built. *(Per Jensen)*

The pub onboard the ***Norröna*** (2) as built. Almost all of the public rooms have since been redecorated. *(Per Jensen)*

collaborate with Smyril Line on booking through voyages to the Faroes and Iceland from the UK (or vice versa), unlike P&O Scottish Ferries had done.

The matter eventually went to court, with the Shetland Development Trust claiming Smyril Line were contractually obliged to continue serving Lerwick until at least 2008. Smyril Line's view won the day, and traffic via the Shetland Islands

The ***Norröna*** (2) passes Travemünde, Germany on her sea trials in February 2003. At this time, the company name on her sides was still rendered simply as Smyril-Line (although the non-hyphenated form is used in all other marketing). Later on, www. and .com were painted around the company name. *(Marko Stampehl)*

The ***Norröna*** (2), seen here in May 2010, dwarfs all buildings in the city when she calls at Tórshavn. (Kalle Id)

Today, Eimskip provides cargo connections from Iceland and the Faroe Islands to the UK on their container ships, such as the ***Lagarfoss,*** seen here during her delivery voyage in 2014, with Eimskip containers strategically placed on the side of each row. *(Hilmar Snorrison)*

ceased at the end of the 2006 summer season. This did not end Smyril Line's services to the UK. Instead, the *Norröna* (2) initiated a weekly summer service from Tórshavn to Scrabster in 2007. This proved more attractive to passengers than the calls at Lerwick, but at the same time problematic for scheduling, as the *Norröna* now made return trips from Tórshavn to four different destinations during the summer seasons: Hanstholm, Bergen, Seydisfjördur and Scrabster, all in different directions from Tórshavn and thus with no chance of combining two ports into a single itenary. When most passengers during the tourist season were en-route to Iceland, the stay at Tórshavn imposed on many of them by this schedule was less than welcome. This, combined with the Scrabster service developing less well than had been hoped for, made Smyril Line abandon their services to UK (and also to Norway) for good at the end of the 2008 summer season. From 2009, the Norröna has sailed on the Hirtshals-Tórshavn-Seydisfjördur route during the summers, with the service trunkated to Hirtshals-Tórshavn during the winter. Afterwards, regular cargo services linking Iceland and the Faroes to the UK have been left primarily to Eimskip's container vessels – at the time of writing, no roro cargo service exists from the UK to the two island nations. Smyril Line does operate three roro cargo vessels, but these link to the Faroe Islands to Iceland, Denmark and Netherlands, not the UK ports.

Occasional negotiations have been carried out between the Shetland authorities and Smyril Line to re-instate the calls at Lerwick (the *Norröna*'s (2) route between Hirtshals and Tórshavn takes her through the Shetland Islands anyway), but these have not resulted in Lerwick being restored to the schedule and 2008 remains the last time Iceland and the Faroe Islands enjoyed a passenger ferry link to the UK.

Chapter six

Denmark to Britain: DFDS Domination

Scheduled passenger services between Denmark and the United Kingdom continued for 194 years, from 1820 until 2014 (excepting times of war). In terms of continuous passenger liner services, Denmark was both the first and last Scandinavian country with a link to the UK, the first to use car-passenger ferries on the link and the only to use ropax tonnage.

In contrast to the other Nordic countries, the Danish link was almost through its entire history dominated by one company, Det Forenede Dampskibsselskab, or DFDS for short. Due to the central location of Copenhagen as a gateway from the Baltic Sea to the outside world, many services linking the UK to countries along the Baltic Sea coast called at Copenhagen en-route, which meant the Danish capital was particularly well-connected, especially during the mid-19th century. However, as including all those numerous services even in briefest detail would make this book excessively long, this chapter concentrates mostly on the dedicated Denmark-UK services, which were also the most important for the subject at hand.

From Copenhagen to the UK

Regular liner service from Copenhagen to the UK ports begun in 1820 in the form of intermediate calls by mostly British steamers on lines linking the UK to ports along the Baltic Sea coast. The first Danish entry into the services was made in 1856, when Det almindelige danske Dampskibsselskab (DADD for short, roughly 'The General Danish Steamship Company') took delivery of three purpose-built steamers for routes linking Baltic Sea ports to the UK via Copenhagen. DADD's finances were not on an even keel, however, and in 1866 the company merged with three other Danish shipping operators – Koch & Henderson, H.P. Prior, and the Anglo-Danish and Baltic Steam Navigation Company – to form the aptly named Det Forenede Dampskibsselskab ("The United Steamship Company"), or DFDS for short. The new company quickly developed into the biggest on the Denmark-UK line services. On the UK routes, DFDS initially sailed from Copenhagen to London, Hull and Edinburgh (with ships continuing onwards to the Faroe Islands and Iceland from the latter port starting either 1882 or 1897; these services are discussed in Chapter 5).

Copenhagen remained the central port for Denmark-UK services through the 19th century, although Esbjerg (offering a much shorter crossing time) was opened in 1874, as explained below. The main reason for Copenhagen's dominance were the through services from the Baltic Sea to the UK. An example of these is DFDS' Köningsberg (today Kaliningrad)-Copenhagen-London route, for which a pair of liners, the *Frederik* and *Louise* (both 1,113 grt and 50 passengers) were built in 1872, and naturally the various Finland-Copenhagen-UK services described in Chapter 2.

The opening of the Kaiser-Wilhelm-Kanal (today the Nord-Ostsee-Kanal), known better in English as the Kiel Canal, in 1895 upset Copenhagen's status as the gate to the Baltic Sea. Instead of sailing around the Jutland peninsula and through the Danish straits, ships could now bypass Denmark entirely by taking the canal from the estuary of the Elbe River in the west to the Kiel Fjord in the east. What must have added insult to the injury for the Danes was the fact that the canal was built on former Danish soil, the twin duchies of Schleswig-Holstein (or Slesvig-Holsten in Danish) having been conquered by Prussia and Austria in the Second Schleswig War of 1864. Just two years later, the Austro-Prussian War saw the dutchies pass solely under Prussian control, making the construction of the Canal possible as a purely Prussian venture (the predominantly Danish-speaking northern parts of Slesvig were re-incorporated into Denmark after a plebiscite in 1920 – but this had no effect on the canal).

The opening of the Kiel Canal, and the resulting drop in calls to Copenhagen, prompted DFDS to contract the first ships designed solely for the needs of linking Copenhagen to the UK. These were the *Ficaria* (1,530 grt and 59 passengers) and *Primula* (1,524 grt and 257 passengers), both delivered in 1896 for a Copenhagen-Newcastle link. (The passenger figures here come from DFDS' 125th anniversary history; no explanation was given there as to why the two near-identical vessels had so different passenger capacities).

Of course, not all through services linking the UK to Baltic Sea ports via Copenhagen ceased; Finska Ångfartygs Aktiebolaget's Finland-UK services, discussed in detail in Chapter 2, continued to sail via Copenhagen, as did many services of the UK-based Bailey & Leetham. The latter company was acquired by the Wilson Line in 1903, and the new owners went on the establish dedicated lines from Copenhagen to both Newcastle and Hull. These were operated by the 1899-built *Una* (2; 1,406 grt and 58 passengers) and the 1896-built *Zero* (1,143 grt and 213 passengers). Although Wilson Line's traditional hull colour was forest green, the two ships sailing to Copenhagen retained Bailey & Leetham's grey hulls – perhaps due to the fact they carried refrigerated cargo, for which a lighter hull shade

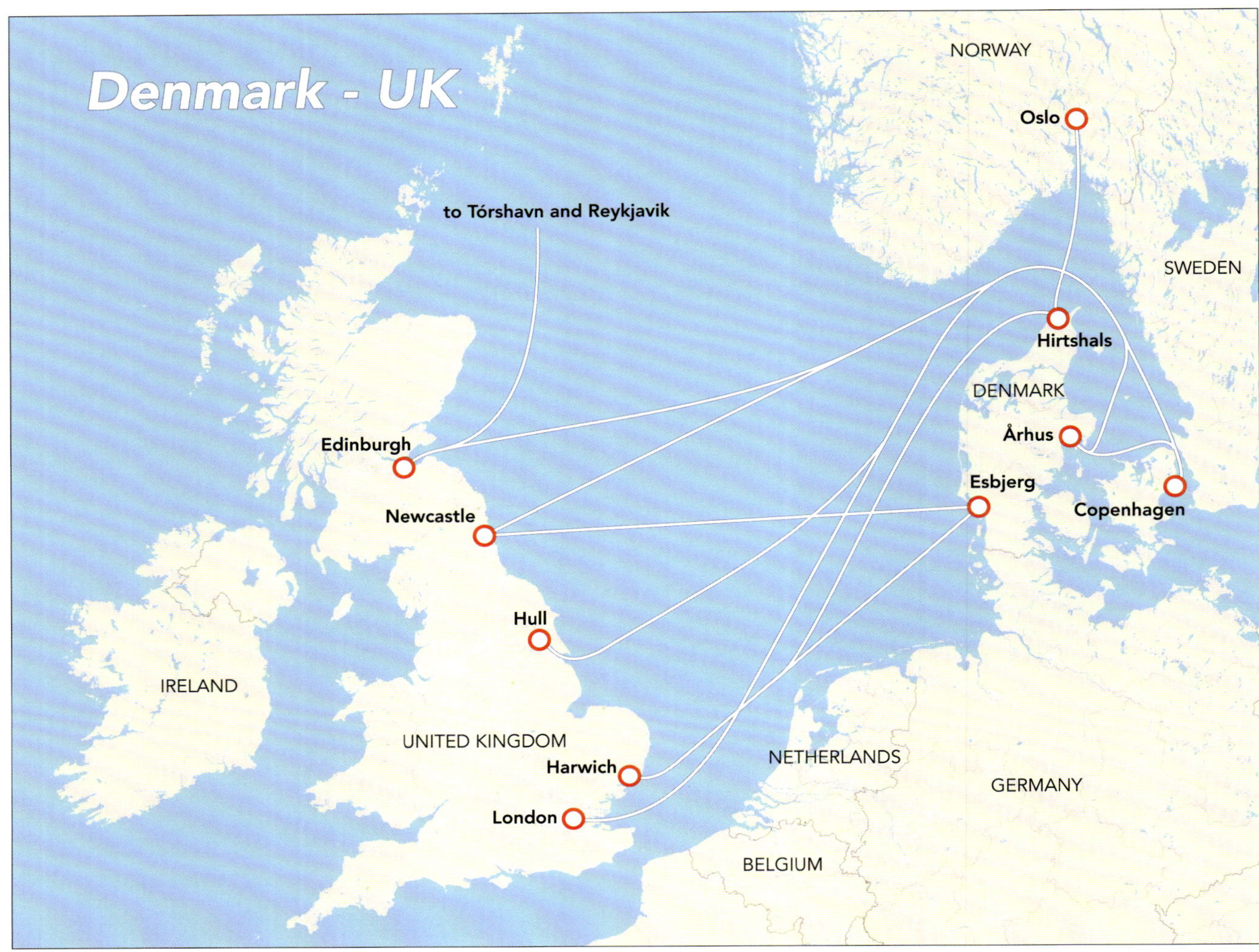

(gathering less heat) was beneficial.

With the acquisition of Bailey & Leetham, Wilson Line had grown to be the largest privately owned shipping company in the World, which gave them much power in negotiations with rivals. DFDS and Wilson Line entered a joint service agreement on the Copenhagen-UK lines, as well as on services from the UK to Saint Petersburg, Reval (present-day Tallinn) and Riga. The warm relationship between the two companies only ended with the bankruptcy of Wilson Line in 1981.

Birth of the Esbjerg-Harwich line

The loss of Schleswig and Holstein had wider ramifications for Danish seafaring than just the construction of the Kiel Canal. Prior to the Second Schleswig War, Denmark's only major port on its North Sea coast had been Tønning in Holstein, due to most of the west coast of Jylland being shallow and riddled with shoals, making safe navigation difficult. Between 1847 and 1860, a Danish company had attempted a cargo and passenger service from the village Hjerting to Lowestoft, but without long-term success.

After the loss of Schleswig and Holstein, the question of creating a major port on Denmark's western coast became acute. The subject was particularly dear to C.F. Tietgen, the leader of Privatbanken in Copenhagen, who had also been a major figure in the formation of DFDS. The construction of a new port at Esbjerg (just south of Hjerting mentioned above – today Hjerting is a district of the Esbjerg municipality) commenced in 1868, but proved more challenging than anticipated. The port was not opened to traffic until 1875, and was only completed in 1878. In 1875, DFDS first initiated passenger services from Esbjerg to Thameshaven with the brand-new paddle steamer *Riberhuus* (615 grt and 28 passengers). In 1880, the UK port of the service was moved to Harwich, where the Great Eastern Railway had built a rail connection and a state-of-the-art port. This move also coincided with a switch on the cargo business from exporting live cattle to exporting food products, such as butter and bacon, which took up less space but also required the ships to have cooled cargo holds.

In 1883, DFDS took delivery of the paddle steamer *Koldinghuus* for the Esbjerg-Harwich service. She was a notable improvement as far as passengers were concerned; whereas the previous ships had accommodated passengers in temporary hammocks, the 1,057 grt *Koldinghuus*' 118 passengers could enjoy relatively well-appointed saloons and cabins. To help keep her refrigerated cargo holds cool, the ship's hull was painted light grey instead of DFDS' usual black. The grey colour would subsequently become synonymous

Above: The ***Primula*** of 1896 was one of DFDS' first ships purpose-built to link Copenhagen to the UK – a fitting name, as primulas tend to be amongst the first flowers to bloom in the spring. *(Museet for Søfart (CC-BY-NC-SA))*

Left: The ***Primula***'s sister ship Ficaria. Today, the names of both sisters live on in the DFDS fleet in the North Sea freight roros ***Ficaria Seaways*** and ***Primula Seaways***. *(F. Baunsgaard collection, Museet for Søfart (CC-BY-NC-SA))*

Middle left: Prior to the opening of the Kiel Canal, most DFDS Denmark-UK services continued further to the Baltic Sea ports of Russia and Germany; the ***Louise*** of 1872 is an example of these ships. Danish shipping companies had a strong presence in the services to Russia's Baltic provinces (today Estonia, Latvia and Lithuania). *(Museet for Søfart (CC-BY-NC-SA))*

Bottom left: Wilson Line's ***Zero***, seen here with the grey hull of Wilson's reefer ships, served the company for 35 years, until sold for scrap after a brief layup in 1932. *(Maritime Museum: Hull Museums)*

Below: The ***Una*** of 1899 was originally a Bailey & Leetham ship, but she is seen here after the 1903 takeover by Wilson Line. The Wilsons sold her to Spain already in 1909, but she went on to have a very long career under Spanish ownership, which ended only with her sinking in 1960. *(Maritime Museum: Hull Museums)*

Above: The ***J.C. la Cour*** was a something of an improvement for the Esbjerg-Harwich route when delivered in 1901. Her namesake, Jørgen Carl la Cour (1838-1898) was an important figure in the modernisation of Danish agriculture and the education of Danish farmers. *(Museet for Søfart (CC-BY-NC-SA))*

Left: A postcard view of Esbjerg harbour, with the 1883-built Esbjerg-Harwich paddle steamer ***Koldinghuus*** moored middle right. *(Museet for Søfart (CC-BY-NC-SA))*

Middle left: : An uncredited painting of the first DFDS Esbjerg-UK passenger and cargo steamer ***Riberhuus***, giving a nice illustration of the original DFDS livery. *(DFDS, Joonas Kortelainen collection)*

Bottom left: An impressive aft view of the ***J.C. la Cour*** at sea. The ship spent her entire 32-year career with DFDS. *(Bruce Peter collection)*

Below: The 1896-built ***N.J. Fjord*** at port. Niels Johannes Fjord (1825-1891) was a professor at the Danish Royal Veterinary and Agricultural University, and a pioneer in dairy and milk research. *(Museet for Søfart (CC-BY-NC-SA))*

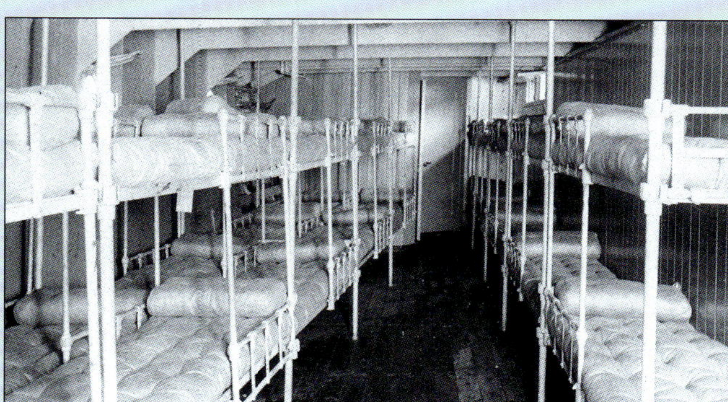

Above: The ***A.P. Bernstorff***, delivered in 1913, presented a more substantial exterior look than her predecessors. Andreas Peter Graf von Bernstorff (1735-1797) had been a pro-British diplomat, but was also known as a proponent of personal and political freedoms. *(Museet for Søfart (CC-BY-NC-SA))*

Left: The first class passengers of the ***J.C. la Cour*** travelled in plush comfort, such as in the lounge seen here. *(Museet for Søfart (CC-BY-NC-SA))*

Middle left: But the sleeping accommodation for the lower classes on the ***J.C. la Cour*** was of a quite different standard. *(Museet for Søfart (CC-BY-NC-SA))*

Bottom left: The ***Botnia*** of 1891, already familiar from Chapter 5, sailed on the Esbjerg-Harwich route between 1902 and 1909. *(Museet for Søfart (CC-BY-NC-SA))*

Below: Another view of the classically proportioned ***A.P. Bernstorff***. As we shall see, her career with DFDS lasted until her scrapping in 1955. *(Hans J. Hansen, Museet for Søfart (CC-BY-NC-SA))*

with DFDS' Denmark-UK service, while the other routes retained the black hulls. DFDS used numerous small steamers on the route alongside the *Koldinghuus*, but the next ship of note was the 1,425 grt *N.J. Fjord* delivered in 1896. She was a near-sister of the *Ficaria* and *Primula* mentioned above, but with capacity for 347 passengers.

In 1901, DFDS took delivery of another purpose-built passenger steamer *J.C. la Cour* (1,615 grt and 112 passengers) for the Esbjerg-Harwich route, now offering three weekly departures from both ports with the diverse trio of *Koldinghuus*, *N.J. Fjord* and *J.C. la Cour* (fittingly for a route carrying so many agricultural products, both *N.J. Fjord* and *J.C. la Cour* were named after 19th century figures important for the development of Danish agriculture). The *Koldinghuus* grounded and sunk outside Fanø in 1903; as a replacement,

The passenger-reefer ***Spero*** (2) of 1922 was not a lucky ship, grounding after just four months in service, being damaged in an air raid in 1943 and hitting a mine in 1947. Yet she served EWL until 1958. *(Postcard, Ian Boyle collection)*

An ice-encrusted ***Hroar*** at Hanko, Finland. The Finland-UK liner ***Arcturus*** (2) can be seen in the background on the left. *(Rami Wirrankoski collection)*

the 1891-built *Botnia* (1 032 grt and 243 passengers) was transferred to the route. She was no stranger on the service, having made occasional sailings on it since 1892 in addition to her primary Copenhagen-Hanko route. However, the *Botnia* was transferred to the Copenhagen-Edinburgh-Faroe Islands-Iceland service already in 1909, as discussed in Chapter 5. A proper running mate for the *J.C. la Cour* and *N.J. Fjord* was completed in 1913 in the form of the *A.P. Bernstorff*, named after an 18th century Danish diplomat, of 2,316 brt and 407 passengers.

World War I and stagnation in Copenhagen

The First World War interrupted sailings on most of the through services from the UK to the Baltic Sea via Copenhagen, and after the war many were converted to cargo-only services. Although passenger services from Copenhagen to British ports continued for decades, as we shall see below, there was little to no growth in passenger numbers – whereas on the Esbjerg routes, ship sizes would continue to grow and Esbjerg became the undisputed leading port on passenger lines to the UK.

As noted in the previous chapters, Wilson Line ended up under the personal ownership of Sir John Ellerman during World War I, and was resultingly renamed Ellerman's Wilson Line (EWL). Whereas increased competition from Nordic companies forced EWL to downsize and eventually abandon their passenger services to Sweden and Norway, the joint service agreement with DFDS guaranteed a continuation of EWL's presence on the Copenhagen-Hull route, despite the fact EWL had no usable passenger ships after the war. DFDS similarly suffered heavy losses: 26 vessels were lost, despite Denmark's neutrality in the conflict.

DFDS and EWL jointly ordered a pair of combined reefer-passenger vessels for the Copenhagen-Hull route in the early 1920s. EWL's *Spero* (2) was a 1,589 grt and 60 passenger vessel delivered in 1922, with DFDS' *Hroar* of 1,401 grt, but capacity for just 39 passengers, following a year later. DFDS' cargo vessels also carried a limited number of passengers from Copenhagen to London and Newcastle during the 1920s and 1930s.

EWL also took delivery of a second newbuilding for Copenhagen in 1922: the *Tasso* of 3,540 grt and 407 passengers was designed for the Danzig-Copenhagen-Hull service. The route was envisioned to carry Polish migrants on the first sea leg of their journey to North America. However, when the United States radically curtailed the number of immigrants allowed into the country the same year, the *Tasso* was superfluous from the start. She was sold to Poland in 1929, leaving the *Spero* (2) as EWL's only passenger vessel serving Denmark (and, eventually, the company's sole passenger vessel overall).

Furthermore, Copenhagen gained a new connection to the UK in the late 1920s, when the Soviet Union's Baltiyskoye Morskoye Parokhodstvo (Балтийское морское пароходство, BMP), opened a long-haul passenger-cargo service linking Leningrad to London via, amongst other ports, Copenhagen. This is covered in more detail in Chapter 2.

Growth in Esbjerg

Amongst the vessels DFDS lost during World War I was the Esbjerg-Harwich -steamer *N.J. Fjord*. Thus, when the service was re-initiated in December 1919 (the somewhat late date dictated by the need to clear mines blockading Esbjerg), sailing on it were the already familiar *J.C. la Cour* and *A.P. Bernstorff*, joined for the 1920 summer season by the 1906-vintage *Dronning Maud* (1,761 grt and 422 passengers), which had previously served the Stettin-Copenhagen-Christiania

Above left: The ***Dronning Maud*** was built in 1906 for the Stettin-Copenhagen-Frederikshavn-Kristiania route, but sailed between Esbjerg and Harwich 1920-1929. She remained with DFDS (excluding wartime service with the German Navy as the ***Almuth***) until 1947, when she was sold to Finnish owners as the ***Bore II*** and subsequently fitted with a dummy funnel forward of the real one. She was later sold to FÅA and scrapped in 1967 as the ***Silja II*** in the ripe age of 61. *(Museet for Søfart (CC-BY-NC-SA))*

Above right: The lead ship of DFDS' new class of the UK steamers, the ***Parkeston***, was externally near-identical to the older ***A.P. Bernstorff.*** She was the only ship of the class to resume DFDS service after World War II. After being sold by DFDS in 1964, the ***Parkeston*** saw a further service as an accommodation ship in Oslo, until scrapped in 1975. *(Bruce Peter collection)*

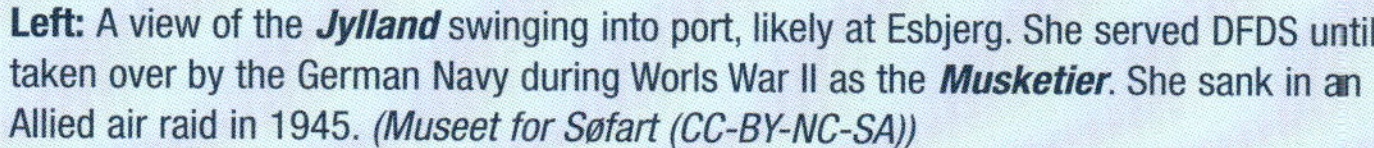

Left: A view of the ***Jylland*** swinging into port, likely at Esbjerg. She served DFDS until taken over by the German Navy during Worls War II as the ***Musketier***. She sank in an Allied air raid in 1945. *(Museet for Søfart (CC-BY-NC-SA))*

Middle left: The 1929-built ***Esbjerg*** was another World War II loss, but her wreck was sold to Spain for repairs, where she reappeared as the Trasmediterránea steamer ***Ciudad de Ibiza***, outliving her sisters by only being scrapped in 1978. *(Museet for Søfart (CC-BY-NC-SA))*

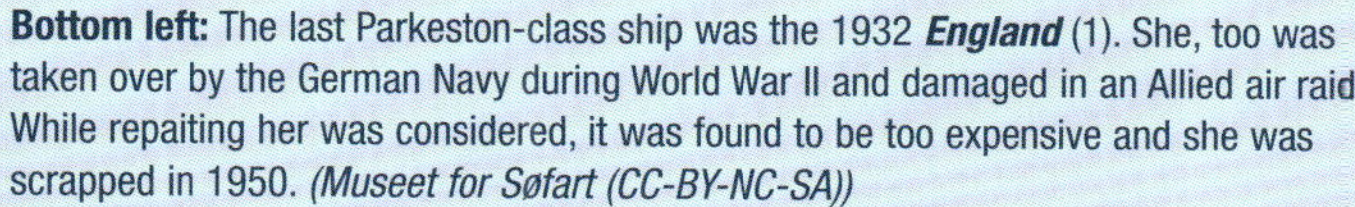

Bottom left: The last Parkeston-class ship was the 1932 ***England*** (1). She, too was taken over by the German Navy during World War II and damaged in an Allied air raid. While repaiting her was considered, it was found to be too expensive and she was scrapped in 1950. *(Museet for Søfart (CC-BY-NC-SA))*

Below: The first-class lounge of the ***England*** (1), decorated in somewhat uninspired neoclassical style – more than a bit out of touch for the era, considering she was delivered in 1932. *(Museet for Søfart (CC-BY-NC-SA))*

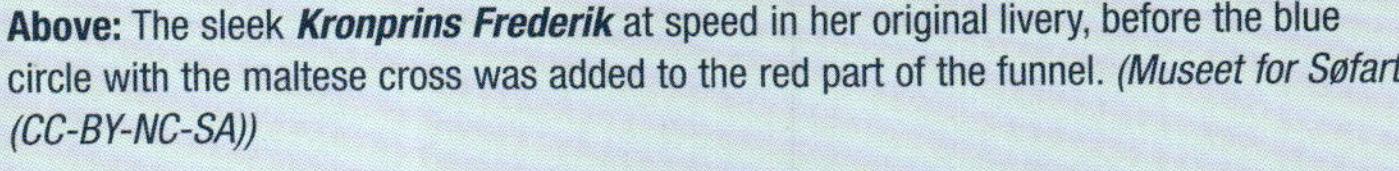
Above: The sleek ***Kronprins Frederik*** at speed in her original livery, before the blue circle with the maltese cross was added to the red part of the funnel. *(Museet for Søfart (CC-BY-NC-SA))*

Left: The first class dining room of the ***Kronprins Frederik***, with Scandinavian modernist stylings featuring plentiful wood panelling. *(Museet for Søfart (CC-BY-NC-SA))*

Middle left: The first class smoking room offered very impressive forward views from plush armchairs and sofas. *(Museet for Søfart (CC-BY-NC-SA))*

Bottom left: Waiters set the tables for service in the second class dining room – comfortable, but clearly more simply decorated than the first class counterpart. *(Museet for Søfart (CC-BY-NC-SA))*

Below: The launch of the ***Kronprins Frederik***'s sister ***Kronprinsesse Ingrid*** at the Helsingør shipyard in 1948. *(Museet for Søfart (CC-BY-NC-SA))*

An aerial view of the ***Kronprins Frederik*** towards the end of her DFDS career. She was laid up in 1974 and sold to Egyptian owners two years later. She caught fire and sank on the Red Sea on Christmas Eve 1976, with the loss of 102 lives – a sad fate for a ship that had been already near-destroyed by fire once in her career. *(FotoFlite)*

route. The *Dronning Maud* was made a permanent fixture on the Esbjerg-Harwich route in 1922 and for this she was refitted with refrigerated cargo holds. The *Dronning Maud*'s sister ship *Kong Haakon* of 1906 (1,761 grt and 336 passengers) also occasionally visited the route.

Soon, it seemed that the older tonnage could not cope with the growth projections. Thus, between 1925 and 1932, a quartet of new, larger vessels were delivered from the Helsingørs Jernskips og Maskinbyggeri shipyard in Helsingør (indeed, almost all of DFDS' new passenger ships discussed in this chapter came from that yard). What makes these four ships notable is the adoption of diesel engines, for the first time on passenger routes of this length, although in other respects they drew heavily from the *A.P. Bernstorff*. The *Parkeston* of 1925, *Jylland* of 1926, *Esbjerg* of 1929 and *England* (1) of 1932 had gross register tonnages of approximate 2,800. However, emphasis was more on cargo than in the previous vessels, and thus this quartet only had accommodation for 190 to 320 passengers, depending on the individual ship, and the passenger areas, designed by the Copenhagen architect Carl Brummer, were relatively basic. The quartet replaced the older ships on the route and offered daily departures from both ports – although the older ships would occasionally return to provide extra capacity. Initially, the *Parkeston*-class, particularly the latter two examples, seemed something of a mis-investment, due to the Great Depression that started in 1929 in the United States. During the early 1930s, the Esbjerg-Harwich route was operated at a notable loss.

As was the case with Copenhagen, it was also possible to sail from Esbjerg to other UK ports, such as London and Grimsby, on DFDS' cargo vessels, which often had limited passenger capacity.

An extended period of political wrangling took place during the early 1930s on whether or not DFDS would receive a massive state subsidy to build a new transatlantic liner for their Skandinavien-Amerika Linien subsidiary (DFDS were only willing to invest three million kroner but demanded an 18 million kroner subsidy). In the end, no subsidiary was forthcoming and DFDS closed down Skandinavien-Amerika Linien in 1935. This had a positive effect on passenger numbers of the Esbjerg-Harwich route, as DFDS now offered passengers bound to North America a crossing to Harwich, followed by an overland journey to Southampton, where they could join the ships of Cunard-White Star Line. Combined with improved rail links from Copenhagen to Esbjerg, this radically increased passenger numbers on the Esbjerg-Harwich route. During the late 1930s, DFDS begun planning a trio of larger liners with more emphasis on passenger accommodation, modelled after the 1937-built Copenhagen-Oslo ship *Kronprins Olav*. The intention was for the first ship to enter service in 1940, but war again broke out in Europe before this.

World War II and reconstruction

Denmark was invaded by Germany in April 1940, as a part of the latter's campaign to gain control of the iron ore shipments from Narvik in Norway. The Danish army was overrun in just six hours and Denmark became a German

The ***Kronprinsesse Ingrid*** photographed somewhere on the North Sea in 1966. Unusually, she left the DFDS earlier than her older sister, being sold in 1969. After a brief career with different Danish owners, she was sold to Greek owners and had a successful career in Greek waters from 1970 until 1983. She was scrapped in Pakistan in 1985. *(FotoFlite)*

Onboard the ***Kronprinsesse Ingrid***, the first class smoking room furniture was given different upholstery from her older sister, making them appear more modern – despite being otherwise identical. *(Museet for Søfart (CC-BY-NC-SA))*

Crates of butter are loaded onboard the ***Kronprinsesse Ingrid*** at Esbjerg in 1963. The safety equipment of the dockworkers seems decidedly inadequate for the job by today's standards. *(Museet for Søfart (CC-BY-NC-SA))*

protectorate. All passenger services between Denmark and the UK were terminated.

The new Esbjerg-Harwich ship, the *Kronprins Frederik*, was launched in June of the same year, after which construction was halted and she was laid up; DFDS even considered cancelling the contract altogether. According to the legend, several crucial parts of her engines were "misplaced" by the local resistance to stop the Germans from completing and making use of Denmark's to-be flagship. When Denmark was liberated in May 1945 by British and Soviet forces, these parts miraculously reappeared and completion of the *Kronprins Frederik* proceeded swiftly, with the ship able to enter service between Esbjerg and Harwich already in 1946. (The story is somewhat dubious, as nothing would have stopped the Germans from making suitable replacement parts themselved had they wanted to press the ship into service). The *Kronprins Frederik* could accommodate a maximum of 358 passengers, spread evenly between first and second class, in her 3,895 grt volume; the passenger accommodation, designed by Kay Fisker, was of a particularly good quality for the immediate post-war years.

The swift delivery of the *Kronprins Frederik* was a boon for DFDS, who had suffered heavy losses during the war; amongst the 27 lost vessels were the *Jylland, Esbjerg* and *England* (1). Thus, the *Kronprins Frederik* initially entered service alongside the *Parkeston* and, during the high season, the raged *A.P. Bernstoff*. To rectify the situation, DFDS quickly contracted a near-identical sister ship to the *Kronprins Frederik*, the *Kronprinsesse Ingrid* of 3,968 grt and 334 passengers, which was delivered in 1949. Her interiors were, at least arguably, more luxurious than those of the *Kronprins Frederik*. With the arrival of the *Kronprinsesse Ingrid*, both the *Parkeston* and *A.P. Bernstorff* were redeployed on a new

On the ***Kronprins Frederik*** and ***Kronprinsesse Ingrid***, the funnel was actually painted red with a black top, the top deck of the superstructure below the funnel painted black to give the effect of the full DFDS funnel colours. In views such as this one, the ships look almost like they are in the colours of EWL instead. *(FotoFlite)*

Copenhagen-Ålborg-Newcastle route – but this was a summer-only service, and both would occasionally return to Esbjerg-Harwich to cover for dockings. As mentioned above in Chapter 5, the services from Copenhagen to the Faroes and Iceland via Edinburgh were not restarted until 1952, and were again discontinued in 1955, which marked the final time passenger services from Denmark to Scottish capital were operated.

Meanwhile, services from Copenhagen were not entirely forgotten. In 1950, EWL took delivery of a new passenger-cargo steamer for their Copenhagen-Århus-Hull route. The *Borodino* of 3,206 grt and facilities for 57 passengers (plus large refrigerated cargo holds) would prove the last purpose-built passenger vessel for the Copenhagen-UK routes. The new ship replaced the older *Spero* (2), which was converted to a cargo-only vessel. Other Copenhagen-UK passenger services were offered by the Baltiyskoye Morskoye Parokhodstvo, whose vessels continued to sail via Copenhagen on their Leningrad-London line (discussed in more detail in Chapter 2). From 1947 until 1987, it was also possible to sail from Copenhagen to Southampton (until 1969) and later London Tilbury (from 1969) on the ships of the Polskie Linje Oceaniczne (Polish Ocean Lines) as a part of their longer services from Poland to North America and India.

Disaster struck DFDS in April 1953, when the *Kronprins Frederik* caught fire in Harwich, subsequently capsizing and partially sinking. Fortunately there were no passengers onboard at the time and the entire crew could be safely evacuated. The *Parkeston* was quickly roped in as a temporary replacement, while DFDS pondered what to do with their sunken ship. Simultaneously, the *A.P. Bernstoff* moved to a new Esbjerg-Newcastle service, with the Copenhagen-Ålborg-Newcastle passenger service abandoned. Meanwhile, DFDS

The 1950-vintage ***Borodino*** was the last conventional passenger-cargo steamer built for EWL. Her career lasted for just 17 years, being sold for scrap by EWL in 1967. *(Postcard, Ian Boyle collection)*

Polskie Linje Oceaniczne's ***Batory*** of 1936 photographed in Helsinki on the occasion of the 1952 Olympic Games. The ***Batory*** was replaced in 1968 with the former Holland America Line ship ***Stefan Batory***, which continued to offer a Copenhagen-UK connection as the part of longer liner services from Poland. *(Olympia-kuva, Helsingin kaupunginmuseo (CC BY 4.0))*

The capsized ***Kronprins Frederik*** at Harwich port, 1953. Notice people standing on the ship's side. *(Museet for Søfart (CC-BY-NC-SA))*

The battered ***Kronprins Frederik*** under tow from Harwich back to her builders at Helsingør for repairs. *(Museet for Søfart (CC-BY-NC-SA))*

decided to repair the *Kronprins Frederik*, despite the severity of the damage. In August, the ship was raised, and after temporary repairs in Harwich, the hulk was towed to Helsingør for rebuilding. The *Kronprins Frederik* returned to service after repairs in May 1954, allowing for the *Parkeston* to take over the Esbjerg-Newcastle line, with the *A.P. Bernstorff* left as a reserve ship. The latter's remaining career was short, being scrapped in 1955.

Dawn of the car ferry era

The 1960s was the era of the car ferry revolution on the services linking the Scandinavian countries to Britain. DFDS was the pioneer in adapting car ferries on these long-haul routes: the *England* (2), delivered in 1964 from Helsingør (where else?), was the first car ferry on the trans-North Sea routes. She was designed jointly by DFDS' own technical department, led by Brian P.C. Walker, and the builders. In profile, she heavily resembled the 1957-built Copenhagen-Oslo ferry *Prinsesse Margarethe*; indeed, this was DFDS' "company look" until the late 1960s.

The 8,221 grt *England* (2) could transport 467 passengers (some sources quote 399) in two classes, as well as a side-loading car deck 100 cars – but the deck height was too low to transport trucks or buses, and cargo was carried in conventional holds below the car deck. Despite the specification of a car deck, the cargo arrangements made the ship old-fashioned from the start. This was the result of DFDS chairman J.A. Kørbing's suspicion of the safety of the full-height, bow and stern loading car ferry designs favoured by most Scandinavian shipowners at the time. While Kørbing was not the only shipping company leader with such reservations, the fact they were allowed to override commercial concerns at such a relatively late date is surprising.

Inside, passenger areas were divided into two classes, with first class forward and second aft. On the saloon deck (the main public room deck) the galley was placed between the areas for the two classes, filling the entire width of the ship and making later conversion into one-class ship difficult. The interiors were designed by the Danish architect Kay Kørbing, the son of J.A. Kørbing, who worked on many DFDS newbuilds of the 1950s and 60s. On arrival, the *England* (2) replaced the *Kronprins Frederik*, which was cascaded to the Esbjerg-Newcastle service, replacing the *Parkeston*. During the winter season, the *England* (2) sailed on the Esbjerg-Harwich route alone, while the *Kronprinsesse Ingrid* was sent on long cruises from Copenhagen to the Canary Isles and the Western Mediterranean.

The *England* (2) was, despite her limitations, an immediate success and soon after her entry into service DFDS begun planning a sister ship. This was not immediately acted on, however, as the company wanted first to evaluate the success of the ship during the entire operational year and make improvements for the next vessel. Briefly, a joint ownership of the second ferry was discussed with Fred. Olsen, who suggested that the ship should sail on the Esbjerg-Harwich route during the summer season with DFDS and on a combined cargo and cruise operation from Northern Europe to

Above: A postcard view of the ***England*** (2) as built, with her original DFDS livery. As we shall see, she would go on to carry no less than four different liveries during her relatively short time with the company! *(Joonas Kortelainen collection)*

Left: Passengers disembarking from the ***England*** (2) at Harwich, possibly on the occasion of her maiden voyage to the port (she made several introductory cruises from Copenhagen before entering regular service). *(Museet for Søfart (CC-BY-NC-SA))*

Middle left: : A view from the first class hallway of the ***England*** (2) to the first class smoking room, decorated in fashionable hues of brown, orange, blue and white. *(Helsingør Skibsværft, Museet for Søfart (CC-BY-NC-SA))*

Bottom left: The ***England*** (2)'s second-class dining room was nearly identical to the first class counterpart in terms of decor, an indicator of the egalitarian trends in Scandinavia at the time. Here, the dominant colours we dark wood and turquise. *(Helsingør Skibsværft, Museet for Søfart (CC-BY-NC-SA))*

Below: The launch of the ***England*** (2) at Helsingør Skibsværft og Maskinbyggeri in December 1963. *(Berlingske Tidende, Museet for Søfart (CC-BY-NC-SA)*

the Canaries under the Fred. Olsen flag during the winter. No agreement was reached, apparently due to disagreements about the design, and, as we have seen above in Chapter 4, Fred. Olsen eventually chose collaboration with Det Bergenske Dampskibsselskab instead.

Thus, DFDS were left to realise the running mate to the *England* (2) alone. An order was placed in 1965, soon after DFDS discovered Lion Ferry and Wallenius had contracted overnight ferries for a new Bremerhaven-Harwich route, which DFDS saw as a competitor for their Esbjerg-Harwich route. In a break from tradition, the order was placed at the Riva Trigoso shipyard in Italy. The new, 8,657 grt, 462 passenger and 180 car vessel was delivered in 1967 as the *Winston Churchill*. In addition to being slightly larger, the *Winston*

The ***England*** (2) loading at Esbjerg. Her unusually high side-loading car deck required the construction of special ramps, restricting her use in other services. *(Museet for Søfart)*

A view of the ***England*** (2)'s car deck as built, with just three lanes for cars. The crew member standing in the distance gives an impression of how low the deck height was. *(Helsingør Skibsværft, Museet for Søfart (CC-BY-NC-SA))*

Churchill differed from the *England* (2) by having gates at bow and stern for loading and unloading cars and cargo, as well as sufficient deck height to carry trucks in parts of the car deck. While an improvement over the *England* (2), the limited freight-carrying capacity was still a retrograde choice compared to the new trans-North Sea ferries of Tor Line, Fred. Olsen and BDS, described in the previous chapters, and indeed also the aforementioned new Prinzen Linie Bremerhaven-Harwich ferry *Prinz Hamlet* (1).

Coinciding with the arrival of the new ship, a new terminal was taken into use in Esbjerg. The *Winston Churchill*'s delivery also allowed for another tonnage cascade, with the *Kronprinsesse Ingrid* moved to the Esbjerg-Newcastle route, replacing the *Kronprins Frederik*, which now moved to a Denmark-Faroe Islands-Iceland service. Winter-season cruising continued, but now the *England* (2) was sent cruising to the Mediterranean and even Caribbean, while the *Winston Churchill* remained on the Esbjerg-Harwich route. The *England* (2) was refitted with an outdoors swimming pool and, unlike the *Kronprinsesse Ingrid* before her, was very popular as a cruise ship – despite the fact her rigid class separation made her interiors somewhat ill-suited for the role.

A further development in 1967 was the withdrawal of the *Borodino* from EWL's Copenhagen-Århus-Hull route, ending their involvement in Denmark-UK passenger trades. Now, only Soviet and Polish shipping companies offered passenger connections from Copenhagen to the UK.

Ships on the secondary Esbjerg-Newcastle service were shuffled around somewhat during the following years: the *Kronprinsesse Ingrid* was sold ahead of the 1969 summer season, and her place was taken over by the broadly similar but newer *Prinsessen*, a 5,061 grt, 1,200 passenger and 35 car ferry originally built in 1957 as the *Prinsesse Margrethe* for the Copenhagen-Oslo run. The *Prinsessen* was, in turn, sold in late 1971. To continue the summer service to Newcastle, the *Kronprins Frederik*'s previous service – which linked Copenhagen to Reykjavik via three intermediate calls in the Faroe Islands – was altered to Esbjerg-Newcastle-Tórshavn. The move of the company's oldest surviving passenger ship to the Esbjerg-Newcastle service was an interesting, if not perhaps entirely welcome, development.

The 1970s newbuildings

The Esbjerg-Harwich link was DFDS' prime passenger service from the 1960s until the 1980s, and it experienced constant growth in both cargo and passenger numbers. Passenger numbers were affected by the fact that, since the arrival of the *Winston Churchill*, return trips on the route were marketed as minicruises. As the premiere route, Esbjerg-Harwich usually enjoyed DFDS' newest and largest vessels.

Soon after the delivery of the *Winston Churchill*, DFDS begun planning a replacement for the *England* (2). The original intention was for a ship very similar to the *Winston Churchill*, with a limited cargo capacity and a relatively small passenger capacity of 609. The appointment in 1969 of a new director of passenger operations, Rudolf Bier, resulted in a change of plans: instead of contracting a new ship already in 1969, the projected ship was entirely redesigned, resulting ina delay of several years.

Bier envisioned DFDS morphing into a modern cruise and ferry operator with a product similar to Stena Line and Prinzen Linie, describing the future ships as "floating Tivolis" (after the famous amusement park in central Copenhagen). As an initial update, the *England* (2) and *Winston Churchill* were converted into single-class ships and rebuilt with additional cabin accommodation in the former cargo holds in 1971, increasing

Above: An impressive view of the ***Winston Churchill*** at sea during the early years of her career. Unusually, she had an aft visor to hide the aft car ramp, giving her the appearance of a traditional liner, when she was, in reality, a drive-through ferry with ramps both forward and aft. *(Suomen laivahistoriallinen yhdistys)*

Below left: The Saga Lounge onboard the ***Winston Churchill***, photographed during the 1980s but still largely unchanged from the original. *(Andrew Kilk, Bruce Peter collection)*

Bottom left: A 1983 view of the Tivoli Restaurant of the ***Winston Churchill,*** decorated in bright colours fashionable in the late-1960s, but perhaps somewhat outdated for the early 1980s. *(Bruce Peter collection)*

Below right: The ***Winston Churchill*** under construction on the slipway of the Riva Trigoso shipyard in Italy. Although she looks relatively complete on the outside, after launching she was towed to Genoa for outfitting. *(Museet for Søfart (CC-BY-NC-SA))*

A 1969 aerial view of the ***England*** (2, closer to the camera) and ***Winston Churchill*** passing at sea. This photo nicely illustrates how similar the ships appeared externally, despite the ***Winston Churchill*** being notably larger and having different car deck arrangements. *(FotoFlite)*

The ***England*** (2) in the twilight of her DFDS career in the all-white DFDS Seaways livery. Although she had been the car-ferry pioneer of the North Sea, her nonstandard car deck arrangement meant she was quickly outdated – and unlike, for example, the ESL ships discussed in Chapter 3, she could not be easily modified. *(FotoFlite)*

The 1957-built ***Prinsessen*** (ex-***Prinsesse Margrethe***), seen here in sore need of a new lick of paint, served on the Esbjerg-Newcastle route during summers 1969-1971. In the latter year she became the ***Prinsessan*** (note the different Swedish spelling), the first ship of the successful Finnish shipping company Birka Line. *(Knud Fredfeldt, Museet for Søfart (CC-BY-NC-SA))*

their passenger capacities to 566 and 590, respectively. At the same time they were painted in a new white-hulled livery, with the DFDS Seaways brand name painted on in blue letters.

Meanwhile, the design of the new Esbjerg-Harwich ferry continued under the project name "Dana Futura", taking the form of a combined ferry and cruise ship. When finally delivered in 1974 from Aalborg Værft in Ålborg, the ship was named *Dana Regina* (the name *Dana Futura* was used on a 1975 cargo vessel instead) and replaced the *England* (2) as the *Winston Churchill*'s running mate. Compared to the 1960s-built vessels, the *Dana Regina* was an entirely different animal: at 12,192 grt, combined with a capacity for 975 passengers and 250 cars, she was a superlative ship – and the first Danish-flagged passenger vessel to surpass the 1914-built transatlantic liner *Frederik VIII* in size. Her interiors, again designed by Kay Kørbing, were built to a standard suitable for upmarket cruising, drawing from the recent *Queen Elizabeth 2* and the also-Kørbing-designed Norske Amerikalinje luxury cruise ship *Vistafjord*. Although envisioned as the first of several sister ships, in the end the *Dana Regina* was a one-off. The first Oil Crisis radically increased her construction price, which was already inflated by the luxurious fittings. According to Bruce Peter's book *DFDS 150*, the contract price of a more conventional North Sea ferry of the same capacity would have been circa 70 million Danish kroner, but the cruise-quality fittings combined with inflation raised the final price to 140 million. At the same time, the new ships' champion Rudolf Bier had fallen out of favour with DFDS' owners and left the company in 1973. With Bier's departure, all thoughts of cruise service for the *Dana Regina* were abandoned, and the previous off-season cruising using the Esbjerg-Harwich vessels also ceased.

The fleet redeployments allowed by the arrival of the *Dana*

The ***Winston Churchill*** seen in the first variation of the DFDS Seaways livery. Her captain K.T. Greaki supposedly said the blue band made the ship look like a tub of margarine, and the livery was quickly altered to the all-white seen on the facing page. *(Postcard, Joonas Kortelainen collection)*

DFDS's 1974-built flagship ***Dana Regina*** differed very much from the previous generation in terms of design. *(Postcard, Joonas Kortelainen collection)*

Above: An aerial view of the ***Dana Regina***, likely taken outside Harwich. *(FotoFlite)*

Left: Thanks to the latest safety regulations, the ***Dana Regina***'s interiors were mostly decorated in colourful synthetic materials. The Mermaid Bar seen here was clad in purple leather. *(Knud Fredfeldt, Museet for Søfart (CC-BY-NC-SA))*

Middle left: The foyer onboard the ***Dana Regina*** – naturally, as a single-class ship, there was no longer any need for duplication of spaces. *(Museet for Søfart (CC-BY-NC-SA))*

Bottom left: The cocktail bar and sitting lounge, also referred to as the restaurant arcade, outside the Codan Restaurant onboard the ***Dana Regina***, with the spiral staircase leading up to the Bellevue Lounge on Boat Deck. *(Knud Fredfeldt, Museet for Søfart (CC-BY-NC-SA))*

Below: The ***Dana Regina***'s night club, the Compass Club, with fashionable furniture by Jan Ekselius. *(Bruce Peter collection)*

The ***Dana Regina*** passes the Prinzen Linie Hamburg-Harwich ferry ***Prinz Hamlet*** (2). DFDS's worries about Prinzen Linie proved exaggerated – the original ***Prinz Hamlet*** (1) by proved too large for the service, despite the original vision for two ships, and was quickly replaced by a smaller vessel. Eventually, the entire service passed to DFDS in 1981. *(FotoFlite)*

Regina meant the *England* (2) replaced the *Kronprins Frederik* on the summer services from Esbjerg to Newcastle and Tórshavn. Instead of running to Tórshavn via Newcastle, route was broken into two separate services, with alternating departures from Esbjerg to both other ports. At the same time, the *England*'s car capacity was increased to 120, when interior cabins flanking the car deck were removed. This was not enough to meet demand, however, and additional cars were often stored on the aft outer decks. During the winter of 1974-75, the *England* (2) was chartered to Det Bergenske Dampskibsselskab for Bergen-Newcastle service, as explained in Chapter 4.

The *Dana Regina* and *Winston Churchill* made another mismatched part, and plans to replace the latter were soon underway. Rather than opt for a sister ship to the *Dana Regina*, which on top of her huge cost was already proving too small (DFDS had perhaps failed to foresee the growth of business following from Denmark and the UK both joining the European Communities in 1973), DFDS' new leadership wanted a much larger ferry. Initially, the plan was to contract a sister ship the recent TT-Line 'jumbo ferries' *Peter Pan* (1; 1974) and *Nils Holgersson* (1975) from Werft Nobiskug in West Germany. A contract had already been negotiated, when DFDS were advised by their owners to instead build the ship at Aalborg Værft, which was owned by the same interest – despite a higher contract price. To decrease costs, DFDS sent the drawings prepared by Werft Nobiskug to Aalborg Værft, but without permission from the German yard. Fortunately, the shipyards were eventually able to agree on compensations.

The result, delivered in 1978 as the *Dana Anglia*, was in many ways an "economy version" of the TT-Line ships she was modelled on, and certainly not as well-appointed as the *Dana Regina*. However, at 14,400 grt, with space for 1,372

The ***Dana Anglia*** was clearly the product of a new era, an early example of the jumbo ferry that was to become common in Northern Europe in the next decade. However, as the ***Dana Anglia*** was the last newbuilt ship for the Nordics-UK routes of the century, jumbo ferries never had a big impact on the route. *(Postcard, Joonas Kortelainen collection)*

A view of the ***Dana Anglia*** outside Harwich, displaying her unusual looks with an angular superstructure and very high funnel. *(Krzysztof Brzoza collection)*

passengers (1,249 had cabin berths) and no less than 470 cars, the *Dana Anglia* was very efficient. Efficiency had also been the keyword of her final design process, with the cheapest possible constructions chosen for her exterior, resulting in the unusually high funnel (it was cheaper to build a high funnel than add the smoke-deflecting fin that had been originally planned). To keep costs down, the interior design and provision of artworks was entrusted to the artist Hannelore Lauritzen – the wife of DFDS chairman Knud Lauritzen – working together with the shipyard's drawing office.

The arrival of the *Dana Anglia* allowed for the *Winston Churchill* to be moved to a new summer service between

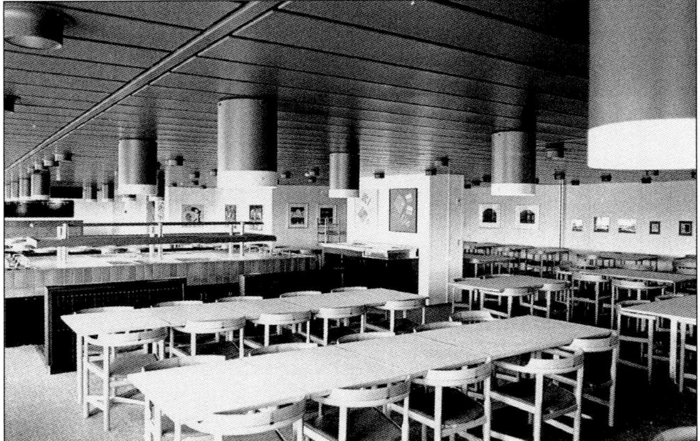

The Tivoli Restaurant onboard the ***Dana Anglia*** is representative of the minimalist interior design. The ceilings were painted dark brown to keep the unavoidable nicotine stains from showing. *(Museet for Søfart (CC-BY-NC-SA))*

The port side of the ***Dana Anglia***'s car deck, with the hoistable platforms allowing the carriage of more cars in the process of being raised or lowered. *(Museet for Søfart (CC-BY-NC-SA))*

Gothenburg and Newcastle operated jointly with Tor Line, discussed in detail in Chapter 3. After this ended in a serious grounding accident in the Gothenburg archipelago in late summer 1979, the *Winston Churchill* joined the *England* (2) on the Esbjerg-Newcastle and Esbjerg-Tórshavn routes. Prior to the arrival of the *Dana Anglia*, the *Dana Regina* was rebuilt to increase her car capacity, albeit it still fell short of the larger running mate.

Renaissance and end of services from Copenhagen

Although almost entirely forgotten today, the *Dana Anglia* was not the only new ferry to appear on Denmark-UK routes during 1978, as Copenhagen also (briefly) gained a car-passenger ferry link to Britain. Polska Żegluga Bałtycka (better known with the marketing name Polferries), the 1976-established Polish state-owned ferry operator, took delivery of their first newbuilt vessel, the *Pomerania*, from the Stoczni Szczecińskiej im. A. Warskiego yard in Szczecin. In a somewhat unusual move, the new 7,414 grt, 984 passenger (436 cabin berths) and 277 car vessel opened a new service, linking Świnoujście in Poland to Felixstowe via Copenhagen.

The service was unsuccessful: although prices on the Copenhagen-Felixstowe route were similar to those asked by DFDS on the Esbjerg-Harwich route, the sailing time wasn't: Esbjerg-Harwich on DFDS took only 19 hours, but Copenhagen-Felixstowe crossing on the *Pomerania* took a leisurely 44 hours. Already in 1979, the route was abandoned and the *Pomerania* moved to the Gdynia-Nynäshamn-Helsinki line. A contributing factor may have been the existence of the Gdynia-Felixstowe cargo route operated by a different Polish state-owned shipping company, the aforementioned Polskie Linie Oceaniczne. It is perhaps of interest to note that PLO's 1980-delivered newbuilding for the service, the *Inowrocław*, was designed with provisions for conversion into a car-passenger ferry, although this never took place.

After the closure of Polferries' link from Copenhagen to Felixstowe, it was still possible to sail from the Danish capital to Britain on the service offered by the Soviet's Baltiyskoye Morskoye Parokhodstvo (BMP) onboard the aged *Baltika* on the Leningrad-London (Tilbury) route (see Chapter 2), and onboard PLO's *Stefan Batory* as a part of her lengthy Gdynia-Montreal service, which called in both Copenhagen and London (Tilbury) along the way. BMP's Leningrad-London service was closed at some point between 1977 and 1986, while PLO closed down their transatlantic service in 1987, which finally meant the end of Copenhagen's passenger link to the UK.

Growth and difficulties

The early 1980s would prove the golden era for Denmark-UK routes, with passenger numbers reaching their all-time high in 1982. At the same time DFDS was aggressively expanding in other fronts, and much of the investments on other routes proved ill-advised. While the Denmark-UK routes flourished, the difficulties faced by the company elsewhere would prove to have a knock-on effect on their most profitable services.

As explained in detail in the previous chapters, in 1981 DFDS took over the Norway-UK services of Fred. Olsen-Bergen Line (see Chapter 4), Tor Line's Sweden-UK services (see Chapter 3) and the Bremerhaven and Hamburg to Harwich operator Prinzenlinie (being a West Germany-UK operation, it falls outside the scope of this book). At the same time, DFDS started its North American ferry cruising arm, Scandinavian World Cruises, which would prove to be a

The **Dana Gloria** (1) was originally the FÅA-owned Silja Line ferry **Wellamo**, one of three identical sisters built in France in 1975 for the Helsinki-Stockholm route. She was later lenghtened by DFDS for the Copenhagen-Oslo route, and in that guise she later enjoyed a long career on the Bergen-Newcastle route, as discussed in Chapter 4. *(FotoFlite)*

mistake of colossal dimensions and nearly bankrupted the company.

The Denmark-UK services also got their share of new investment: in 1981 DFDS purchased the 1975-built Silja Line ferry *Wellamo* (2) from Effoa (formerly Finska Ångfartygs Aktiebolaget, encountered previously in Chapter 2).The 12,348 grt vessel had a well-appointed accommodation for 1,200 passengers, but a relatively small car deck for 240 cars. She was renamed *Dana Gloria* (1) and placed on the Esbjerg-Newcastle and Gothenburg-Newcastle lines, replacing the *Winston Churchill*. The latter now took over the Denmark-Faroe Islands service, whereas the *England* (2) spent the summers sailing from both Esbjerg and Oslo to Newcastle.

The *England*'s (2) last involvement with the UK routes was the 1982 summer season, her inability to carry commercial vehicles having made her obsolete after less than two decades. In early 1983 she was sold to Cunard for use as a troopship in the construction efforts following the Falklands War, without a change of name. At the same time six other DFDS ships, including the *Winston Churchill*, were put up for sale. While Cunard had ambitions to rebuild the *England* (2) as a cruise ship, she subsequently had a brief career as an accommodation ship until laid up at Eleusis in Greece in 1987. There she lingered, butchered after an abandoned rebuilding into a private yacht, before sinking en-route to scrappers in 2001.

Decline

DFDS' near-fatal expansion was followed by a vigorous rationalisation programme. The *Dana Regina* and *Dana Gloria* (1) were transferred to the Copenhagen-Oslo run at the end of the 1983 summer season, and would not return to the Denmark-UK routes again (although the *Dana Gloria* (1) later

The **Dana Gloria** (1)'s Compass Club discotheque as it appeared in 1986, after she had been moved to the Copenhagen-Oslo route. *(Bruce Peter collection)*

A 1986 of the **Dana Gloria** (1)'s Mermaid Restaurant. The original interior design by Vuokko Laakso had favoured tubular steel furniture, but by this time DFDS had replaced these Borge Morgensen-designed furniture also used on the **Dana Anglia**. *(Bruce Peter collection)*

Above: : DFDS's 1980s policy of using ships sailing from the UK hubs of Harwich and Newcastle on alternating sailing to several Scandinavian ports brought the Sweden-service sisters ***Tor Britannia*** (pictured) and ***Tor Scandinavia*** to the Esbjerg-Harwich route, alongside the Gothenburg-Harwich service, between 1983 and 1990. *(FotoFlite)*

Top left: The ***England*** (2) in Cunard Line funnel colours; she never entered commercial service with the company, rather being used as a military transport after the Falklands war. She was never used in normal ferry service after leaving the DFDS fleet in 1982. *(Krzysztof Brzoza collection)*

Middle left: The use of ships on alternating sailing from the UK also brought the Norway-UK ships, such as the ***Jupiter*** (3) seen here, to the Esbjerg-Newcastle summer sailings. *(Krzysztof Brzoza collection)*

Bottom left: The former ***Prinz Hamlet*** (2) sailed from Newcastle to Esbjerg and Gothenburg as the ***Prins Hamlet*** in 1987 and 1988. *(FotoFlite)*

Bottom right: The ***Braemar*** (2) offered an unusual connection from the northern Jutland port of Hirtshals to Harwich, and later Newcastle, as a part of a longer service from Oslo, during the second half of the 1980s. *(FotoFlite)*

sailed between Norway and the UK for Color Line and Fjord Line, as discussed in Chapter 4). Neither received a full-time replacement. Instead, the *Tor Britannia* and *Tor Scandinavia* purchased from Tor Line started making Esbjerg-Harwich sailings alongside their previous Gothenburg-Harwich route. A similar arrangement for the Esbjerg-Newcastle route was made using the *Jupiter* (2) and *Venus* (3) chartered from Fred. Olsen-Bergen Line (see Chapter 4) during the 1984 summer season.

At the same time, a threat loomed for DFDS' monopoly on the Denmark-UK services. The previously state-owned UK ferry operator Sealink was sold to Sea Containers, a Bermuda-based company owned by the American-born businessman James Sherwood. When the new owners took over Sealink at the end of July 1984, they made public their intention to open a service from Harwich to Denmark. This, like many other plans made public following privatisation, was never realised – although, as noted in Chapter 4, Sealink did not abandon their ambitions for a service to Scandinavia.

With no competition forthcoming, things continued very much as before. For the summers of 1985 and 1986, the *Jupiter* (2) was joined by the *Winston Churchill*, as the *Venus* (3) left the fleet due to DFDS' gradual divesting of the Norway-UK operations (and no buyer had been found for the *Winston Churchill* in the interim). For the 1987 and 1988 summer seasons, the *Jupiter* (2) was replaced by the *Prins Hamlet* (originally *Prinz Hamlet* (2) acquired with Prinzenlinie earlier in the decade), a 5,829 grt, 1,100 passenger and 225 car ferry built in 1973. At the same time, the *Winston Churchill* began part-time cruising in North European waters. The *Prins Hamlet* was sold at the end of the 1988 summer season, and the next year *Winston Churchill* was again the sole Esbjerg-Newcastle ship. By this time the service was far from regular, as the ship also continued Esbjerg-Torshavn sailings and cruising.

The middle of the decade did see competition for DFDS' services appear, but from ports in northern Jutland and not by Sealink. As explained above in Chapter 4, Fred. Olsen Lines operated their impressive cruise ferry *Braemar* (2) on a service linking Oslo to Harwich via Hirtshals in Denmark from Autumn 1985 onwards. Around the same time, it was also been possible to sail to Lerwick on the Shetland Islands from Hanstholm (also in northern Jutland) with Smyril Line's *Norröna* (1) during the summer seasons, as explained in Chapter 5. The route of the *Braemar* (2) was altered in 1989 to Oslo-Hirtshals-Newcastle, but the service was discontinued in Autumn 1990. Smyril Line suspended their Lerwick calls in 1993, after which DFDS were again the sole Denmark-UK passenger operator.

From the mid-1980s DFDS initiated a protracted rebranding effort. First, the livery was changed to all white with diagonal blue stripes (this had been the livery of the ill-fated Scandinavian World Cruises) in 1985 and the marketing name of the passenger operations was altered to Scandinavian Seaways in 1989. At the same time, a gradual renaming of the passenger vessels with *of Scandinavia* -suffixes began.

Increased competition from airlines was a part reason for

The ***Dana Anglia*** in port, showing the new Scandinavian Seaways branding and "racing stripes" livery taken into use in the mid-1980s – DFDS leadership at the time believed the DFDS name was too strange for non-Danes, particularly Britons, hence the rebranding. *(Miles Cowsill)*

A 1992 aerial view of the *Winston Churchill* at sea. Despite the fact she had a limited cargo capacity, the ship survived in the DFDS fleet for 29 years – and even then her career was cut short by an engine fire, which put hold to plans to use her on a new Norway-Netherlands service. (FotoFlite)

SCANDINAVIAN
SEAWAYS

The ***King of Scandinavia*** (2) was acquired in a ship swap with Color Line in 1994. Built in 1974, she had been employed on the Sweden-West Germany routes of Sessanlinjen and Stena Line, followed by a series of charters in the late 1980s, before a sale to Norway Line for Bergen-Newcastle services in 1990, as discussed in Chapter 4. *(FotoFlite)*

A spring 1999 view of the ***Dana Anglia*** at Esbjerg, now painted in the recently re-introduced DFDS Seaways branding. She was rebuilt with large side sponsons for added stability the following year. *(Marko Stampehl)*

The ***King of Scandinavia*** served on a variety of routes; here she is seen in 1995 at Hamburg. The ship survives in service today as the European Seaways ferry ***Prince***. *(Marko Stampehl)*

the rebranding. Dropping passenger figures also resulted in a route reorganisation on the services from Gothenburg. For the Denmark-UK services this had the knock-on effect of the *Tor Britannia* and *Tor Scandinavia* no longer sailing on the Esbjerg-Harwich route after 1990. The service was thus reduced to just one ship, the *Dana Anglia*.

In 1993, the *Winston Churchill*'s summer ferry service was changed to alternating sailings from Newcastle to Esbjerg and Hamburg. For the 1995 summer season, she was replaced by the new *King of Scandinavia* (2), which DFDS had acquired by selling the *King of Scandinavia* (1), previously the *Dana Gloria* (1), to Color Line, and accepting Color's Norway-UK ferry *Venus* (4) as part payment. The new *King of Scandinavia* (2) was not actually that new, dating from 1974 (see Chapter 4 for details about her career on Norway-UK routes). She was 13,336 grt with capacity for 1,230 passengers and 300 cars. The *Winston Churchill* went on to serve one further season with DFDS, on the Newcastle-Amsterdam line, but a fire in one of the auxiliary engines stopped her planned further career with the company. She was instead sold in 1996 to a new operator planning to use her on the Caribbean, but this never materialised and she was scrapped in 2004. The remaining time of the Esbjerg-Newcastle service was short – the *King of Scandinavia* (2) sailed on it only during the 1995 summer season, after which the route was closed down and the *King of Scandinavia* (2) became a reserve vessel.

In autumn 1995, DFDS had just one passenger vessel left sailing between Denmark and Britain: the venerable *Dana Anglia*, which had faithfully continued on the Esbjerg-Harwich service despite all the changes taking place around her. In late 1998, the *King of Scandinavia* (2) briefly covered for a docking of the *Dana Anglia*, marking one last appearance on the Denmark-UK routes (despite her age, the former *King of*

The ***Dana Anglia***'s Blue Riband restaurant as it appeared after the 1993 refit, with opulent interiors from Tillberg Design – a stark contrast to the original interior as seen on page 142. *(Bruce Peter collection)*

The ***Dana Gloria*** (2) updated the Esbjerg-Harwich route to the ropax era, but she was known to be a temporary solution from the start. *(John Bryant)*

This aft view of the ***Dana Gloria*** (2), taken on her first departure from Harwich with passengers, nicely illustrates how much of her was dedicated to the carriage of freight. Note also the unique DFDS Ro-pax branding on her side, illustrating that she truly was a ship of a new breed for the Scandinavia-UK routes. *(John Bryant)*

Trailers packed tight on the ***Dana Gloria*** (2)'s weather deck as she prepares to depart Harwich. In the background is the Cuxhaven-Harwich ferry ***Admiral of Scandinavia*** (ex-***Hamburg***), which was withdrawn shortly after the ***Dana Gloria*** (2) entered service. *(John Bryant)*

Scandinavia (2) still exists in active service in the Mediterranean at the time of writing). 1998 also marked a change in DFDS Group's company structure, which led to the abandoning of the Scandinavian Seaways brand name in favour of the old form DFDS Seaways.

However, the *Dana Anglia* did not remain the only Denmark-UK passenger ferry for long: the 1999 summer season saw the restoration of Smyril Line's services from Hanstholm to Lerwick, as a part of the longer Denmark-Faroe Islands-Iceland route, as explained in Chapter 5.

The ropax era and the end

After the end of tax free sales in intra-European Union ferry services in July 1999, the passenger-oriented *Dana Anglia* was no longer profitable on the Esbjerg-Harwich route. DFDS felt there was a future for the service, if a vessel to more suitable to the demands of the new era could be found. A solution was discovered at the Stocznia Szczecinska im. A. Warskiego shipyard in Poland in 2002: the Italian shipping company Lloyd Sardegna had contracted two ropax ferries, to be named *Golfo dei Coralli* and *Golfo dei Delfini*, but had cancelled the contract after severe delays, which had caused the yard to go bankrupt. The ships were now in the hands of the shipyard's creditors, Bank Polska Kasa Opieki, from whom DFDS purchased them in July 2002. The near-complete *Golfo Dei Coralli* was renamed *Dana Gloria* (2). During the rest of the 2002 summer season she was used on the Esbjerg-Harwich route as a cargo ferry, then in the autumn her passenger accommodation was completed, and in the beginning of October the *Dana Gloria* (2) replaced the *Dana Anglia* as the passenger vessel on the Esbjerg-Harwich service. Following the finalisation of her construction, the *Dana Gloria* (2) was 20,140 gross tons (under the new measurement rules) with capacity for just 308 passengers but 2,600 lane metres of cargo. Having been supplanted on her original route, the *Dana Anglia* was renamed *Duke of Scandinavia* and used to open a new (but short-lived) Denmark-Poland service. She remains in service today in the Mediterranean as the *Moby Corse*.

A change of guard at Esbjerg, June 2003: the ***Dana Gloria*** (2, left) arrives on her last crossing from Harwich, while the ***Dana Sirena*** (2) waits to start on her maiden voyage on the same route. The latter sister is easily identifiable by the round windows of the public rooms added to the original cargo deck, missing from the older sibling. *(Søren Lund Hviid)*

The ***Dana Sirena*** (2) photographed at Harwich, 2008, showing her unusual hybrid livery: the white hull and blue funnel in the style of DFDS LISCO combined with the DFDS Tor Line brand name on the side – and all this on a ship marketed as a part of the DFDS Seaways fleet! *(John Bryant)*

An aft view of the ***Dana Sirena*** (2). Compare with the similar view of the ***Dana Gloria*** (2) on page 150 to get an idea of the extent of her superstructure expansion done after her takeover by DFDS. Note also the impressive panoramic windows of the Commodore Lounge between the lifeboats. *(John Bryant)*

The Lighthouse Café on the ***Dana Sirena*** (2), located in the area that was originally conceived as a part of the cargo decks. *(Sverre Andread Rud)*

The Columbus bar of the ***Dana Sirena*** (2) was decorated in the relatively simple style also used onboard the ***Dana Gloria*** (2). Elsewhere, the ***Dana Sirena*** (2) was given interiors more in style of the rest of the DFDS Seaways fleet. *(John Bryant)*

The *Dana Gloria* (2) was known to be a temporary solution from the start. After DFDS purchased her sister, the incomplete *Golfo dei Delfini*, the latter ship was taken to the Remontowa shipyard in Gdansk, Poland, for completion in revised form, with a notable larger passenger accommodation than originally projected. Named *Dana Sirena* (2), the second ship's larger superstructure increased her gross tonnage to 22,382, while the passenger capacity increased to 600. Due to conversion of a part of the upper cargo deck into passenger areas, the cargo capacity decreased to 2,060 lane metres. In June 2003, the *Dana Sirena* (2) replaced the *Dana Gloria* (2). Unusually, both the *Dana Gloria* (2) and *Dana Sirena* (2) were painted all-white with a blue funnel and DFDS Ropax and DFDS Tor Line, respectively, on the sides in place of the DFDS Seaways brand name – despite the fact they were marketed to passengers as DFDS Seaways ships (although both were owned by the DFDS Tor Line branch of the group). On arrival of the *Dana Sirena* (2), the *Dana Gloria* (2) was transferred to the DFDS subsidiary DFDS Lisco and renamed *Lisco Gloria* for service on the Baltic Sea. She was destroyed in a fire in 2010.

From the end of the 2006 summer season, the *Dana Sirena* (2) was the sole passenger vessel sailing from Denmark to the UK, as Smyril Line discontinued their intermediate calls at Lerwick on the Shetland Islands on the Hanstholm-Tórshavn-Seydisfjördur route operated by the *Norröna* (2). In 2008, the *Dana Sirena* (2) became the only passenger vessel in service between the Nordic Countries and the UK, as the Faroes-UK and Norway-UK routes were closed down, as explained in Chapters 4 and 5.

While the *Dana Sirena* (2) sailed on the Esbjerg-Harwich route for over a decade, she was not the success as DFDS had hoped for. A former DFDS employee explained to the author that a part of the problem was running the Esbjerg-

The former ***Dana Sirena*** (2) photographed in 2013, after repainting in the new blue-hulled DFDS Seaways livery and renaming into ***Sirena Seaways*** in accordance to the new naming convention. However, she carried this livery and name for only a short while, as the service closed at the end of the 2014 summer season. *(John Bryant)*

Harwich route as a single-ship service; with no possibility of daily departures, both prospective passengers and freight hauliers shied away from the route, despite a timetable that theoretically made it a good option to, for example, Denmark-UK business travellers as an alternative to flying. It seems that fixing this issue, for instance by bringing the *Dana Gloria* (2) back as the *Dana Sirena*'s running mate, was never seriously considered.

In 2013, DFDS reorganised and simplified their brand structure, unifying all the different operations under a single DFDS Seaways brand, with the ships given new, Seaways-suffixed names and a blue-hulled livery (this was in part a cost-saving measure, as the largest DFDS sub-brand, DFDS Tor Line, already carried a blue-hulled livery and thus for the majority of the fleet only minimal repainting was necessary). With the rebranding, the white-hulled *Dana Sirena* (2) became the blue-hulled *Sirena Seaways* (also marking the end of the elegant Dana-prefixed names, first taken into use in the 1970s).

Time was running out for the Esbjerg-Harwich service, however. With the impending arrival of the new International Maritime Organisation (IMO) regulations capping the amount of sulphur oxides in marine fuel due to come into effect in 2015 on the North Sea, the Baltic and the coasts of North America (often erroneously claimed to be a directive of the European Union, when in reality the EU only ratified the already binding IMO regulation as a directive), DFDS forecasted the service would no longer be profitable. In April 2014, the company made known that the service would close down at the end of the summer season. Cargo services would be maintained with a six times per week connection from Esbjerg to Immingham (which is still operated today). This sole remaining roro link between the west coast of Denmark and the UK carries no passengers, although this ships have 12 berths, due to the restrictions placed on the cargo port of Immingham by the UK Border Force.

The ***Ark Dania*** and her sister ship ***Ark Germania*** today, built in 2014 by the P+S Werften but completed by Fayard in Odense after the builder's bankruptcy, operate DFDS' Esbjerg-Immingham route, the main roro cargo link between Denmark and the UK. *(DFDS)*

Alarmists warned that all long sea routes in Northern Europe were under threat dye to "the sulphur directive," but the closure of the Esbjerg-Harwich route turned out to be an oddity; most northern European long-haul ferry routes were able to adapt, either by alternative fuels or by installation of scrubbers that remove the sulphur from the exhausts. The *Sirena Seaways*, however, received no scrubber at the time, the installation having been deemed too expensive to pay itself back on the Esbjerg-Harwich -route (she did receive one after being transferred to a different route, however). On 29 September 2014, the *Sirena Seaways* arrived in Esbjerg from Harwich for the last time. The scheduled passenger link

Chapter seven

Dreams of Restoration

between Scandinavia and Britain was broken after 194 years of service.

End of the passenger link between the Nordic Countries and Britain have aroused surprisingly many passions. Hopeful start-ups have occasionally made public plans to restart the services and – in Britain – local authorities have shown interest in the services, with promises of financial support. In a situation where cargo is king and flying is cheap, is there any realistic hope of a restored passenger link?

Pipe dreams and false starts

Years after the closure of the last link, there are still numerous petitions, social media groups, and discussion forums calling for the restoration of these connections. Occasionally, a group of enthusiastic entrepreneurs make the news with their upstart company that has *almost* secured funding – or in some cases just by stating they are *hoping* to secure funding.

While outfits such as Regina Line and the oddly named North Sea Cruiseline appeared nothing more than pipe dreams by individuals or small groups, more realistic plans for the restoration of the service have been made public – and it is likely that similar plans have been made under wraps and never reach the knowledge of the public. One of the more publicized (and more realistic) plans was originally known as Norwegian Seaways, a company with the intention of re-initiating Newcastle-Bergen services in 2013 using the *Ikarus Palace* chartered from Minoan Lines. The 1997-built ropax ferry would have been fairly well suited for the route, carrying 1,500 passengers and 2,195 lane metres of cargo in her 30,010 grt hull and capable of a 26.4 knot service speed. Modified photos of her in a projected light blue -dominated livery were published, but Norwegian Seaways failed to secure funding and service never happened. Subsequently, the venture rebranded, first into Project Norse and then into British Norwegian. In 2015, British Norwegian reported they had secured half of the funding needed. After that, nothing concrete has been heard from them.

Politicians have also shown occasional interest in the restoration of the service, at least in Britain. In March 2015, the Newcastle municipality received funds from the British state budget to study the possibility of restoring a link to Norway. In Scotland, meanwhile, the Scottish National Party demanded a study into establishing a link from a Scottish port to Norway. As recently as 2018, P&O Ferries made it known they were "willing to enter talks with the Scottish Government about a new ferry route between Scotland and Scandinavia."

Despite thesoccasional interest, no realistic plans are known to exist for the restoration of a Norway-UK service at the time of writing (nor one linking the other Scandinavian countries to the UK).

Similarly, the decision-makers of the Shetland Islands have been keen for the restoration of the *Norröna*'s (2) calls in Lerwick, as already touched on in Chapter 5. High-level negotiations were held in 2014 and more recently in 2018, but with no positive results. Even so, the restoration of the *Norröna*'s (2) Lerwick calls does seem the most likely way of restoring a link between the Nordic countries and Britain (albeit in a very limited manner), as the *Nörrona*'s (2) route between Denmark and the Faroes takes her thought the Shetland Islands – the restoration of a call there would be a simple matter, if an economic case can be made for it.

Travel trends – hope or despair?

With Britain's divorce from the European Union, or Brexit, looming in the horizon, many hopefuls have claimed the restoration of tax free sales on ferry services from British ports would provide the impetus to restore the Scandinavia-UK links. What these commentators fail to recall is that both Norway-UK and Sweden-UK services had tax-free sales onboard right until the end, as Norway is not a member of the EU (as noted in Chapter 3, the Gothenburg-Newcastle route calling in Kristiansand, Norway en-route to gain the right to continue selling tax-free goods). In fact, the most persistent of the services, Esbjerg-Harwich, was also the only one that didn't have tax free sales onboard after the end of intra-EU tax free in 1999. At the same time, the mini cruise culture – that was once almost synonymous with tax free sales – has been in decline for decades. As noted in the previous chapters, on the Nordics-UK routes the mini cruise product was losing popularity already in the 1980s. Today, a handful of routes reliant on mini cruise passengers remain, in northern Europe, but they are increasingly anachronistic. If there is a future of the Scandinavia-UK routes, it is not in a return to the past.

If there is a future, it lies in different type of tonnage and in emerging travel trends. In an earlier version of this chapter, dating from mid-2018, I wrote that when it comes to travelling today, the ferry simply cannot compete with the airplane on the cross-North Sea services when it comes to price, speed, or comfort, and that especially when considering the fact that the big Scandinavian population centers are located away from the convenient seaways to Britain (apart from Bergen and Gothenburg), ferries could have no chance of competing – unless outside forces radically diminish the attractiveness of flying, for example by tighter regulations of the air travel industry, end to the tax free status of aviation fuel in the EU, or a 'carbon tax' on flying.

Since then, however, a rising travel trend in the Nordic countries has given me reason to re-evaluate my opinion: the no-fly movement, which has arisen from increased awareness

The former ***Sirena Seaways*** as she is at the time of writing as the ***Baie de Seine***, under charter from DFDS to Brittany Ferries since 2015. Her charter is due to end in Spring 2020, and rumours indicate DFDS will employ her in their own fleet on the Baltic Sea routes afterwards. *(Miles Cowsill)*

of pollution caused by airplanes and their detrimental effect on the climate, has already caused travel companies in the Nordic countries to alter their offerings to have more no-fly options. If this movement becomes more wide-spread – and developments in Finland and Sweden, at least, point to it being on the verge of becoming mainstream – there maybe hope for the restoration of passenger services linking the Nordic countries and Britain. But, as has been the case with all passenger services discussed in this book, such a service is only possible if it also carries large amounts of cargo alongside passengers. As it is with other long-haul European ferry services, the possible future lies in ropax tonnage.

In 2013, the ***Icarus Palace*** on Minoan Lines was advertised as Norwegian Seaways' new Norway-UK ship, with advertising showing a planned livery where the red parts of the existing livery altered sky blue. However, the service never happened. *(Marko Stampehl)*

Cargo is king

Despite ubiquity of the ropax, the Esbjerg-Harwich route was the only Scandinavia-UK connection converted to ropax operation. As we have seen in Chapter 3, initial studies did show "promising figures" for converting the Gothenburg-Newcastle route to ropax running, even if this option was not taken up. Indeed, it could be argued that a part of the reason why the services linking Sweden and Norway to the UK failed was the operators' continuing reliance on a cruise ferry product at a time when almost all similar long-haul routes in Europe converted to ropax.

Even with the potential renewed interest in sea travel caused by the no-fly movement, it is immensely more difficult to start a new route (or restart an old one after a long absence) than it is to develop a new one. It is even more difficult to do so for both passengers and cargo at the same time, especially considering how strong the market positions of the existing operators of cargo tonnage between British ports and those in Scandinavia are – and how relatively small the cargo flows are.

Denmark, Norway and Sweden all enjoy six weekly roro cargo connection to ports in the UK – primarily the freight hub in Immingham (not counting the ships exclusively serving the needs of Sweden's Gulf of Bothnia forest industry, that take no cargo from outside customers). For Denmark and Sweden, the services are concentrated on "trunk routes": Esbjerg-Immingham and Gothenburg-Immingham. For Norway, the connections are more spread out, with three weekly from ports in western Norway and another three from the southern part of the country. Any newcomer company would face difficulties in trying to find enough cargo to support a frequent ropax operation, especially considering any such company would have to wrestle that cargo from strong existing companies, DFDS and Sea-Cargo. For the other Nordic countries, the picture is bleaker: there are no roro cargo connections from Iceland and the Faroes to the UK, the services being handled by container vessels, while for Finland – from which there is a surprisingly frequent service, mostly for the needs of the forest

A large number of former Scandinavia-UK ferries survive in the fleet of Italy's Moby Lines, all naturally painted in the cartoon liveries favoured by the company. Seen here is the former ***Dana Anglia***, which after a brief charter and later sale to Brittany Ferries she became the ***Moby Corse*** in 2009. She is seen here in Livorno in 2010. *(Marko Stampehl)*

The last Norway-UK ferry ***Queen of Scandinavia*** became the St. Peter Line (SPL) Helsinki-St. Petersburg ferry ***Princess Maria*** in 2010. When financial difficulties forced SPL to form a joint venture with Moby in 2016, she too joined the Moby fleet, sailing today as the ***Moby Dada***. *(Kalle Id)*

The ***Moby Otta***, ex-***Tor Scandinavia*** and ***Princess of Scandinavi***a, and her sister are also members of the Moby fleet, employed to provide additional capacity in the summer season. The ***Moby Otta*** is seen here in Livorno, May 2009. *(Kalle Id)*

industry, again with six weekly return departures to UK ports – the sheer distance makes a direct passenger service unlikely, as a single vessel can only practically provide a weekly service. And, again, securing enough cargos for a new company would mean going against long-established competitors with financial resources to withstand competition.

Thus, the most likely – perhaps only possible – scenario for a restoration of a Scandinavia-UK passenger link is one involving the existing cargo operators. In terms of routes and schedules, the company best poised to convert existing roro cargo routes to ropax operation is the one that closed down all three Scandinavia-UK passenger links: DFDS. The company has shown increased interest for the passenger trades in the years following the closure of the Esbjerg-Harwich -route in 2014… but whether they or any other company is willing to (re-)start a Scandinavia-UK passenger service depends on one thing only: money.

Whether we like it or not, we live in a world dominated by market forces where profitability is the sole criteria for making investment decisions (and is often allowed to override all other concerns, even if the outcome is detrimental to people or the environment). In order for a passenger service to exist, it must have enough passengers willing to pay high enough prices. In the past, this has not been the case – hence all the closures described in this book. Will the circumstances change in the future and we will see a passenger vessel sailing between the Nordic countries and the UK again? As things stand when I'm writing this, the business case doesn't seem to exist, but travel trends and political decisions can change things. For the moment, this book compiles the entire history of the passenger services between the Nordic countries and the UK – but maybe one day a new chapter needs to be added to it.

A delightful deck scene from the twilight years of both the ***Princess of Scandinavia*** and the Sweden-UK passenger service. Alas, today it's no longer possible to make such a pleasant crossing from Scandinavia to the UK. Instead, travellers are forced to choose between crowded confines of airplanes, or lengthy and impractical overland journeys through central Europe. *(Søren Lund Hviid)*

The former Leningrad-London liner *Estoniya* makes a fine sight as the motors through the sea in spring 1989. Much like the her home country was about to become shortly afterwards, the Leningrad-UK was by this time a memory (albeit less unpleasant than the single-party state had been). Notice the cars – including a Soviet-made Lada Niva – secured on the forward sun deck. *(FotoFlite)*

Bibliography

Archives

The National Library of Finland, Helsinki, Finland
The archives of The Ship Historical Society of Finland, Helsinki, Finland
The author's personal archives
The personal archives of Anders Bergenek, Halmstad, Sweden
The personal archives of Harald Oanes, Stavanger, Norway

Books

Dag Bakka Jr: *Bergenske – byen og selskapet.* Seagull Publishing: Bergen 1993.
Anders Bergenek & Klas Brogen: *Passagerare till sjöss – Den svenska färjesjöfartens historia.* ShipPax Information: Halmstad 2006.
Bruno Bock & Klaus Bock: *Soviet Block Merchant Ships*. Jane's Publishing Company: London–Sydney 1981.
N.R.P. Bonsor: *North Atlantic Seaway – volume 4.* Brookside Publications: Jersey 1979.
John Bryant: *Hurtigruten 120 – The Complete Story.* Ferry Publications: Ramsey 2013.
Richard Clammer: *Marco Polo – Celebrating Fifty Golden Years of Ocean Travel.* Ferry Publications: Ramsey 2014.
Anthony Cooke: *Liners & Cruise Ships – Some notable smaller vessels.* Carmania Press: Huddersfield 1996.
Anthony Cooke: *The Fred. Olsen Line and its Passenger Ships.* Carmania Press: London 2009.
Miles Cowsill & John Hendy: *Winston Churchill*. Ferry Publications: 1991.
Miles Cowsill & John Hendy: *DFDS – The Fleet*. Ferry Publications: Narberth 1998.
Arthur C. Credland & Michael Thompson: *The Wilson Line of Hull 1831-1981.* Hutton Press: Cherry Burton 1994.
Arthur Credland & Richard Greenwood: *Bailey and Leetham*. Ships in Focus Publications: Preston 2002.
Rolf Danielsen & Olav Vedeld: *Det Nordenfjeldske Dampskibsselkab 1857-1957.* Det Nordenfjeldske Dampskibsselkab: Trondheim 1957.
Ambrose Greenway: *A Century of North Sea Passenger Steamers.* Ian Allard: London 1986.
Gunnar Karlsson: *A Brief History of Iceland.* Mál og menning: Reykjavík 2010. 2nd, revised edition.
Paavo Haavikko: *Vuosisadan merikirja – Effoan sata ensimmäistä vuotta*. Effoa: Helsinki 1983.
Morten Hahn-Pedersen (ed.): *North Sea Passenger Lines.* Association of North Sea Cities – Maritime Museums Network & The Fisheries and Maritime Museum: Esbjerg 2009.
John Harrower: *Wilson Line – The history and fleet of Thos. Wilson, Sons & Co. and Ellerman's Wilson Lines Ltd.* The World Ship Society: Gravesend 1998.
Kalle Id & Bruce Peter: *Innovation and Specialisation – The Story of Shipbuilding in Finland.* Nautilus: Copenhagen 2017.
Helge Jääsalo: *Pohjoiset satamat auki*. Kustannusosakeyhtiö Pohjoinen: Oulu 1980.
Yrjö Kaukiainen: *Ulos maailmaan! Suomalaisen merenkulun historia.* Suomalaisen kirjallisuuden seura: Hämeenlinna 2008.
Wilhelm Keilhau: *Norges eldste linjerederi.* Bergen: 1952.
Wilhelm Keilhau: *Norway and the Bergen Line.* Bergen Line: Bergen 1953.
Dick Keys & Ken Smith: *Ferry Tales – Tyne-Norway Voyages 1864-2001.* Tyne Bridge Publishing: Newcastle 2002.
Kimmo Kiljunen: *Leijonasta siniristiin – Suomen liput ja historia.* Into Kustannus: Helsinki 2018.
Thure Malmberg: *Valkeat laivat.* Suomen Höyrylaivaosakeyhtiö: Helsinki 1970.
Thure Malmberg: *Laivoja ja ihmisiä – kuvia ja kertomuksia Effoan satavuotistaipaleelta.* Effoa: Helsinki 1983
Thure Malmberg & Peter Raudsepp (eds.): *Passenger Ships of the World: A History in Posters.* Raud Publishing: Helsinki 2004.
Thure Malmberg & Marko Stampehl: *Siljan viisi vuosikymmentä.* Frenckellin Kirjapaino Oy: Espoo 2007.
Matthew Murtland and Richard Seville: *Sealink and beyond.* Ferry Publications: Ramsey 2014.
Kai Ortel: *TT-Line Through Five Decades.* Ferry Publications: Ramsey 2014.
Bruce Peter: *Passengers Liners Scandinavian Style.* Carmania Press: London 2003.
Bruce Peter: *DFDS Sailing in Style.* Ferry Publications: Ramsey.
Bruce Peter: *Knud E. Hansen – Ship Design Through Seven Decades.* Nautilus Forlag: Frederiksværk 2010.
Bruce Peter: *Knud E. Hansen A/S – 75 Years of Ship Design.* Ferry Publications: Ramsey 2012.
Bruce Peter: *DFDS 150*. Nautilus: Copenhagen 2016.
Bruce Peter & Philip Dawson: *The Ferry – A Drive-Through History.* Ferry Publications: Ramsey 2011.
Bruce Peter & Oddbjörn Fastesson: *Tor Line and The Battle of the North Sea.* Nautilus: Copenhagen 2016.
Lauritz Pettersen Jr: *Opprettelsen av Englandsruten – (Trondheim)-Bergen-Newcastle.* A.S. John Griegs Boktrykkeri: Bergen 1954.
Matti Pietikäinen: *The Ships of our First Century – The Effoa Fleet 1883-1983.* Effoa: Helsinki 1983.
Matti Pietikäinen: *The Finnlines Fleet 1947-1997 – 50 Years at Your Service.* Finnlines: Helsinki 1998.
Matti Pietikäinen: *Vain yksi palasi takaisin – höyrylaiva Turson 70 ensimmäistä vuotta.* Satamajäänsärkijä S/S Turso Yhdistys ry: 2016.
Henrik Ramsay: *Jääsaarron murtajat.* Werner Söderström Osakeyhtiö: Helsinki 1949.
Peter Raudsepp (ed.): *Höyrylaivalla Tallinnaan – Matkustajahöyrylaivaliikenne Suomenlahden yli vuodesta 1837 alkaen.* Raud Publishing: Helsinki 2018.
Ture Rinman: *Svenska Lloyd genom etthundra år.* Zindermans:

Uddevalla 1969.
Bo Rosén (ed.): *Laivojen kirja.* Werner Söderström Osakeyhtiö: Porvoo 1959.
Claus Rothe: *Welt der Passagierschiffe unter Hammer und Sichel.* DSV-Verlag: Hamburg 1994.
Bruno Suviranta: *Suomen Höyrylaiva Osakeyhtiö 1883-1958.* Tilgmannin kirjapaino: Helsinki 1958.
William Taubman: *Hruštšov – Mies ja hänen aikansa.* Art House: Helsinki 2007.
Søren Thorsøe, Peter Simonsen, Søren Krogh-Andersen, Frederik Frederichsen, Henrik Vaupel: *DFDS 1866-1991. Ship Development Through 125 Years – from Paddle Steamer to Ro/Ro Ship.* DFDS: 1991.
Henrik Vidén: *Wasa-Nordsjö Ångbåts A.B. 1873-1923.* Mercators Tryckeri Aktiebolag: Helsingfors 1923.
Nick Widdows (ed): *Ferries 2019*. Ferry Publications: Ramsey 2018.
E.A. Wilson: *Soviet Passenger Ships 1917-1977.* World Ship Society: Kendal 1978.

Unpublished manuscripts

James Pedersen: *Den ældre norske dampskibsfart*. 1907.
Rami Wirrankoski: *USSR – Morpasflot Fleet List*.

Articles

Aferry.co.uk 9.6.2006: "Tórshavn court backs Smyril Line in battle to quit Lerwick"
Aftenbladet 2.12.2014: "Planer om ny englandsferje"
Associated Press 11.10.1986: Andrew Rosenthal: "Mrs. Gorbachev in Public Spotlight as Blacked-Out Summit Begins"
BBC News 11.11.2008: "Summer ferry sailings cancelled"
Båtologen, unknown issue: Anders Bergenek: "Från Biscaya till Kattegatt"
Båtologen, unknown issue: Anders Bergenek: "Nordsjöns trogna parhästar"
Båtologen, unknown issue: Anders Bergenek: "De sista Londonbåtarna" (part 1)
Båtologen, unknown issue: Anders Bergenek: "De sista Londonbåtarna" (part 2)
Båtologen 2/1985: Ragnar Ödman: "Ett Emigrantfartyg"
Båtologen 2/1986: Anders Bergenek: "ESL's Spero"
Båtologen 6/1986: Gören Freiholtz: "Leda åter i Bergen"
Båtologen 6/1997: Anders Bergenek: "Moderna färjor på 'gamla Nordsjön'"
Båtologen 1/1998: Anders Bergenek: "Hårda tider på 'gamla Nordsjön'"
Båtologen 6/2000: Anders Bergenek: ""En sjökapten i det 20:e århundraet"
Car Ferry Info 4/1984: "North Atlantic". pp. 65-66.
Car Ferry Info 11/1984: "The Winter Cruises of Fred. Olsen". p. 48.
Car Ferry Info 11/1985: "Sealink/British Ferries' Route to Scandinavia". pp. 31-32.
Car Ferry Info 11/1985: "The Great Success of Fred. Olsen Lines on the Oslo-Hirtshals-Harwich Route". p. 32.
Car Ferry Info 2/1986: "Norway Line's First, Profitable Year".
Edinburgh Evening News 4 January 2018: Ian Swanson: "P&O willing to consider new ferry routes from Scotland to Scandinavia"
Herald Scotland 12.11.2008: "Blow as ferry link with Scandinavia faces the axe"
The Journal 19.3.2015: "Norway to Newcastle Ferry route given fresh hope after budget announcement"
Laiva 4/2007: Tuukka Laakso: "Epäonnistunut yritys – Jättimäinen FÅA söi pienen Nordin". pp. 44-47.
Laiva 1/2018: Rami Wirrankoski: "Vanhin Wasa-Nordsjö". pp. 24-39.
Laiva 2/2018: Rami Wirrankoski: "Wasa-Nordsjön laivasto". pp. 22-35.
Länspumpen 1/2019: Anders Bergenek: "En nästan glomd Saga".
Scandinavian Shipping Gazette 4/1978: "Polish ferry service to Felixstowe opened". p. 13.
Shetland News 7 May 2014: Neil Riddel: "Norröna return?"
Shetland News 18 October 2018: Chris Cope: "Renewed call for Norröna to return to isles"
Skipet Juni 1988: "Englandsruten skjæres til beinet"
Suomen Kuvalehti, unknown issue 1925: "Oberon – Suomen höyrylaivayhtiön suurin laiva valmistunut"
Suomen Kuvalehti 25-26/2019: Vesa Vares: "Englantiin päin rähmällään". pp. 58-61.
Ulkomatala 2/2014: Kalle Id: "Dannebrogin alla New Yorkiin". pp. 34-43.
Ulkomatala 3/2014: Kalle Id: "Vuonoilta Amerikkaan". pp. 36-45.
Ulkomatala 4/2015: Jussi Littunen: "Color Linen värikkäät vuodet". pp. 23-33.
Vapavahti–Frivakt 2/2013: Peter Raudsepp: "Avomeriliikenteen matkustaja-höyrylaivoja Suomessa Krimin sodan jälkeen". pp. 24-25.

Websites

Britain2Norway (www.facebook.com/pages/Britain2Norway/305745318325)
Eimskip (eimskip.is)
Fakta om Fartyg (www.faktaomfartyg.se)
Ferry to Norway (ferrytonorway.com)
Kommandobryggan (kommandobryggan.se)
Maritime Timetable Images (www.timetableimages.com/maritime/index.html)
Norway-Heritage – Hands Across the Sea. (www.norwayheritage.com)
Pörssitieto (www.porssitieto.fi)
TheShipsList (www.theshipslist.com)
Simplon Postcards (www.simplonpc.co.uk)
Smyril Line (www.smyrilline.com)
Водный транспорт (fleetphoto.ru)
Wikipedia (en.wikipedia.org, fi.wikipedia.org and no.wikipedia.org)
Äänimeri (www.aanimeri.fi)

Other

Matkakuume radio programme. Yle 2015.
Tilastokeskus / Statistics Finland (www.stat.fi)
Statistiska centralbyrån / Statistics Sweden (www.scb.se)